The Key to History

Eric Harbinger

ISBN: 978-1-77961-901-3
Imprint: Electric Tree Pulp
Copyright © 2024 Eric Harbinger.
All Rights Reserved.

Contents

Introduction	**1**
Overview of the importance of contemporary history	1
Scope and purpose of the textbook	1
Methodology and approach used in the book	1
Structure of the textbook	1
Chapter 1: The World in the Aftermath of World War II	**3**
Section 1: The Political Landscape	3
Section 2: Economic Developments	33
Section 3: Social and Cultural Transformations	61
Chapter 2: The Information Age and Digital Revolution	**89**
Section 1: The Birth of the Internet	89
Section 2: The Impact of Technology on Society	118
Section 3: Challenges and Opportunities in the Information Age	149
Chapter 3: Globalization and the Interconnected World	**179**
Section 1: The Rise of Global Trade	179
Section 2: Migration and the Movement of People	210
Section 3: Global Challenges and Collaborative Solutions	240
Bibliography	**245**
Index	**273**

Introduction

Overview of the importance of contemporary history

Scope and purpose of the textbook

Methodology and approach used in the book

Structure of the textbook

Chapter 1: The World in the Aftermath of World War II

Section 1: The Political Landscape

Subsection: The Formation of the United Nations

The formation of the United Nations (UN) marked a significant turning point in the aftermath of World War II. As the world grappled with the devastation and destruction caused by the war, there was a growing realization that a new international organization was needed to prevent future conflicts and foster global cooperation. This subsection explores the origins, principles, and structure of the UN, as well as its role in promoting peace and addressing global challenges.

Origins of the United Nations

The idea of an international organization to maintain peace and security emerged during the war itself. In 1942, representatives from the United States, the Soviet Union, China, and the United Kingdom signed the Declaration by United Nations, pledging to uphold principles such as collective security and respect for human rights. This declaration laid the foundation for the eventual establishment of the UN.

Principles and Objectives

The UN is guided by a set of core principles aimed at promoting peace, fostering cooperation, and addressing global challenges. These principles include sovereign equality of all member states, peaceful settlement of disputes, non-interference in internal affairs, and respect for human rights. The overarching objective of the UN

4 CHAPTER 1: THE WORLD IN THE AFTERMATH OF WORLD WAR II

is to maintain international peace and security, develop friendly relations among nations, and promote social progress, better living standards, and human rights.

Structure of the United Nations

The UN is composed of multiple organs and specialized agencies that work together to achieve its goals. The main organs of the UN are the General Assembly, the Security Council, the Economic and Social Council, the Secretariat, the International Court of Justice, and the Trusteeship Council (which has been inactive since 1994). Each organ has specific roles and responsibilities within the organization. Additionally, the UN has specialized agencies, such as the World Health Organization (WHO) and the United Nations Educational, Scientific and Cultural Organization (UNESCO), which focus on specific areas like health, education, and culture.

Functions of the United Nations

The UN performs a wide range of functions to fulfill its objectives. These include:

1. Peacekeeping: One of the most important roles of the UN is peacekeeping, where UN forces are deployed to conflict zones to maintain peace and stability. This involves monitoring ceasefires, facilitating negotiations, and providing humanitarian assistance.

2. Conflict Resolution: The UN plays a significant role in mediating and resolving conflicts between nations through diplomatic channels. The Security Council, in particular, can authorize sanctions or military actions to address threats to international peace and security.

3. Development Assistance: The UN promotes global development in areas such as education, healthcare, poverty reduction, and gender equality. It provides technical support, financial aid, and expertise to member states to help them achieve sustainable development goals.

4. Humanitarian Aid: The UN coordinates and provides humanitarian assistance in response to natural disasters, conflicts, and other emergencies. It supports relief efforts, provides food aid, medical assistance, shelter, and works to protect the rights of refugees and displaced persons.

5. Promotion of Human Rights: The UN is committed to protecting and promoting human rights worldwide. It works to prevent human rights abuses, supports initiatives for gender equality, fights against discrimination, and advocates for the rights of marginalized groups.

SECTION 1: THE POLITICAL LANDSCAPE 5

Challenges and Limitations

While the United Nations has made significant contributions to global peace and development, it also faces various challenges and limitations. These include:

1. Limited Enforcement Power: The UN relies on member states' voluntary compliance with its resolutions and decisions. Lack of enforcement mechanisms can limit its effectiveness in addressing global conflicts and human rights violations.

2. Political Divisions: The diverse membership of the UN, with different political ideologies and national interests, can pose challenges to consensus-building and decision-making. Issues such as veto power in the Security Council can hinder effective action.

3. Funding Constraints: The UN's work relies heavily on member states' financial contributions. Limited funding can constrain its capacity to carry out essential programs and respond to global crises effectively.

4. Reform and Adaptation: The world has undergone significant changes since the establishment of the UN, and there is a need for ongoing reform to ensure the organization remains relevant and responsive to emerging challenges.

Overall, the formation of the United Nations has played a crucial role in promoting global peace and cooperation. By bringing together nations and fostering dialogue, the UN seeks to address common challenges and promote a more peaceful and equitable world. While it faces various challenges, the UN continues to evolve and adapt to meet the complex needs of the contemporary global landscape.

Example: A Contested Security Council Decision

To better understand the functioning of the United Nations, let's consider a hypothetical scenario where the Security Council deliberates on a contentious issue. Suppose there is an ongoing conflict between two neighboring countries, Alpha and Omega, over territorial disputes. After several failed attempts at negotiations, the situation escalates, leading to violence and the displacement of thousands of civilians.

Both Alpha and Omega bring their case to the Security Council, seeking a resolution that favors their respective positions. The Security Council, consisting of 15 members with five permanent members (USA, UK, China, France, Russia) and ten non-permanent members elected for two-year terms, deliberates on the matter.

The permanent members, known as the P5, each possess veto power, which means any one of them can block a resolution, making consensus-building a challenging task. In this case, the P5 members hold differing views on the conflict, with some having historical alliances or interests with either Alpha or Omega.

6 CHAPTER 1: THE WORLD IN THE AFTERMATH OF WORLD WAR II

The Security Council discusses various proposals, including imposing sanctions, deploying peacekeeping forces, or advocating for a diplomatic resolution. Intense negotiations take place, with representatives from Alpha, Omega, and other member countries passionately presenting their cases and advocating for their interests.

Ultimately, a resolution is proposed that recommends a ceasefire, the initiation of peace talks, and the deployment of UN peacekeeping forces to monitor and maintain the truce. However, reaching consensus proves difficult due to political divisions and conflicting interests among the permanent members.

After extensive debates, negotiations, and possible amendments to the resolution, a compromise is achieved, and the resolution is passed with the required majority of at least nine affirmative votes and no vetoes from the P5. While it may not completely satisfy all parties involved, the resolution provides a framework for a peaceful resolution and sets the stage for further dialogue and engagement.

This example highlights the intricate dynamics and challenges faced by the United Nations, particularly within the Security Council. It showcases the complex process of decision-making and the delicate balance required to address conflicts and promote international peace and security.

Subsection: The Rise of Superpowers: USA and USSR

The aftermath of World War II marked the beginning of a new era in global politics, with the United States and the Soviet Union emerging as superpowers. This subsection will delve into the factors that contributed to the rise of these two nations and the subsequent bipolarity that shaped international relations during the Cold War.

Background

The end of World War II left much of Europe and Asia devastated, providing an opportunity for new powers to rise and exert their influence. The United States, having emerged from the war relatively unscathed and possessing a strong industrial base, became an economic powerhouse. The Soviet Union, on the other hand, had suffered immense human and material losses but managed to consolidate its power over Eastern Europe. Both countries sought to establish their dominance and ideologies in global affairs.

The United States: Superpower by Economic Might

The United States' ascendancy to superpower status was largely driven by its economic strength. In the aftermath of World War II, the U.S. experienced a

SECTION 1: THE POLITICAL LANDSCAPE 7

period of unprecedented economic growth, fueled by technological advancements, the expansion of consumer culture, and government initiatives such as the Marshall Plan. Key factors in the rise of the U.S. as a superpower include:

1. **Industrialization and Technological Advancements:** The U.S. had a highly developed industrial base and was at the forefront of technological innovations. Industries such as automobile manufacturing, aviation, and electronics drove economic growth and contributed to the country's global influence.

2. **Mass Production and Consumer Culture:** The U.S. embraced mass production techniques, allowing for the efficient production of consumer goods at affordable prices. This led to the growth of a prosperous middle class and fueled domestic consumption.

3. **The Marshall Plan:** In 1948, the U.S. launched the Marshall Plan to provide economic assistance to war-torn European countries. This initiative not only helped in the reconstruction of Europe but also positioned the U.S. as a benevolent global power, garnering influence and support.

4. **Establishment of International Financial Institutions:** The U.S. played a leading role in the establishment of international financial institutions like the International Monetary Fund (IMF) and the World Bank. This allowed the U.S. to exert significant influence over global economic policies and aid recipient nations.

The Soviet Union: Superpower by Ideology

While the Soviet Union did not possess the same level of economic might as the United States, it rose to the status of a superpower through its ideology and its ability to effectively project its power. Key factors in the rise of the Soviet Union as a superpower include:

1. **Communist Ideology:** The Soviet Union advocated for the spread of communism, an ideology that resonated with many oppressed nations seeking to break free from colonial rule. This ideology appealed to a broad range of populations, giving the Soviet Union an influential position on the world stage.

2. **Military Power:** The Soviet Union built a formidable military, characterized by its large standing army, advanced weaponry, and a focus on

8 CHAPTER 1: THE WORLD IN THE AFTERMATH OF WORLD WAR II

industrial capacity for defense production. This military strength allowed the Soviet Union to assert its influence and protect its interests.

3. **Control over Eastern Europe:** The Soviet Union established control over Eastern European countries that had been liberated from Nazi occupation. This led to the formation of the Eastern Bloc, a buffer zone that provided security for the Soviet Union and extended its sphere of influence.

4. **Nuclear Weapons:** The Soviet Union successfully developed nuclear weapons, matching the United States in terms of destructive capability. This strategic parity established the concept of Mutually Assured Destruction (MAD), which prevented direct conflict between the two superpowers.

The Bipolar World and the Cold War

The rise of the United States and the Soviet Union as superpowers set the stage for a bipolar world dominated by two opposing ideological and political blocs. This period, known as the Cold War, was characterized by political and military tensions between the two superpowers, despite the absence of direct armed conflict. The key aspects of the Cold War include:

1. **Arms Race:** The United States and the Soviet Union engaged in a competition to develop and stockpile nuclear weapons, leading to an arms race that escalated tensions and raised the specter of global annihilation. This period saw the development of larger and more destructive weapons systems, which further solidified the superpowers' dominance.

2. **Proxy Wars:** The United States and the Soviet Union supported proxy wars in various regions across the globe, using client states as pawns to advance their respective ideologies. Examples include the Korean War, the Vietnam War, and conflicts in Africa and Latin America. These proxy wars allowed the superpowers to exert their influence and gain strategic advantages without direct confrontation.

3. **Space Race:** The United States and the Soviet Union competed in the exploration and conquest of space. This race was not only a symbol of technological prowess but also a demonstration of ideological superiority. The Soviet Union achieved significant milestones, including the launch of the first artificial satellite and the first human in space.

SECTION 1: THE POLITICAL LANDSCAPE

4. **Political and Economic Confrontation:** The United States advocated for a free-market capitalist system, while the Soviet Union promoted a centrally planned command economy. This political and economic rivalry created deep divisions, leading to economic embargoes, ideological propaganda, and a constant struggle for global influence.

Conclusion

The rise of the United States and the Soviet Union as superpowers in the aftermath of World War II shaped the geopolitical landscape for decades to come. The United States' economic strength and the Soviet Union's ideology-driven power were the driving forces behind their ascent. This bipolarity resulted in a tense and competitive relationship marked by an arms race, proxy wars, and ideological confrontations. The stage was set for a new world order, where the actions of these superpowers would determine the course of global history. Understandably, the rise of the superpowers was not without its challenges and complexities, which will be explored further in subsequent sections of this textbook.

10CHAPTER 1: THE WORLD IN THE AFTERMATH OF WORLD WAR II

The Cold War and the Division of Europe

The Cold War, which lasted from the late 1940s to the early 1990s, was a period of intense geopolitical tensions and ideological conflict between the United States and the Soviet Union. This global standoff had a profound impact on the world, particularly on Europe, which became the epicenter of the struggle between the two superpowers. In this subsection, we will explore the causes, key events, and consequences of the Cold War in Europe, with a particular focus on the division of the continent.

Causes of the Cold War

The origins of the Cold War can be traced back to the aftermath of World War II. The ideological differences between the capitalist democracy of the United States and the communist regime of the Soviet Union fueled competition and mistrust. The Yalta Conference in 1945, where the victorious Allied powers discussed the post-war settlement, marked the first signs of tension between the two nations.

One of the primary causes of the Cold War was the differing visions for the future of Europe. The Soviet Union aimed to establish a buffer zone, known as the Eastern Bloc, consisting of satellite states in Eastern and Central Europe to protect its western borders. The United States, on the other hand, sought to promote democratic governments and free-market economies across Europe, which conflicted with Soviet expansionism.

Key Events of the Cold War in Europe

The Cold War had a profound impact on Europe, and the continent became divided into two opposing camps: the Western Bloc, led by the United States, and the Eastern Bloc, dominated by the Soviet Union. Here are some of the key events that shaped the division of Europe:

1. **The Iron Curtain Speech (1946):** British Prime Minister Winston Churchill's famous speech in Fulton, Missouri, is considered a seminal moment in the Cold War. He highlighted the ideological divide in Europe and warned of the emerging "Iron Curtain" separating the East and the West.

2. **The Marshall Plan (1948-1952):** The United States' initiative to provide economic aid to war-torn European countries was met with opposition from the Soviet Union. While the Marshall Plan aimed to foster economic recovery

SECTION 1: THE POLITICAL LANDSCAPE 11

and prevent communism from spreading, the Eastern Bloc countries, under Soviet control, rejected the aid due to fears of increased Western influence.

3. **The Berlin Blockade and Airlift (1948-1949):** In response to the introduction of a new currency in the Western-controlled sectors of Berlin, the Soviet Union initiated a blockade, cutting off all land and water access to the city. In a remarkable display of cooperation and determination, the United States, along with its allies, conducted a massive airlift to supply the western sectors of Berlin for almost a year, ultimately undermining Soviet efforts.

4. **The Formation of NATO (1949):** The North Atlantic Treaty Organization (NATO) was established as a defensive alliance among Western European countries and the United States and Canada. NATO's primary goal was to counter the Soviet Union and ensure collective security against any potential threat.

5. **The Warsaw Pact (1955):** In response to the integration of West Germany into NATO, the Soviet Union formed the Warsaw Pact, a military alliance comprising the Eastern Bloc countries. This move further solidified the division of Europe into two opposing military blocs.

6. **The Construction of the Berlin Wall (1961):** In an attempt to stem the flow of defections from East to West in Berlin, the German Democratic Republic (GDR) built a heavily fortified wall that physically divided the city. The Berlin Wall became a symbol of the Cold War and remained a powerful symbol of the division of Europe until its fall in 1989.

7. **The Cuban Missile Crisis (1962):** The closest the Cold War came to a direct confrontation between the United States and the Soviet Union occurred during the Cuban Missile Crisis. The Soviet Union's deployment of nuclear missiles in Cuba, within striking distance of the United States, brought the world to the brink of nuclear war. The crisis was eventually resolved through diplomatic negotiations, but it highlighted the dangerous escalation of tensions between the two superpowers.

8. **Detente and the Helsinki Accords (1975):** In an effort to reduce tensions and mitigate the risk of nuclear war, both the United States and the Soviet Union pursued a policy of detente in the 1970s. As a significant step towards increased cooperation, the Helsinki Accords were signed by member states

of NATO and the Warsaw Pact, recognizing borders and human rights in Europe and promoting dialogue between East and West.

9. **The Fall of the Berlin Wall (1989):** The collapse of communist regimes in Eastern Europe in the late 1980s led to a wave of popular uprisings demanding political reform and an end to one-party rule. The opening of the Berlin Wall on November 9, 1989, symbolized the reunification of East and West Germany and marked a pivotal moment in the eventual peaceful end of the Cold War.

10. **The Dissolution of the Soviet Union (1991):** The Soviet Union, facing economic and political challenges, disbanded in 1991. The dissolution of the Soviet Union led to the establishment of independent nations across Eastern Europe and Central Asia, marking the end of the Cold War and the division of Europe.

Consequences of the Division of Europe

The division of Europe during the Cold War had lasting geopolitical, social, and economic consequences. Here are some of the key consequences:

+ **NATO and Warsaw Pact:** The formation of military alliances, such as NATO and the Warsaw Pact, entrenched the division of Europe and heightened tensions between the superpowers. This division not only had a profound impact on European security dynamics but also shaped the global balance of power for decades.

+ **Proxy Wars in Europe:** Europe became an arena for proxy wars, where the United States and the Soviet Union supported rival factions in conflicts such as the Greek Civil War, the Hungarian Revolution, and the proxy wars in Afghanistan and Vietnam. These conflicts highlighted the ideological struggle and power projection of the superpowers in the region.

+ **Economic Disparities:** The division of Europe created stark economic disparities between the prosperous capitalist countries in the West and the centrally planned economies of the East. Western Europe experienced remarkable economic growth, while the Eastern Bloc lagged behind, leading to a significant divergence in living standards.

+ **Suppression of Liberties:** The Eastern Bloc countries, under Soviet influence, experienced suppression of political dissent, restricted freedom of

SECTION 1: THE POLITICAL LANDSCAPE

speech, and limited civil liberties. The division of Europe not only divided the continent physically but also created stark contrasts in terms of democratic governance and individual freedoms.

- **Technological Competition:** The division of Europe propelled a technological race between the superpowers, particularly in the fields of space exploration and military technology. The competition between the United States and the Soviet Union led to significant advances in science and technology but also posed the risk of catastrophic consequences in the event of a conflict.

In Brief

The Cold War and the division of Europe had a far-reaching impact on the continent. The ideological struggle between the United States and the Soviet Union shaped the political, economic, and social landscape of Europe for several decades. While the fall of the Berlin Wall and the dissolution of the Soviet Union marked the end of the Cold War, the effects of this era still reverberate in Europe today. It is important to study and understand this historical period to comprehend the complexities of our modern world and the ongoing geopolitical challenges we face.

Subsection: Decolonization and the End of Empires

Decolonization refers to the process by which colonies gained their independence from colonial powers. It marked a significant shift in the balance of power and had far-reaching consequences for both the colonized nations and the former colonial powers. This subsection explores the causes, process, and consequences of decolonization, as well as the challenges faced by newly independent nations.

Causes of Decolonization

The decolonization movement gained momentum in the aftermath of World War II. The war weakened the colonial powers, both economically and politically, and exposed the inherent contradictions of colonial rule. Some key causes of decolonization are as follows:

- **Nationalist Movements:** Nationalist sentiments and movements in colonized regions grew stronger, fueled by the desire for self-determination and political freedom. Leaders like Mahatma Gandhi in India and Kwame Nkrumah in Ghana played instrumental roles in mobilizing their people towards independence.

14 CHAPTER 1: THE WORLD IN THE AFTERMATH OF WORLD WAR II

- **Global Anti-Colonial Sentiment:** The rise of global anti-colonial sentiment, driven by the principles of self-determination and equality propagated by the United Nations, put pressure on colonial powers to grant independence to their colonies. The Atlantic Charter of 1941, for example, promoted the right to self-determination.

- **Economic Factors:** The economic cost of maintaining colonies became increasingly burdensome for the colonial powers. The devastation caused by World War II further strained their resources, making it difficult to sustain colonial administrations and defend their imperial interests.

- **Shift in International Power Dynamics:** The emergence of new power centers, such as the United States and the Soviet Union, challenged colonial powers' traditional dominance. The Cold War rivalry between these two superpowers prompted them to support anti-colonial movements, further pressuring the colonial powers to grant independence.

Process of Decolonization

Decolonization unfolded differently in different regions of the world, but it typically followed a series of stages:

1. **Rise of Nationalist Movements:** Nationalist leaders and movements emerged, demanding independence from colonial rule. They mobilized their people through protests, strikes, and civil disobedience campaigns.

2. **Negotiations and Peaceful Transfers of Power:** In some cases, negotiations took place between colonial powers and nationalist leaders, resulting in the peaceful transfer of power. For example, India gained independence from Britain through negotiations led by Mahatma Gandhi and the Indian National Congress.

3. **Armed Struggle:** In other instances, particularly where colonial powers resisted granting independence, armed struggle and guerrilla warfare were employed to achieve independence. The Algerian War of Independence against France and the Mau Mau Uprising in Kenya are examples of armed struggles for liberation.

4. **Granting of Independence:** Ultimately, colonial powers had to recognize the futility of maintaining their colonies and began the process of granting independence. This often took the form of official declarations or the passage of legislation in the colonial powers' parliaments.

SECTION 1: THE POLITICAL LANDSCAPE 15

5. **Formation of New Nations:** With independence, new nations were born. They faced the challenge of establishing stable governments, formulating constitutions, and building national identities and institutions.

Consequences and Challenges of Decolonization

Decolonization had profound and lasting consequences for both the former colonies and the former colonial powers. Although decolonization was a triumph for self-determination and independence, it also brought significant challenges:

- **Nation Building:** Newly independent nations faced the immense task of nation-building. They had to establish effective governance systems, create inclusive political structures, and forge national identities in diverse societies. This often involved overcoming ethnic, religious, and regional divisions.

- **Economic Challenges:** Many newly independent countries inherited economic systems that were heavily dependent on their former colonial rulers. They had to navigate the legacy of economic exploitation and develop sustainable economies. However, the unequal global economic order and neocolonial practices sometimes hindered their progress.

- **Political Instability:** The transition to independence was not always smooth, and many newly independent countries experienced political instability, including military coups, civil wars, and ethnic conflicts. The struggle for power and challenges in establishing democratic systems created barriers to stability and development.

- **Legacy of Colonialism:** Decolonization did not erase the deep-rooted social, cultural, and economic impacts of colonialism. The legacy of colonial policies, such as arbitrary borders, unequal resource distribution, and discriminatory social structures, continued to shape post-colonial societies.

- **International Relations:** The end of empires transformed the geopolitical landscape, with new nations seeking their place in the international community. They had to navigate complex relationships with their former colonial rulers and other global powers, balancing between alliances and asserting their independence.

16 CHAPTER 1: THE WORLD IN THE AFTERMATH OF WORLD WAR II

Case Study: Decolonization in Africa

The decolonization process in Africa provides an insightful case study. Many African countries gained independence in the 1950s and 1960s, following years of resistance to colonial rule. The continent faced unique challenges and opportunities during the decolonization era.

Challenge: Ethnic Divisions A major challenge faced by African nations was the existence of diverse ethnic groups within their borders. Colonial powers often exploited ethnic divisions to maintain control, leading to tensions and conflicts among different ethnic groups. As a result, forging national unity and overcoming these divisions was a significant challenge for newly independent African nations.

Opportunity: Pan-Africanism Pan-Africanism, a movement advocating for the unity and cooperation of African nations, played a crucial role during decolonization. Prominent leaders like Kwame Nkrumah of Ghana and Julius Nyerere of Tanzania championed the idea of a united Africa, transcending ethnic and national boundaries. Pan-Africanism provided a platform for collective action, solidarity, and the promotion of African identity.

Challenge: Economic Dependency Many African nations inherited economic systems that were designed to serve the interests of the colonial powers, leaving them economically dependent. The exploitation of natural resources and the lack of diversification hindered economic development. African leaders faced the challenge of establishing self-sufficient economies and reducing dependency on former colonial powers.

Opportunity: Non-Aligned Movement The Non-Aligned Movement, a coalition of newly independent nations from Africa, Asia, and Latin America, provided an opportunity for African nations to assert their independence on the global stage. By aligning with neither the United States nor the Soviet Union during the Cold War, African countries sought to pursue their own development agendas and maintain their sovereignty.

Challenge: Post-colonial Conflicts Decolonization in Africa was not immune to conflicts and struggles for power. In some cases, ethnic tensions, political rivalries, and struggles over resources led to civil wars and instability. The Congo Crisis, for example, erupted shortly after the Democratic Republic of the Congo gained

SECTION 1: THE POLITICAL LANDSCAPE 17

independence, highlighting the complex challenges faced by newly independent nations.

Opportunity: Pan-African Institutions To address the challenges of decolonization, African nations established pan-African institutions such as the Organization of African Unity (OAU), now known as the African Union (AU). These institutions provided a platform for collective decision-making, conflict resolution, and cooperation on issues of common concern. They played a pivotal role in fostering unity and facilitating regional integration.

In conclusion, decolonization marked a transformative era in modern history. The end of empires and the birth of newly independent nations reshaped global dynamics and ignited a wave of hope for self-determination. However, decolonization also presented numerous challenges for these nations, including nation-building, economic development, and social cohesion. It is essential to study and understand the complex process of decolonization to comprehend the trajectory of the modern world.

Subsection: The Creation of Israel and Middle East Conflict

The creation of Israel and the ongoing conflict in the Middle East has been a pivotal event in contemporary history. This subsection will explore the historical background, key figures, and factors that led to the establishment of the State of Israel and the subsequent conflicts in the region.

Historical Background

The roots of the Israeli-Palestinian conflict can be traced back to the late 19th and early 20th centuries, during the period of intense nationalism and political upheaval in the Middle East. The Zionist movement, led by Jewish intellectuals and activists, emerged with the aim of establishing a Jewish homeland in Palestine, which was then under Ottoman rule.

The Balfour Declaration, issued by the British government in 1917, expressed support for the establishment of a Jewish national home in Palestine. This declaration, combined with other geopolitical factors, set the stage for the eventual creation of Israel.

The Zionist Movement

The Zionist movement gained momentum in the early 20th century, with Jews from Europe and other parts of the world immigrating to Palestine in increasing numbers.

18 CHAPTER 1: THE WORLD IN THE AFTERMATH OF WORLD WAR II

Theodor Herzl, considered the father of modern political Zionism, played a crucial role in advocating for the establishment of a Jewish state.

The Zionist movement faced resistance from the Arab population in Palestine, who saw the establishment of a Jewish state as a threat to their own national aspirations. Tensions between Jews and Arabs escalated over time, leading to clashes and violence.

The British Mandate

Following the end of World War I, the League of Nations granted Britain a mandate over Palestine. The British government struggled to balance the competing interests of Jews and Arabs, as the Zionist movement continued to gather support while the Arab population sought self-determination.

During the British Mandate period, Jewish immigration to Palestine increased, leading to demographic shifts and further exacerbating tensions. The Arab population felt marginalized and oppressed by British policies, leading to widespread protests and uprisings.

The United Nations Partition Plan

In 1947, the United Nations proposed a partition plan for Palestine, dividing the territory into separate Jewish and Arab states. Jerusalem was to be governed separately as an international city.

The partition plan was accepted by Jewish leaders but rejected by Arab leaders, who believed it unfairly favored the Jewish population. The plan failed to bring about a peaceful resolution to the conflict, and instead, it intensified hostilities between the two sides.

The Establishment of Israel

On May 14, 1948, the State of Israel was officially established, leading to immediate military conflicts with neighboring Arab countries. The War of Independence, as it came to be known, resulted in Israel gaining control over a larger portion of Palestine than originally proposed in the UN partition plan.

The establishment of Israel led to the displacement of hundreds of thousands of Palestinians, who became refugees in neighboring Arab countries. This mass displacement remains a central issue in the Israeli-Palestinian conflict today.

SECTION 1: THE POLITICAL LANDSCAPE 19

The Arab-Israeli Conflicts

The creation of Israel sparked a series of conflicts between Israel and its Arab neighbors. The first Arab-Israeli war was followed by a series of wars and conflicts, including the Suez Crisis, the Six-Day War, the Yom Kippur War, and the Lebanon War.

These conflicts have been characterized by territorial disputes, border conflicts, and political tensions. Issues such as the status of Jerusalem, the rights of Palestinian refugees, and the establishment of a Palestinian state continue to be major points of contention.

Peace Process and Challenges

Efforts to resolve the Israeli-Palestinian conflict have been ongoing for decades, with various peace processes and negotiations taking place. The Oslo Accords, signed in 1993, aimed to establish a framework for achieving peace and a two-state solution, but progress has been limited.

Challenges to the peace process include the construction of Israeli settlements in the occupied territories, the status of Jerusalem, the right of return for Palestinian refugees, and the issue of security for both Israelis and Palestinians.

Resources and Further Reading

For further exploration of this topic, the following resources are recommended:

1. "The Arab-Israeli Conflict" by Ian J. Bickerton and Carla L. Klausner: This comprehensive book provides an in-depth analysis of the historical background and key events in the Arab-Israeli conflict.

2. "Palestine: Peace Not Apartheid" by Jimmy Carter: Former President Jimmy Carter offers his perspective on the Israeli-Palestinian conflict and suggests solutions for achieving peace.

3. "A History of Israel: From the Rise of Zionism to Our Time" by Howard M. Sachar: This book provides a detailed account of the history of Israel, from its early Zionist roots to the present day.

4. "The Israel-Arab Reader: A Documentary History of the Middle East Conflict" edited by Walter Laqueur: This collection of primary source documents offers a comprehensive overview of the Arab-Israeli conflict from various perspectives.

In conclusion, the creation of Israel and the Middle East conflict have shaped the modern world in significant ways. Understanding the historical background,

20 CHAPTER 1: THE WORLD IN THE AFTERMATH OF WORLD WAR II

key figures, and ongoing challenges is crucial for gaining insights into this complex issue.

Subsection: The Korean War and the Domino Theory

The Korean War, which took place from 1950 to 1953, was a significant event in contemporary history that had far-reaching consequences on the political landscape of East Asia and the world. This section explores the key aspects of the Korean War and its connection to the Domino Theory.

Background: The Division of Korea

To understand the Korean War, it is essential to examine the context of the division of Korea after World War II. At the end of the war, Korea, which was previously under Japanese rule, was divided into two separate parts along the 38th parallel. The Soviet Union occupied the north, establishing a communist regime under Kim Il-sung, while the United States occupied the south, supporting a democratic government led by Syngman Rhee.

Causes of the Korean War

The Korean War was ignited by a surprise attack launched by North Korea on South Korea on June 25, 1950. However, the underlying causes of the conflict were rooted in the political and ideological divisions between the communist and capitalist powers.

One of the key factors leading to the outbreak of the war was the Domino Theory. This theory, popularized by American policymakers during the Cold War, asserted that if one country in a region fell to communism, neighboring countries would also follow suit, like a row of falling dominos. The fear of communism spreading throughout Asia was a significant concern for the United States, which viewed the Korean War as a crucial battleground in the fight against the spread of communism.

Course of the Korean War

The Korean War can be divided into three distinct phases: the North Korean offensive, the UN counteroffensive, and the stalemate.

The North Korean offensive began with a swift advance by the North Korean People's Army, which quickly captured most of South Korea. The United Nations, led by the United States, intervened to support the South Korean forces. Over

SECTION 1: THE POLITICAL LANDSCAPE

time, the UN counteroffensive managed to push back the North Korean forces and recaptured Seoul.

As the conflict escalated, China entered the war in support of North Korea, vastly increasing the scale of the conflict. The United States responded by carrying out a series of strategic bombing campaigns and naval blockades. Despite heavy fighting and high casualties on both sides, neither the North Korean nor the South Korean forces were able to gain a decisive advantage.

Consequences of the Korean War

The Korean War had significant consequences both regionally and globally. Firstly, it resulted in the maintenance of the division between North and South Korea along the 38th parallel. The two countries remain divided to this day, with tensions and occasional skirmishes persisting.

Secondly, the Korean War solidified the United States' commitment to containing communism and led to its increased military presence in East Asia. The war also served as a catalyst for the formation of alliances, such as the Southeast Asia Treaty Organization (SEATO), which aimed to counter the spread of communism in the region.

Furthermore, the Korean War highlighted the limitations of the global superpowers in pursuing their ideological objectives through direct confrontation. The war demonstrated that the United States and the Soviet Union were unwilling to engage in a direct military conflict, leading to a shift towards proxy wars and covert operations during the Cold War.

Contemporary Relevance: North Korea

The Korean War left a lasting impact on the geopolitical landscape in East Asia, particularly concerning North Korea. The war further isolated North Korea from the international community and solidified its position as a communist regime under dynastic rule.

Today, North Korea continues to be a source of concern due to its pursuit of nuclear weapons and intercontinental ballistic missiles. The ongoing tensions between North Korea and the United States, South Korea, and other regional powers necessitate diplomatic efforts to prevent a resurgence of hostilities.

Conclusion

The Korean War, fueled by Cold War tensions and the Domino Theory, played a critical role in shaping the contemporary history of East Asia. The conflict

22 CHAPTER 1: THE WORLD IN THE AFTERMATH OF WORLD WAR II

highlighted the complexities of ideological confrontation and the limitations of military force in achieving strategic objectives. The legacy of the Korean War continues to reverberate in the current geopolitical dynamics surrounding North Korea, emphasizing the importance of diplomatic efforts and regional stability.

Subsection: The Cuban Revolution and the Spread of Communism

The Cuban Revolution, led by Fidel Castro, is a pivotal event in contemporary history that had a significant impact on the spread of communism in the Western Hemisphere. The revolution, which began in 1953 and culminated in Castro's victory in 1959, marked a turning point in Cuba's political, economic, and social landscape. In this subsection, we will explore the key factors that led to the Cuban Revolution, its aftermath, and its implications for the spread of communism in the region.

Background and Causes

To understand the Cuban Revolution, it is essential to examine the socio-political climate that prevailed in Cuba before Castro's rise to power. For decades, Cuba had been under the authoritarian rule of General Fulgencio Batista, whose regime was marked by corruption, repressive policies, and economic inequality. Additionally, Cuba was heavily influenced by the United States, which maintained close ties with the Batista government and had significant economic interests in the country.

These conditions created a breeding ground for discontent and revolutionary sentiment, especially among the working class and rural population who felt marginalized and exploited. Castro, a young lawyer and Marxist-Leninist, emerged as a charismatic leader who promised to address these grievances and overthrow the Batista regime.

The Cuban Revolution

The Cuban Revolution can be divided into three main phases: the guerrilla war, the seizure of power, and the consolidation of the revolutionary government.

During the guerrilla war, which began in 1956, Castro and a small group of revolutionaries, including Ernesto "Che" Guevara, launched a military campaign against the Batista regime from the Sierra Maestra mountains. Despite facing initial setbacks and a lack of resources, Castro's guerrilla fighters gained popular support and gradually expanded their influence.

In 1959, the revolutionary forces successfully overthrew Batista, leading to Castro assuming power as the Prime Minister of Cuba. The revolution was met

SECTION 1: THE POLITICAL LANDSCAPE

with widespread enthusiasm from the Cuban population, who hoped for radical political and socio-economic changes.

Policies and Ideology

After seizing power, Castro implemented a series of radical policies and reforms that aimed to transform Cuba into a socialist state. The Cuban government nationalized industries, confiscated large landholdings, and implemented agrarian reforms to distribute land to peasants. These measures aimed to address the economic inequality that had plagued Cuba for decades.

Castro's revolutionary government also pursued a foreign policy that aligned with communist ideology. Cuba established close ties with the Soviet Union, receiving economic and military support. This alliance with the Soviet Union and Castro's adoption of Marxist-Leninist principles led to the spread of communism in Cuba and heightened tensions with the United States.

Impact and Legacy

The Cuban Revolution had a profound impact not only on Cuba but also on the geopolitical landscape of the Western Hemisphere. The establishment of a socialist government in a region dominated by capitalist systems challenged the existing power dynamics and sparked fear among anti-communist forces, most notably the United States.

The United States reacted to the Cuban Revolution by imposing economic sanctions, cutting off diplomatic relations, and even attempting to overthrow the Castro government through the failed Bay of Pigs invasion in 1961. This hostile response further solidified Cuba's alignment with the Soviet Union and intensified the Cold War rivalry between the United States and the Soviet bloc.

The Cuban Revolution also served as a source of inspiration for other communist movements in Latin America and beyond. It demonstrated that a small, determined revolutionary force could successfully challenge the status quo and achieve radical social and political change. Throughout the 20th century, several revolutionary movements in Latin America, such as the Sandinista National Liberation Front in Nicaragua and the Farabundo Marti National Liberation Front in El Salvador, drew inspiration from the Cuban Revolution.

Despite its enduring legacy and inspiration for leftist movements, the Cuban Revolution also faced criticism for its authoritarian practices, limitations on civil liberties, and failure to deliver on some of its promises, particularly in the areas of economic development and political pluralism. The revolution's impact on Cuban

24 CHAPTER 1: THE WORLD IN THE AFTERMATH OF WORLD WAR II

society and its relationships with other nations continues to be debated and analyzed.

Contemporary Relevance

The Cuban Revolution and the subsequent spread of communism in the Western Hemisphere have enduring contemporary relevance. The revolution serves as a case study for understanding the dynamics of revolutionary movements, the complexities of ideology and governance, and the geopolitical implications of shifts in power.

Furthermore, the Cuban Revolution reminds us of the enduring tensions and ideological divisions between socialism and capitalism. The ideological struggle between communism and capitalism continues to shape global politics, economic policies, and social movements.

Additionally, the Cuban Revolution raises important questions about the balance between state control and individual freedoms, the role of external powers in supporting or suppressing political movements, and the legacy of revolutions for future generations.

Students of contemporary history can explore these themes and debates, critically analyzing the Cuban Revolution and its implications for the modern world. By studying this pivotal event, students can develop a deeper understanding of the transformative power of revolution and the complexities of socio-political change.

Subsection: The Space Race and the Race for Technology

In the aftermath of World War II, two superpowers emerged: the United States and the Soviet Union. With tensions running high between them, a new competition emerged that would shape the course of history: the Space Race. This subsection explores the significance of the Space Race and how it propelled advancements in technology.

Background: The Cold War Context

The Space Race took place during the Cold War, a time of intense ideological and political rivalry between the United States and the Soviet Union. The two superpowers were locked in a battle for supremacy, seeking to demonstrate their technological prowess and dominate the global stage.

SECTION 1: THE POLITICAL LANDSCAPE 25

The Launch of Sputnik 1

The Space Race officially began on October 4, 1957, when the Soviet Union successfully launched the world's first artificial satellite, Sputnik 1, into space. This achievement stunned the United States and the rest of the world, as it marked the first time a man-made object orbited the Earth.

Implications and Reactions

The launch of Sputnik 1 had profound implications. It demonstrated that the Soviet Union had achieved a significant technological milestone and could potentially launch intercontinental ballistic missiles capable of reaching the United States. This sparked fear and concern within the American government and fueled a sense of urgency to catch up.

In response, the United States established NASA (National Aeronautics and Space Administration) in 1958, with a mission to regain American dominance in space exploration. The U.S. government allocated substantial funding towards scientific research and development, aiming to surpass the Soviet Union in space-related achievements.

Advancements in Technology

The Space Race spurred rapid advancements in various fields of technology that had far-reaching impacts. Some key areas of technological progress include:

1. **Rocket Technology:** Both the United States and the Soviet Union made significant strides in rocket technology. The development of more powerful and efficient rocket engines enabled the launch of manned spaceflight missions.

2. **Satellites and Communication Technology:** The race to put satellites into orbit led to the development of advanced communication technologies. Satellites revolutionized global communication and provided platforms for transmitting television signals, telephone calls, and internet connectivity across vast distances.

3. **Spacecraft and Navigation Systems:** The construction of manned spacecraft, such as the Soviet Union's Vostok and the United States' Mercury capsules, paved the way for human space exploration. Innovations in navigation systems ensured precise guidance and control of spacecraft during missions.

26 CHAPTER 1: THE WORLD IN THE AFTERMATH OF WORLD WAR II

4. Materials Science and Engineering: To withstand the harsh conditions of space, new materials were developed, such as heat-resistant ceramics and lightweight alloys. These advancements in materials science found applications not only in space exploration but also in various other industries.

5. Computers and Data Processing: The need for complex calculations and data analysis during space missions accelerated the development of computers and data processing capabilities. The miniaturization of computers made them more accessible and paved the way for further technological advancements.

Legacy and Lasting Impacts

The Space Race left a lasting legacy and numerous impacts on society and technology:

1. Technological Spin-offs: Many of the technologies developed during the Space Race found applications in everyday life. For example, advancements in miniaturization led to the creation of smaller and more powerful consumer electronics, including laptops and smartphones.

2. Scientific Discoveries: Space exploration provided valuable scientific insights. The study of celestial bodies, the Earth's atmosphere, and the effects of microgravity on the human body contributed to our understanding of the universe and sparked advancements in fields such as astronomy and medicine.

3. National Pride and Unity: The Space Race fostered a sense of national pride and unity within both the United States and the Soviet Union. The achievements in space exploration symbolized the technological prowess and capabilities of the nations, boosting morale and inspiring future generations of scientists and engineers.

4. International Cooperation: While the Space Race was characterized by intense competition, it also led to some collaborative efforts. In later years, the United States and Soviet Union, along with other nations, worked together on projects such as the Apollo-Soyuz Test Project, which served as a symbol of detente and cooperation during the Cold War.

SECTION 1: THE POLITICAL LANDSCAPE

5. Space Exploration: The Space Race laid the foundation for further exploration of space. It paved the way for subsequent manned missions to the Moon, the building of the International Space Station, and the ongoing pursuit of human exploration of Mars and beyond.

Conclusion

The Space Race between the United States and the Soviet Union was a pivotal moment in history that fueled rapid technological advancements. It had wide-ranging impacts, from advancements in rocket technology to the development of communication systems and materials science. The legacy of the Space Race continues to shape our understanding of the universe and inspire future generations to push the boundaries of scientific and technological exploration.

Resources:

1. John M. Logsdon, *The Decision to Go to the Moon: Project Apollo and the National Interest*

2. Walter A. McDougall, *The Heavens and the Earth: A Political History of the Space Age*

3. Roger D. Launius, *Historical Perspectives on the Space Race and Its Legacy*

Exercises:

1. Research and discuss one key technological advancement that resulted from the Space Race and explain its impact on modern society.

2. Compare and contrast the motivations behind the United States and the Soviet Union's participation in the Space Race.

3. Debate the ethics and implications of allocating substantial funding towards space exploration when there are pressing issues on Earth, such as poverty and environmental degradation.

4. Imagine you are living during the Space Race era. Write a diary entry expressing your thoughts about the launch of Sputnik 1 and its implications for the future.

Caveat:

The Space Race was a product of the geopolitical climate of its time. While it yielded significant technological advancements, it is essential to recognize that the competition between nations also had its drawbacks, such as diverting resources from other pressing societal needs. As we explore the history of the Space Race, it

28 CHAPTER 1: THE WORLD IN THE AFTERMATH OF WORLD WAR II

is crucial to critically examine both its achievements and the broader context in which it occurred.

Subsection: The Nuclear Arms Race and the Threat of Mutually Assured Destruction

The Nuclear Arms Race and the concept of Mutually Assured Destruction (MAD) were defining features of the Cold War era. This section explores the historical context, principles of nuclear deterrence, and the potential consequences of nuclear weapons proliferation.

Historical Context

The Nuclear Arms Race can be traced back to the end of World War II when the United States became the first and only country to use atomic bombs. The bombings of Hiroshima and Nagasaki in 1945 demonstrated the devastating power of nuclear weapons and marked the beginning of the nuclear age.

Following the war, the geopolitical landscape was characterized by the ideological divide between the United States and the Soviet Union. Both superpowers sought to build their nuclear arsenals as a means of deterrence and maintaining a balance of power. This competition led to a rapid escalation of nuclear weapons development and the development of strategic doctrines based on the principle of MAD.

Principles of Nuclear Deterrence and MAD

At the core of the Nuclear Arms Race was the concept of nuclear deterrence. The idea behind deterrence theory is that a country possessing a credible and devastating retaliatory capability will deter potential adversaries from launching a nuclear attack. This was the fundamental principle that underpinned MAD.

MAD, which emerged as a theory during the Cold War, posited that if both the United States and the Soviet Union possessed enough nuclear weapons to inflict unacceptable damage on each other, neither would risk launching a first strike. The fear of massive retaliation and the certainty of mutual destruction acted as a deterrent and maintained a delicate balance of power.

Under MAD, the emphasis was on maintaining second-strike capabilities. Both superpowers developed intercontinental ballistic missiles (ICBMs), submarine-launched ballistic missiles (SLBMs), and strategic bombers to ensure survivability and the ability to retaliate even after a devastating first strike. This state of equilibrium became known as the "balance of terror."

SECTION 1: THE POLITICAL LANDSCAPE   29

Consequences of the Nuclear Arms Race

The Nuclear Arms Race had profound implications for international relations and global security. While it prevented a direct military confrontation between the United States and the Soviet Union, it created a state of tension and fear that permeated the entire world.

One of the most significant concerns during the Arms Race was the possibility of accidental or unauthorized nuclear launches. The inherent risks associated with such a high-stakes competition heightened the need for effective command and control systems to prevent unauthorized use and limit the risk of accidental nuclear war.

Moreover, the Arms Race had a detrimental effect on global disarmament efforts. The United States and the Soviet Union amassed vast nuclear arsenals, making it difficult for other countries to argue for nuclear disarmament with any credibility. This led to the proliferation of nuclear weapons, as additional countries sought to acquire nuclear capabilities for their own security.

The Arms Race also had severe economic consequences. Both superpowers allocated significant resources to their nuclear programs, diverting funds away from social and economic development. This diversion of resources contributed to heightened tensions and exacerbated the ideological divide between capitalist and communist states.

Contemporary Challenges and the Future of Nuclear Weapons

While the Cold War ended with the dissolution of the Soviet Union, the threat of nuclear weapons remains a significant concern in the contemporary world. The spread of nuclear technology and the potential for non-state actors to acquire nuclear weapons pose new challenges to global security.

Efforts to curb the proliferation of nuclear weapons have led to the establishment of international treaties and nonproliferation regimes such as the Treaty on the Non-Proliferation of Nuclear Weapons (NPT). However, the existence of nuclear weapons in the hands of several states, including those in geopolitical hotspots, creates ongoing uncertainties.

The threats of nuclear terrorism, accidental launches, and the potential for regional conflicts to escalate into nuclear confrontations continue to be major concerns. International cooperation, diplomatic negotiations, and comprehensive disarmament efforts are vital for mitigating these risks.

In conclusion, the Nuclear Arms Race and the concept of Mutually Assured Destruction shaped the geopolitical landscape of the Cold War era. The principles

30 CHAPTER 1: THE WORLD IN THE AFTERMATH OF WORLD WAR II

of nuclear deterrence and the fear of mutual destruction influenced the actions and strategies of both superpowers. While the end of the Cold War brought some relief, the challenges posed by nuclear weapons in the contemporary world require a renewed commitment to nuclear disarmament and global cooperation.

Subsection: The Fall of the Berlin Wall and the End of the Cold War

The fall of the Berlin Wall in 1989 marked a turning point in contemporary history. This event symbolized the end of the Cold War, a period of political tension and ideological conflict between the United States and the Soviet Union. The fall of the wall not only led to the reunification of East and West Germany but also had far-reaching effects on global politics, economics, and society. In this subsection, we will explore the factors leading to the fall of the Berlin Wall, its significance, and the consequences of the end of the Cold War.

Background: The Division of Berlin

To understand the fall of the Berlin Wall, we must first examine its historical context. After World War II, Germany was divided into two separate nations: the Federal Republic of Germany (West Germany) and the German Democratic Republic (East Germany). The city of Berlin, located deep within East German territory, was also divided into East and West Berlin. West Berlin became an enclave surrounded by the communist East German regime and was supported by the Western Allies, particularly the United States.

The division of Berlin represented a microcosm of the broader East-West divide during the Cold War. The Iron Curtain, a metaphorical barrier separating the communist nations of Eastern Europe from the democratic nations of Western Europe, passed through Berlin. East Berlin was the capital of East Germany, while West Berlin became a symbol of the capitalist West's determination to protect democracy and freedom.

Factors Leading to the Fall of the Berlin Wall

The fall of the Berlin Wall was the result of a combination of internal and external factors. Some of the key factors include:

1. **Internal Opposition:** The East German regime faced increasing opposition from its own citizens due to its repressive policies, lack of political freedom,

SECTION 1: THE POLITICAL LANDSCAPE 31

and economic stagnation. Dissidents and human rights activists played a crucial role in mobilizing public sentiment against the government.

2. **Economic Challenges:** East Germany faced significant economic challenges, with a struggling socialist economy and a large wealth disparity compared to its western counterpart. This further fueled discontent among the East German population.

3. **Soviet Policy Changes:** Mikhail Gorbachev, the General Secretary of the Communist Party of the Soviet Union, introduced a series of reforms known as perestroika (economic restructuring) and glasnost (openness). These policies fostered a more liberal environment and contributed to the overall weakening of the communist ideology.

4. **Mass Protests:** In the months leading up to the fall of the Berlin Wall, mass protests erupted in East Germany. The largest of these protests took place in Leipzig, where thousands of citizens demanded political reform and the right to travel freely.

5. **International Pressure:** Western countries, especially the United States, put pressure on the East German government to address human rights concerns and political reforms. The support of the West played a crucial role in emboldening the opposition movement.

The Fall of the Berlin Wall: A Symbolic Moment

On the evening of November 9, 1989, the East German government announced that citizens would be allowed to travel freely to West Berlin. Thousands of East Berliners flocked to the border crossings, and the overwhelmed border guards eventually opened the checkpoints. As people started crossing the wall, it became apparent that the barriers of division were crumbling.

The fall of the Berlin Wall not only represented the physical reunification of East and West Berlin, but it also symbolized the end of the Cold War. The event captured the imagination of people worldwide and embodied the desire for freedom and the rejection of oppressive regimes. The fall of the Berlin Wall came to represent the triumph of democracy and the power of ordinary citizens to effect change.

Consequences of the End of the Cold War

The end of the Cold War and the fall of the Berlin Wall had significant implications for global politics, economics, and society. Some of the key consequences include:

32 CHAPTER 1: THE WORLD IN THE AFTERMATH OF WORLD WAR II

1. **End of the Bipolar World:** With the collapse of the Soviet Union, the world transitioned from a bipolar world, defined by the competing ideologies of capitalism and communism, to a unipolar world dominated by the United States. This shift in power dynamics reshaped international relations.

2. **Expansion of NATO and the European Union:** The end of the Cold War led to the expansion of NATO, as former Eastern Bloc countries sought to join the alliance. The European Union also expanded, absorbing several former communist countries. These developments aimed to promote stability and cooperation in the region.

3. **Economic Restructuring:** The end of the Cold War brought about significant economic changes. Former socialist countries transitioned to market-oriented economies, leading to both opportunities and challenges. The integration of the global economy accelerated, with the spread of liberal economic policies and free trade agreements.

4. **Democratization and Human Rights:** The end of the Cold War created opportunities for democratization and the promotion of human rights. Former Soviet bloc countries embarked on democratic reforms, although progress varied. Civil liberties expanded, and political participation increased in many parts of the world.

5. **New Security Challenges:** While the end of the Cold War brought about a reduction in nuclear arms, it also gave rise to new security challenges. Non-state actors, such as terrorist organizations, emerged as significant threats. Regional conflicts and ethnic tensions escalated in some regions, requiring new approaches to peacekeeping and conflict resolution.

The Legacy of the Berlin Wall

The fall of the Berlin Wall became a powerful symbol of hope, change, and the resilience of humanity. Today, fragments of the wall are preserved as reminders of the division and subsequent reunification of Germany. The reunified Berlin serves as a testament to the triumph over division and a symbol of the enduring desire for freedom and unity.

The fall of the Berlin Wall and the end of the Cold War continue to shape our world today. It serves as a reminder of the power of grassroots movements, the importance of promoting democracy and human rights, and the need for international cooperation in addressing global challenges. As we navigate the

SECTION 2: ECONOMIC DEVELOPMENTS 33

complexities of the contemporary world, understanding the historical significance of these events can provide valuable insights for building a more peaceful and inclusive future.

Key Takeaways

- The fall of the Berlin Wall in 1989 marked the end of the Cold War and symbolized the reunification of East and West Germany.

- Internal opposition, economic challenges, changes in Soviet policies, mass protests, and international pressure contributed to the fall of the Berlin Wall.

- The event had far-reaching consequences, including the end of the bipolar world, the expansion of NATO and the European Union, economic restructuring, democratization, and new security challenges.

- The fall of the Berlin Wall represents a powerful symbol of hope and unity, reminding us of the need for democracy, human rights, and international cooperation in building a better world.

Summary

The fall of the Berlin Wall in 1989 was a pivotal moment in contemporary history. This subsection examined the background and factors leading to the fall, the significance of the event, and the consequences of the end of the Cold War. The fall of the Berlin Wall marked the reunification of East and West Germany and symbolized the triumph of freedom over oppression. It had wide-ranging effects on global politics, economics, and society, reshaping the world order and paving the way for new challenges and opportunities in the contemporary era.

Section 2: Economic Developments

Subsection: The Bretton Woods System and the Creation of International Financial Institutions

The Bretton Woods system, established in 1944 during the United Nations Monetary and Financial Conference held in Bretton Woods, New Hampshire, played a crucial role in shaping the global financial landscape after World War II. This subsection explores the origins, principles, and impact of the Bretton Woods

34 CHAPTER 1: THE WORLD IN THE AFTERMATH OF WORLD WAR II

system, as well as the creation of international financial institutions that emerged from this landmark agreement.

Background

After the devastation caused by World War II, the international community recognized the need for a new framework for economic cooperation to prevent widespread economic instability and currency fluctuations. The collapse of the gold standard and the rise of economic protectionism during the interwar period highlighted the importance of international monetary cooperation.

The conference at Bretton Woods aimed to establish a stable and predictable monetary system that would facilitate global economic recovery and development. Delegates from 44 countries participated in the negotiations, leading to the creation of the International Monetary Fund (IMF) and the International Bank for Reconstruction and Development (IBRD), now part of the World Bank Group.

Principles of the Bretton Woods System

The Bretton Woods system operated based on several core principles:

1. Fixed Exchange Rates: Under this system, participating countries agreed to fix the value of their currencies to the U.S. dollar, which was pegged to gold. This pegged exchange rate regime aimed to provide stability and prevent competitive devaluations.

2. Convertibility: The participating countries agreed to maintain the convertibility of their currencies into U.S. dollars at a fixed rate. This allowed for smooth international transactions and promotion of trade.

3. Reserve Currency: The U.S. dollar assumed the role of the world's reserve currency, and the IMF played a key role in managing international reserves and stabilizing exchange rates.

4. IMF Surveillance and Conditionality: The IMF was tasked with overseeing member countries' economic policies and providing financial assistance to countries facing balance of payments difficulties. In exchange for financial support, the IMF imposed conditions aimed at promoting economic stability and reforms.

Creation of International Financial Institutions

The Bretton Woods conference gave birth to two key institutions:

1. International Monetary Fund (IMF): The IMF, with its headquarters in Washington, D.C., was established to promote global monetary cooperation, facilitate international trade, and provide financial assistance to member countries.

SECTION 2: ECONOMIC DEVELOPMENTS 35

It aimed to maintain stable exchange rates and promote economic growth and development.

The IMF's primary functions include surveillance of member countries' economies, provision of financial assistance during balance of payments crises, technical assistance, and capacity development. Its decision-making body, the Executive Board, consists of representatives from its 190 member countries.

2. International Bank for Reconstruction and Development (IBRD): The IBRD, now part of the World Bank Group, was created to provide financial support for the reconstruction of war-torn Europe and the development of other member countries. It aimed to promote economic development by offering loans and technical assistance for infrastructure projects, poverty reduction programs, and social development initiatives.

The IBRD raises funds by issuing bonds in international capital markets and lends them to member countries. It also provides policy advice and research to help countries achieve sustainable development.

Impact and Legacy

The Bretton Woods system and the creation of the IMF and the IBRD had a significant impact on the global financial system:

1. Economic Stability: The fixed exchange rate system provided stability and predictability, facilitating international trade and investment. It contributed to the post-war economic recovery and the subsequent period of unprecedented economic growth known as the "Golden Age of Capitalism."

2. Financial Assistance: The IMF played a crucial role in providing financial assistance to member countries experiencing balance of payments problems. Its conditionality requirements aimed to address underlying economic imbalances, promote structural reforms, and steer countries towards sustainable growth.

3. Development Financing: The IBRD supported the reconstruction of war-ravaged countries and funded projects to promote economic development in member nations. Its mission expanded over time to include poverty reduction, social development, and environmental sustainability.

4. Evolution and Challenges: The Bretton Woods system eventually faced challenges, such as the varying economic priorities of member countries, speculative attacks on currencies, and persistent trade imbalances. These challenges led to the breakdown of the fixed exchange rate system in the early 1970s and the shift towards flexible exchange rates.

Overall, the Bretton Woods system and the creation of international financial institutions laid the foundation for the modern global financial order. These

36 CHAPTER 1: THE WORLD IN THE AFTERMATH OF WORLD WAR II

agreements established rules, mechanisms, and institutions to promote economic stability, financial cooperation, and development on an international scale.

Real-World Example: The Asian Financial Crisis

The Asian Financial Crisis of 1997-1998 serves as a notable example highlighting the role of the IMF and the challenges faced by the Bretton Woods system. The crisis, triggered by the devaluation of the Thai baht, spread rapidly to other Southeast Asian economies.

In response, the IMF provided financial assistance packages to affected countries, including Thailand, South Korea, and Indonesia, in exchange for implementing structural reforms. The crisis revealed vulnerabilities in the fixed exchange rate system and the Asian economies' heavy reliance on short-term foreign capital inflows.

Critics argued that the IMF's conditionality requirements exacerbated the crisis by imposing austerity measures that worsened the economic downturn. This event prompted a reevaluation of the role and effectiveness of international financial institutions in managing financial crises and supporting sustainable development.

Further Resources

For further exploration of the Bretton Woods system and its impact, the following resources are recommended:

- Book: "The Battle of Bretton Woods" by Benn Steil provides an in-depth analysis of the Bretton Woods conference and its historical context.

- Documentary: "The Money Masters" directed by Bill Still offers a comprehensive overview of the history of money and the global financial system.

- Website: The IMF website (`www.imf.org`) provides access to a wealth of information, including research papers, publications, and data on member countries' economies.

- Website: The World Bank website (`www.worldbank.org`) offers resources on development projects, research papers, and data on poverty and development indicators.

SECTION 2: ECONOMIC DEVELOPMENTS 37

Key Takeaways

- The Bretton Woods system, established in 1944, aimed to create a stable international monetary system after World War II.

- The system relied on fixed exchange rates, convertibility, the role of the U.S. dollar as a reserve currency, and the surveillance functions of the IMF.

- The IMF provides financial assistance, oversees economic policies, and promotes global monetary cooperation.

- The IBRD, part of the World Bank Group, supports development projects and offers financial assistance for economic growth and poverty reduction.

- The Bretton Woods system played a crucial role in promoting economic stability, facilitating development financing, and establishing the foundations of the modern global financial system.

Exercises

1. Explain why the establishment of the Bretton Woods system was considered necessary after World War II.

2. Discuss the roles of the IMF and the IBRD in the global financial system and the differences between their functions.

3. Critically analyze the challenges faced by the Bretton Woods system and its eventual collapse. How did this impact the global financial landscape?

4. Explore a recent financial crisis or economic downturn. Discuss the role played by the IMF and the IBRD in addressing the crisis and supporting recovery.

5. Research one of the projects funded by the IBRD and discuss its impact on the development of a specific country or region.

Remember to provide detailed explanations and examples in your answers.

Subsection: The Marshall Plan and European Economic Recovery

The Marshall Plan, officially known as the European Recovery Program (ERP), was an ambitious initiative launched by the United States in the aftermath of World War II. It aimed to provide economic assistance to war-torn European countries, primarily those in Western Europe, to aid in their recovery and prevent the spread of communism. In this subsection, we will explore the background of the Marshall Plan, its implementation, and its impact on European economic recovery.

38 CHAPTER 1: THE WORLD IN THE AFTERMATH OF WORLD WAR II

Background

By the end of World War II, Europe was left devastated, both physically and economically. Infrastructure was destroyed, industries were crippled, and millions of people were displaced or left without basic necessities. Additionally, the threat of communism was looming, with the Soviet Union exerting its influence over Eastern Europe. In this context, the United States recognized the need to assist in the reconstruction of Europe to ensure stability, promote democratic values, and establish markets for American goods.

Implementation

The Marshall Plan was announced by U.S. Secretary of State George C. Marshall in a speech at Harvard University on June 5, 1947. It proposed that the United States would provide substantial financial aid and technical assistance to European countries that were willing to cooperate in the implementation of a comprehensive recovery program.

Under the plan, European nations were invited to submit detailed recovery plans outlining their economic needs. The U.S. Congress eventually passed the Economic Cooperation Act of 1948, which authorized the provision of funds to these countries. Over the course of four years, from 1948 to 1952, the United States allocated approximately $13 billion (equivalent to around $130 billion today) in economic aid to European countries.

The funds provided by the Marshall Plan were used to support a wide range of initiatives, including the reconstruction of infrastructure, the modernization of industry, the improvement of agriculture, and the promotion of trade. Technical assistance was also provided to help European countries develop sound economic policies, improve administrative capacities, and foster regional cooperation.

Impact

The implementation of the Marshall Plan had a profound impact on European economic recovery. It helped stabilize European economies, fostered economic growth, and strengthened political and social stability in the region. The aid provided by the United States not only contributed to the physical reconstruction of Europe but also helped stimulate industrial production, promote trade, and create employment opportunities.

One of the key achievements of the Marshall Plan was the revitalization of European agriculture. The funds provided helped modernize farming techniques, improve infrastructure, and increase agricultural productivity. This not only

SECTION 2: ECONOMIC DEVELOPMENTS 39

ensured food security but also provided a foundation for long-term economic development.

The Marshall Plan also played a crucial role in the development of modern European institutions. The need to coordinate and manage the aid received led to the establishment of the Organization for European Economic Cooperation (OEEC), which served as a platform for cooperation among European countries. The OEEC eventually evolved into the Organization for Economic Cooperation and Development (OECD), which continues to promote economic development and cooperation among its member countries.

Additionally, the Marshall Plan contributed to the formation of a stronger transatlantic alliance and set the stage for the future integration of Europe. The economic interdependence fostered by the plan laid the groundwork for the European Coal and Steel Community (ECSC), which was the precursor to the European Union.

Challenges and Controversies

While the Marshall Plan was generally viewed as a success, it was not without its challenges and controversies. Some European countries were initially skeptical of the plan, fearing that it would lead to American domination or erode their sovereignty. Others, particularly the Soviet Union and its allies, saw it as a tool for American imperialism and a threat to their influence in Eastern Europe.

There were also debates about the conditions attached to the aid provided under the Marshall Plan. The United States required recipient countries to liberalize trade, reduce barriers to investment, and adopt market-oriented economic policies. These conditions were seen by some as an attempt to reshape the economic systems of the recipient countries according to American interests.

Furthermore, the Marshall Plan faced logistical challenges in delivering aid effectively and ensuring its efficient use. Coordinating the distribution of resources, managing complex programs, and addressing the diverse needs of different countries presented significant administrative and logistical hurdles.

Conclusion

The Marshall Plan remains a landmark initiative in the history of international aid and economic development. It demonstrated the United States' commitment to supporting the recovery of war-torn European countries and laid the foundation for the economic and political transformation of the continent. By fostering economic growth, promoting trade, and strengthening ties between nations, the

4CHAPTER 1: THE WORLD IN THE AFTERMATH OF WORLD WAR II

Marshall Plan played a crucial role in Europe's post-war recovery and set the stage for the unprecedented period of peace and prosperity that followed.

Subsection: The Rise of Multinational Corporations and Globalization

The rise of multinational corporations (MNCs) and the phenomenon of globalization have had a profound impact on the modern world. In this section, we will explore how MNCs have transformed the global economy, the challenges they present, and the opportunities they bring.

Overview of Multinational Corporations

A multinational corporation is a company that operates in multiple countries, with a centralized management structure and substantial assets and operations in various locations. These corporations typically have headquarters in one country but conduct business activities in several others.

One of the main drivers behind the rise of MNCs is globalization. Globalization refers to the increasing interconnectedness and interdependence of economies and societies across the world. Advances in technology, transportation, and communication have made it easier for MNCs to expand their operations globally.

MNCs play a crucial role in the global economy by driving economic growth, creating jobs, and facilitating the transfer of technology and knowledge across borders. They often have significant financial resources, advanced technology, and access to international markets, giving them a competitive edge over smaller, locally-based businesses.

Benefits and Opportunities of MNCs

The rise of MNCs has brought numerous benefits and opportunities to both home and host countries. Let's explore some of the major advantages:

1. **Economic Growth and Development:** Multinational corporations contribute significantly to economic growth in host countries by attracting foreign direct investment (FDI). This investment helps to create new industries, improve infrastructure, and enhance productivity, which in turn leads to job creation and higher living standards.

SECTION 2: ECONOMIC DEVELOPMENTS 41

2. **Technological Advancement and Innovation:** MNCs are often at the forefront of research and development, driving technological advancements in various sectors. Their global presence allows them to tap into diverse pools of talent, knowledge, and resources, leading to innovations that benefit both the home and host countries.

3. **Access to International Markets:** MNCs provide access to global markets for host country businesses, enabling them to expand their reach and increase exports. This increased integration into the global economy can lead to higher export revenues, foreign exchange earnings, and improved competitiveness.

4. **Skills and Knowledge Transfer:** MNCs bring with them expertise, best practices, and managerial skills that can be transferred to local employees and businesses. This knowledge transfer contributes to the development of human capital, fostering competitiveness and economic diversification.

Challenges and Concerns

While multinational corporations offer many advantages, they also pose challenges and concerns that need to be addressed. Let's discuss some of the key issues:

1. **Profit Maximization vs. Social Responsibility:** MNCs are primarily driven by profit maximization, which can sometimes lead to unethical practices, such as tax evasion, labor exploitation, or environmental degradation. Balancing profit motives with social responsibility is a crucial challenge that needs to be addressed through regulations and corporate governance mechanisms.

2. **Inequality and Exploitation:** MNCs' operations can exacerbate income inequality within host countries. They often pay higher wages to employees in developed countries while exploiting cheap labor in developing countries. This disparity can lead to social tensions and exploitation of local populations if not properly regulated.

3. **Loss of Local Businesses:** The presence of MNCs may lead to the displacement or closure of local businesses that cannot compete with their global reach and economies of scale. This can have adverse effects on small and medium-sized enterprises, local industries, and cultural diversity.

4. **Environmental Impacts:** MNCs, especially those in resource-intensive industries, can have significant environmental impacts. Issues such as deforestation, pollution, and the depletion of natural resources can arise if

42 CHAPTER 1: THE WORLD IN THE AFTERMATH OF WORLD WAR II

adequate environmental regulations and sustainability practices are not enforced.

Regulations and Mitigation Strategies

To address the challenges associated with the rise of multinational corporations, governments and international organizations have implemented various regulations and mitigation strategies. Let's explore a few:

1. **International Agreements and Standards:** International organizations such as the United Nations, World Trade Organization, and International Labor Organization work towards setting standards and regulations that promote responsible business practices. Agreements like the United Nations Global Compact provide guidelines for ethical behavior in the areas of human rights, labor, environment, and anti-corruption.

2. **Corporate Social Responsibility (CSR):** Many MNCs have adopted CSR initiatives voluntarily to mitigate the negative impacts of their operations. These initiatives involve actions such as environmental sustainability programs, fair labor practices, and community development projects.

3. **Government Regulations:** Governments of both home and host countries can implement regulations to ensure that MNCs operate responsibly. These regulations may cover areas such as labor rights, environmental protection, tax compliance, and intellectual property rights.

4. **Strengthening Local Industries and SMEs:** Governments can support local industries and small and medium-sized enterprises (SMEs) to foster competitiveness. This can be done through access to finance, capacity-building programs, technology transfer, and establishing preferential policies for domestic businesses.

Case Study: The Impact of Multinational Corporations on Developing Countries

To illustrate the impact of MNCs on developing countries, let's consider the case of Nike's manufacturing operations in Southeast Asia. Nike, a leading global sportswear company, sources its products from Asian countries such as Vietnam, Indonesia, and Thailand.

The presence of Nike's manufacturing facilities in these countries has contributed to economic growth by creating employment opportunities and

SECTION 2: ECONOMIC DEVELOPMENTS

attracting foreign investment. However, concerns have been raised regarding labor conditions, such as low wages, long working hours, and poor safety standards.

To address these issues, Nike implemented a series of measures, including the establishment of the Fair Labor Association in 1999. This initiative aimed to improve labor conditions by monitoring and inspecting factories, implementing codes of conduct, and providing training for workers.

The Nike case study highlights the complex nature of MNCs' impact on developing countries. While they bring economic benefits, efforts must be made to ensure fair labor practices and improve working conditions through collaboration between MNCs, governments, and civil society organizations.

Conclusion

The rise of multinational corporations and globalization has revolutionized the modern world. MNCs are powerful economic actors that have the potential to bring numerous benefits through economic growth, technological advancement, and international market access. However, they also raise concerns related to social responsibility, inequality, and environmental impacts.

By implementing effective regulations, fostering responsible business practices, and supporting local industries, governments and international organizations can mitigate the challenges associated with MNCs. This will help maximize the benefits of globalization for both home and host countries, leading to inclusive and sustainable development.

The rise of multinational corporations and the ongoing process of globalization have both positive and negative consequences. It is important for students and scholars to understand the complexities of this phenomenon and its implications for various stakeholders. By critically analyzing these issues, we can strive towards a more equitable and sustainable global economy.

Subsection: The Oil Crisis and the Rise of OPEC

The oil crisis of the 1970s had a profound impact on the global economy, leading to skyrocketing oil prices, energy shortages, and significant geopolitical shifts. This crisis was a pivotal moment in contemporary history, and it marked the rise of the Organization of the Petroleum Exporting Countries (OPEC) as a powerful force in the international oil market. In this subsection, we will explore the causes and consequences of the oil crisis, the role of OPEC in shaping global energy policies, and the long-term implications for both oil-producing and oil-consuming nations.

CHAPTER 1: THE WORLD IN THE AFTERMATH OF WORLD WAR II

Background of the Oil Crisis

The oil crisis of the 1970s was triggered by a series of events that disrupted the stability of the global oil market. One of the main factors was the Arab-Israeli conflict, particularly the Yom Kippur War in 1973. In response to the military support that the United States provided to Israel during the war, the Arab members of OPEC, including Saudi Arabia, imposed an oil embargo on the United States and other Western nations. This embargo led to a significant reduction in oil supply and caused a sudden spike in oil prices.

OPEC: Formation and Objectives

OPEC was founded in 1960 by five oil-producing countries: Iran, Iraq, Kuwait, Saudi Arabia, and Venezuela. Its primary objective was to coordinate and unify the petroleum policies of its member countries and ensure the stabilization of oil markets. However, it was the oil crisis of the 1970s that propelled OPEC into the global spotlight.

Immediate Consequences

The oil crisis had immediate and far-reaching consequences for both oil-producing and oil-consuming nations. The sudden increase in oil prices led to inflation, economic recession, and worsened trade balances for many countries. Oil-consuming nations faced energy shortages and had to implement strict energy conservation measures. The crisis also exposed the vulnerability of industrialized nations, which were heavily reliant on imported oil.

Shift in the Balance of Power

The oil crisis marked a significant shift in the balance of power in the global economy. OPEC emerged as a powerful cartel that could influence oil prices and production levels. By controlling the supply of oil, OPEC member countries gained economic and political leverage over the rest of the world. Additionally, the crisis highlighted the strategic importance of the Middle East, where most of the world's oil reserves were concentrated.

Long-Term Implications

The oil crisis had long-lasting effects on energy policies, international relations, and economic development. It prompted many countries to invest heavily in alternative

SECTION 2: ECONOMIC DEVELOPMENTS 45

energy sources and promote energy efficiency measures. The crisis also led to the diversification of oil-importing countries' energy sources, reducing their dependence on OPEC oil.

In response to the crisis, non-OPEC countries, such as the United States, intensified their domestic oil production efforts to become more self-sufficient. This shift towards energy independence had significant implications for both global geopolitics and environmental concerns.

Contemporary Challenges

While the oil crisis of the 1970s is now a part of history, the challenges it presented are still relevant today. The world continues to grapple with issues such as energy security, the transition to renewable energy sources, and the need to address climate change. Moreover, OPEC remains a key player in the global oil market, and its decisions continue to have a significant impact on oil prices and supply.

Case Study: The Impact on the United States

The United States was one of the most severely affected countries during the oil crisis. The sharp rise in oil prices led to long lines at gas stations, skyrocketing inflation, and a decline in economic growth. As a response, the U.S. government implemented measures to reduce dependence on foreign oil, such as investing in domestic oil production and promoting energy conservation policies. These efforts helped the United States become more energy independent and resilient in the face of future oil shocks.

Conclusion

The oil crisis of the 1970s and the subsequent rise of OPEC had a profound impact on the global economy, energy policies, and international relations. It exposed the vulnerabilities of oil-dependent nations and led to fundamental changes in energy strategies worldwide. The lessons learned from this crisis continue to shape contemporary debates on energy security, sustainability, and the future of global energy markets. As we delve deeper into the transformative events, key figures, and revolutionary ideas that have shaped the modern world, the oil crisis and the rise of OPEC will undoubtedly stand out as a pivotal moment in contemporary history.

CHAPTER 1: THE WORLD IN THE AFTERMATH OF WORLD WAR II

Subsection: The Asian Tigers and the Shift of Economic Power

The Asian Tigers refer to the highly developed economies of Hong Kong, Singapore, South Korea, and Taiwan. These economies experienced rapid industrialization and robust economic growth during the latter half of the 20th century, leading to a significant shift in global economic power. In this subsection, we will explore the key factors that contributed to the rise of the Asian Tigers and the implications of their economic success.

Background

Following World War II, many countries in Asia faced the challenge of rebuilding their economies and achieving sustainable growth. The Asian Tigers emerged as stellar examples of countries that successfully transformed from low-income agrarian societies to high-income industrial economies within a short span of time. Their remarkable economic performance has been attributed to a combination of factors, including strategic government policies, strong focus on export-oriented industries, investment in human capital, and technological advancements.

Government Policies and Market Orientation

One of the critical factors behind the success of the Asian Tigers was their adoption of market-oriented economic policies coupled with robust government intervention. These countries implemented policies that promoted free trade, encouraged foreign direct investment (FDI), and created conducive business environments. They facilitated the growth of export-oriented industries by providing tax incentives, infrastructure development, and streamlined administrative procedures.

Example: Industrial Promotion Policies in South Korea South Korea, for instance, implemented the "Export-Oriented Industrialization" policy, which focused on attracting foreign investment and promoting industries with high export potential, such as electronics, automobiles, and petrochemicals. Government support in the form of tax incentives, subsidies, and financial assistance to exporters played a crucial role in stimulating rapid industrialization.

Investment in Human Capital

Another key factor in the success of the Asian Tigers was their emphasis on education and human resource development. Recognizing the importance of

SECTION 2: ECONOMIC DEVELOPMENTS

skilled labor in driving economic growth, these countries invested heavily in education, vocational training, and research and development (R&D) initiatives. This investment in human capital helped create a highly skilled and productive workforce, fueling innovation and technological advancements.

Example: Singapore's SkillsFuture Initiative Singapore's SkillsFuture initiative is a recent example of investing in human capital. It aims to provide individuals with lifelong learning opportunities, ensuring that the workforce remains adaptable and equipped with the necessary skills to thrive in a rapidly changing economy. By encouraging continuous learning and upskilling, Singapore aims to maintain its competitive edge in the global market.

Technological Advancements and Innovation

The Asian Tigers recognized the importance of technological advancements in driving economic growth and competitiveness. These countries actively promoted research and development, encouraged innovation, and invested in infrastructure to support technological advancements. They focused on developing high-tech industries and leveraging emerging technologies to increase productivity and efficiency.

Example: Taiwan's Semiconductor Industry Taiwan's success in the semiconductor industry is a testament to its commitment to technological advancements. The government actively supported the development of semiconductor manufacturing through the establishment of dedicated research institutes, providing tax incentives, and fostering collaboration between universities, research institutions, and the private sector. Today, Taiwan is one of the leading producers of semiconductors globally.

Implications of the Asian Tigers' Economic Success

The economic success of the Asian Tigers had profound implications for the global economy and the shift of economic power. These countries transformed from aid recipients to major contributors to global trade and investment. Their rapid industrialization and export-oriented growth strategies challenged the dominance of Western economies and reshaped the global economic landscape.

Trade Integration The Asian Tigers' success in export-oriented industries led to their increased participation in global trade networks. Their specialization in

48 CHAPTER 1: THE WORLD IN THE AFTERMATH OF WORLD WAR II

high-value-added manufacturing and technological products contributed to the development of global supply chains.

Example: South Korea's Samsung Electronics South Korea's Samsung Electronics, a prominent player in the global technology market, exemplifies the Asian Tigers' impact on global trade. Samsung's dominance in the smartphone and semiconductor markets demonstrates the ability of these economies to compete on a global scale and challenge traditional industry leaders.

Regional Economic Cooperation The rise of the Asian Tigers also spurred regional economic cooperation in Asia. The Association of Southeast Asian Nations (ASEAN) and other regional frameworks were established to promote trade, investment, and collaboration among Asian economies.

Example: ASEAN Economic Community The ASEAN Economic Community (AEC) aims to create a single market and production base among its member countries. It fosters regional integration, facilitates the movement of goods, services, and skilled labor, and promotes economic cooperation within Southeast Asia. The success of the Asian Tigers has provided a model for the integration and economic development of other Southeast Asian nations.

Conclusion

The Asian Tigers' economic success can be attributed to their adoption of market-oriented policies, investment in human capital, and emphasis on technological advancements. Their rapid industrialization and export-oriented growth strategies have reshaped the global economic landscape and facilitated a shift in economic power. The implications of their success extend beyond their own economies, contributing to global trade integration and regional economic cooperation. Understanding the lessons learned from the Asian Tigers can provide valuable insights for countries aspiring to achieve economic transformation and sustainable growth in the 21st century.

Subsection: The Rise of Neoliberalism and Free Market Ideology

Neoliberalism is an economic ideology that advocates for a free-market system with limited government intervention. It gained prominence in the late 20th century and has been influential in shaping economic policies around the world. This subsection

SECTION 2: ECONOMIC DEVELOPMENTS

will explore the key ideas and factors that contributed to the rise of neoliberalism, as well as its impact on societies and economies.

1. Background and Principles of Neoliberalism: Neoliberalism emerged as a reaction to the perceived failures of Keynesian economics, which advocated for government intervention in the economy to promote stability and ensure economic growth. Neoliberalism challenged this notion and promoted the idea that free markets are the most efficient means of allocating resources. The principles of neoliberalism include:

1.1 Free Market Ideology: Neoliberalism places a high value on free markets, arguing that they lead to efficient resource allocation and economic growth. According to this perspective, the role of the state should be limited to maintaining law and order, enforcing contracts, and protecting property rights.

1.2 Individual Liberty and Choice: Neoliberalism emphasizes individual freedom and choice, believing that individuals should have the freedom to pursue their own economic interests without interference from the state. This includes the freedom to start businesses, enter into contracts, and make choices regarding consumption and investment.

1.3 Deregulation and Privatization: Neoliberal policies often involve reducing government regulations and promoting privatization. The belief is that removing barriers to entry and competition will lead to increased efficiency and productivity.

1.4 Fiscal Responsibility: Neoliberalism emphasizes the importance of balanced budgets and low government debt. It promotes fiscal austerity measures such as reducing government spending and lowering taxes in order to create a favorable business environment.

2. Factors Contributing to the Rise of Neoliberalism: The rise of neoliberalism can be attributed to several key factors:

2.1 Economic Crises: The stagflation of the 1970s and the subsequent economic crises in many countries led to a loss of faith in Keynesian economics. Neoliberalism presented an alternative approach that promised to address these issues through market-based solutions.

2.2 Influence of Economists: Prominent economists such as Milton Friedman and Friedrich Hayek played a significant role in popularizing neoliberal ideas. Their advocacy for free markets and limited government intervention resonated with policymakers and the general public.

2.3 Political Shifts: Political shifts towards conservatism and right-wing ideologies in the 1980s and 1990s created a favorable environment for the implementation of neoliberal policies. Leaders such as Margaret Thatcher in the UK and Ronald Reagan in the US embraced neoliberalism and implemented sweeping economic reforms.

CHAPTER 1: THE WORLD IN THE AFTERMATH OF WORLD WAR II

2.4 Globalization and Advances in Technology: The increasing interconnectedness of economies and rapid technological advancements facilitated the spread of neoliberalism. Free trade agreements and the growth of multinational corporations furthered the adoption of neoliberal policies.

3. Impact of Neoliberalism:

3.1 Economic Growth and Prosperity: Supporters of neoliberalism argue that it has led to increased economic growth and prosperity in many countries. They point to examples such as the rapid economic development of East Asian economies and the success of countries like Chile, which embraced neoliberal reforms.

3.2 Rising Income Inequality: Critics of neoliberalism argue that it has contributed to rising income inequality. The reduction of social welfare programs and the emphasis on market forces can lead to a concentration of wealth in the hands of a few, exacerbating social disparities.

3.3 Financial Crises: Neoliberal policies have also been associated with financial instability. Deregulated financial systems and the pursuit of profit without sufficient oversight can create conditions conducive to speculative bubbles and financial crises, such as the 2008 global financial crisis.

3.4 Social Impacts: Neoliberalism has had varying social impacts across different societies. Some argue that it has led to the erosion of workers' rights, weakened labor unions, and increased job insecurity. Others contend that it has empowered individuals through increased consumer choice and entrepreneurial opportunities.

4. Challenges and Criticisms of Neoliberalism:

4.1 Lack of Social Safety Nets: Critics argue that neoliberalism prioritizes market efficiency over social welfare, leading to insufficient safety nets for vulnerable populations. This has been particularly evident in cases where privatization of public services has resulted in reduced access and affordability.

4.2 Environmental Concerns: Neoliberalism's focus on economic growth and deregulation has been criticized for its negative impact on the environment. The pursuit of profit often comes at the expense of sustainable practices and the protection of natural resources.

4.3 Inequality and Social Justice: Neoliberalism has been criticized for exacerbating income inequality and undermining social justice goals. The concentration of wealth in the hands of a few can limit equal opportunities and social mobility, leading to societal tensions and unrest.

In conclusion, the rise of neoliberalism was influenced by a combination of economic, political, and social factors. While it has been associated with economic growth, it has also faced criticism for its impact on income inequality and social

SECTION 2: ECONOMIC DEVELOPMENTS 51

welfare. The ongoing debate surrounding neoliberalism highlights the complexities and trade-offs involved in economic policymaking.

Subsection: The Dotcom Bubble and the Rise of the Internet Economy

The Dotcom Bubble refers to the speculative frenzy and subsequent collapse of internet-related companies in the late 1990s and early 2000s. This period witnessed an unprecedented surge in the valuation of internet startups, driven by investors' high expectations of future profits. However, many of these companies had flawed business models and inadequate revenue streams, leading to a market correction and significant financial losses.

Background

The emergence of the Dotcom Bubble can be attributed to several factors. First, the rapid growth of the internet in the 1990s fueled a sense of optimism and a belief in the transformative power of technology. The widespread adoption of the World Wide Web opened up new possibilities for e-commerce, communication, and information sharing.

Additionally, the availability of venture capital funding, coupled with the perception that internet startups offered unmatched growth potential, led to a surge in investment in these companies. The allure of quick and substantial returns attracted both traditional investors and individual speculators, creating a speculative bubble.

The Rise of the Internet Economy

The Dotcom Bubble coincided with the rise of the internet economy, which refers to the economic activities and industries enabled by the internet and digital technologies. This period saw the emergence and growth of numerous internet-based companies across various sectors, including e-commerce, online services, content platforms, and technology infrastructure.

E-commerce experienced unprecedented growth during this time. Companies like Amazon and eBay revolutionized retail by offering a convenient and efficient online shopping experience. This led to a shift in consumer behavior, with an increasing number of people opting for online purchases over traditional brick-and-mortar stores. The internet also facilitated the rise of online advertising, as companies realized the potential to reach a global audience through digital platforms.

The Dotcom Bubble also saw the development of online services, such as search engines, social networking sites, and online media platforms. Google emerged as the dominant search engine, while companies like Facebook and YouTube revolutionized social interactions and content consumption. The explosion of online content created new opportunities for advertising and monetization.

Furthermore, the rise of the internet economy necessitated robust technology infrastructure. Companies invested heavily in building data centers, network infrastructure, and software applications to support the growing demands of the internet. This led to the development of cloud computing and scalable technologies, which form the foundation of the modern digital economy.

Issues and Challenges

Despite the immense growth and potential of the internet economy, the Dotcom Bubble revealed several challenges and vulnerabilities within the sector. Many internet companies were driven more by hype and speculation than sound business fundamentals. Business models that relied on continuous user growth and high advertising revenues ultimately proved unsustainable.

Additionally, the Dotcom Bubble exposed the risks associated with overvaluation and market speculation. Investors poured billions of dollars into internet startups without proper due diligence, resulting in significant financial losses when the bubble burst. The subsequent market correction led to a loss of confidence in the internet sector and a decline in investment.

Lessons Learned

The Dotcom Bubble served as a valuable lesson in the importance of sound business strategies and sustainable revenue models. It highlighted the need for prudent investment practices and a critical evaluation of companies' future prospects. Investors became more cautious and focused on companies with solid financial fundamentals, profitability, and a clear path to sustainable growth.

The internet economy, on the other hand, emerged stronger from the Dotcom Bubble. The collapse of numerous internet companies led to a consolidation within the sector, with more robust and sustainable businesses surviving and thriving. This led to a greater emphasis on profitability and economic viability in the internet industry, laying the foundation for the subsequent growth of successful internet giants.

SECTION 2: ECONOMIC DEVELOPMENTS 53

Contemporary Relevance

The lessons learned from the Dotcom Bubble continue to be relevant in today's technology-driven economy. The rise of internet-based companies, such as Uber, Airbnb, and Spotify, demonstrates the ongoing impact of the internet economy on various sectors. Investors, entrepreneurs, and policymakers continue to grapple with questions of valuation, business sustainability, and regulatory frameworks in the digital age.

Moreover, the Dotcom Bubble serves as a reminder of the volatility and risks associated with emerging technologies and rapid market speculation. It underscores the need for responsible investment practices, thorough risk analysis, and a balanced approach to innovation and financial prudence.

Conclusion

The Dotcom Bubble was a pivotal event in the history of the internet economy. It marked the speculative frenzy and subsequent collapse of many internet startups, leading to a market correction and valuable lessons learned. While the bubble exposed vulnerabilities and risks within the sector, it also paved the way for the growth and maturation of the internet economy. Today, the internet economy continues to thrive, with a greater emphasis on sustainability, profitability, and responsible investment practices.

Subsection: The Global Financial Crisis of 2008 and its Aftermath

The Global Financial Crisis of 2008 was one of the most significant economic downturns in history. It had far-reaching effects on the global economy, leading to a recession and causing widespread social and economic distress. In this subsection, we will explore the causes of the crisis, its impact on various sectors, and the measures taken to mitigate its effects.

Causes of the Crisis

The roots of the financial crisis can be traced back to a combination of factors, including deregulation, excessive risk-taking, and unsustainable lending practices. One of the key catalysts was the bursting of the United States housing bubble, which had been fueled by easy access to credit and the securitization of mortgage debt.

Financial institutions began to experience significant losses as mortgage defaults increased, leading to a reassessment of the value of mortgage-backed securities. This, in turn, led to a lack of trust in the financial system as banks became wary of lending to each other. The resulting liquidity crisis shook the global financial markets and triggered a chain reaction that spread to other sectors of the economy.

Impact on the Financial Sector

The crisis had a severe impact on the financial sector, with several major banks and financial institutions facing insolvency or requiring government bailouts to stay afloat. The collapse of Lehman Brothers, one of the largest investment banks, sent shockwaves throughout the industry and further exacerbated the crisis.

Credit markets froze as banks became reluctant to lend, leading to a credit crunch that affected businesses and consumers alike. Stock markets plummeted, wiping out trillions of dollars in market value and eroding investor confidence. The crisis also exposed the interconnectedness of the global financial system, as the failure of one institution could have a cascading effect on others.

Impact on the Real Economy

The crisis had a profound impact on the real economy, with many countries experiencing a sharp decline in economic growth and increased unemployment. As credit became scarce, businesses struggled to secure financing, leading to layoffs and reduced investment. Consumer spending, a key driver of economic activity, declined as households faced tighter credit conditions and falling asset values.

The housing market, which had been at the center of the crisis, also suffered greatly. Home prices declined, leaving many homeowners with negative equity and facing foreclosure. The construction industry, heavily dependent on the housing market, saw a significant downturn, leading to job losses and further economic distress.

Government Intervention and Policy Responses

Governments around the world took swift and decisive action to prevent a complete collapse of the financial system and stimulate economic growth. Central banks injected liquidity into the markets and lowered interest rates to encourage borrowing and investment. Governments implemented fiscal stimulus measures, including increased government spending and tax cuts, to boost demand and support struggling businesses.

Regulatory reforms were also introduced to address the weaknesses in the financial system exposed by the crisis. Stricter regulations were put in place to promote greater transparency, enhance risk management practices, and prevent

SECTION 2: ECONOMIC DEVELOPMENTS 55

excessive risk-taking. International coordination among regulatory authorities was strengthened to ensure a more robust and resilient financial system.

Lessons Learned and Future Implications

The global financial crisis of 2008 highlighted the need for greater oversight and regulation of the financial sector. It exposed the systemic risks posed by interconnected financial institutions and the dangers of excessive leverage and risk-taking. The crisis also emphasized the importance of effective risk management and the need for strong consumer protection measures.

Furthermore, the crisis served as a wake-up call for governments and policymakers to address income inequality and social disparities. It underscored the importance of creating an inclusive and sustainable economy that benefits all segments of society.

In conclusion, the Global Financial Crisis of 2008 had a profound and lasting impact on the global economy. It revealed the vulnerabilities in the financial system and led to significant changes in regulation and policymaking. While the world has since recovered from the immediate effects of the crisis, its lessons continue to shape economic and financial decision-making processes. It serves as a reminder of the importance of sound economic fundamentals, prudent risk management, and the need for ongoing vigilance in safeguarding the stability of the global economy.

Subsection: The Rise of China as an Economic Superpower

The rise of China as an economic superpower has been one of the most significant developments in contemporary history. Over the past few decades, China has experienced remarkable economic growth and has emerged as a major player in the global economy. In this subsection, we will explore the factors that contributed to China's rise, the challenges it faced along the way, and the implications of its ascent for both China and the world.

Background:

China's economic transformation can be traced back to the late 1970s when the country embarked on a series of economic reforms known as "The Four Modernizations." These reforms aimed to shift China from a centrally planned economy to a market-oriented one, promoting economic liberalization, foreign investment, and technological innovation. Deng Xiaoping, China's paramount leader at the time, played a crucial role in initiating these reforms.

CHAPTER 1: THE WORLD IN THE AFTERMATH OF WORLD WAR II

China's Economic Growth:

China's economic growth has been nothing short of astonishing. With an average annual growth rate of around 10% over the past four decades, China has lifted millions of people out of poverty and become the world's second-largest economy. This rapid economic expansion can be attributed to several key factors:

1. **Investment in Infrastructure:** China has heavily invested in infrastructure development, including transportation networks, energy systems, and communication networks. This has facilitated economic activities and attracted foreign investment.

2. **Export-Oriented Economy:** China has adopted an export-oriented approach, becoming the world's largest exporter of goods. Its low-cost labor, large domestic market, and supportive government policies have made it an attractive destination for companies looking to outsource manufacturing.

3. **Foreign Direct Investment (FDI):** China has attracted significant foreign investment, primarily due to its massive consumer market and the availability of cheap labor. Foreign companies have set up production facilities in China to tap into its growing domestic demand.

4. **Technology and Innovation:** China has made significant strides in technological advancements and innovation. It has invested heavily in research and development, leading to breakthroughs in various sectors such as telecommunications, e-commerce, and renewable energy.

Challenges Faced by China:

While China's economic rise has been impressive, it has not come without challenges. Some of the main challenges China has faced in its journey towards becoming an economic superpower include:

1. **Income Inequality:** China's economic growth has resulted in a significant wealth gap between urban and rural areas, as well as between different regions within the country. The government has recognized this issue and has implemented policies to address inequality, but it remains a persistent challenge.

2. **Environmental Concerns:** China's rapid industrialization has taken a toll on its environment. Pollution levels, particularly air pollution, have reached

SECTION 2: ECONOMIC DEVELOPMENTS

alarming levels. The government has taken steps to tackle this issue by implementing stricter environmental regulations and promoting renewable energy sources.

3. **Debt Burden**: China's rapid growth has also led to a surge in debt levels, both at the individual and corporate levels. While debt has been used as a tool to stimulate economic growth, it poses risks to the stability of the financial system and the overall economy.

4. **Geopolitical Tensions**: China's ascent as an economic superpower has caused geopolitical tensions with other countries, particularly the United States. Issues such as trade imbalances, intellectual property theft, and territorial disputes have strained China's relations with other nations.

Implications of China's Rise:

China's rise as an economic superpower has far-reaching implications, both domestically and internationally. Here are some of the key implications:

1. **Shift in Global Economic Power**: China's rise has challenged the traditional dominance of Western economies and shifted the center of global economic power towards the East. It has established itself as a key player in international trade and investment.

2. **Integration into Global Institutions**: China's economic rise has led to its increased integration into global institutions. It has become an influential member of organizations such as the World Trade Organization (WTO) and has initiated its own initiatives like the Belt and Road Initiative (BRI) to expand its influence globally.

3. **Influence on Global Supply Chains**: China's position as the world's manufacturing hub has given it significant leverage over global supply chains. Disruptions in China's manufacturing sector, such as the COVID-19 pandemic, can have wide-ranging implications for global trade and the global economy.

4. **Competition and Cooperation**: China's rise has led to intensified competition with other major economies, particularly the United States. However, it also presents opportunities for cooperation in addressing global challenges such as climate change, cybersecurity, and pandemic response.

58 CHAPTER 1: THE WORLD IN THE AFTERMATH OF WORLD WAR II

Case Study: The Belt and Road Initiative (BRI):

The Belt and Road Initiative (BRI) is a massive infrastructure and development project initiated by China. It aims to strengthen connectivity and economic cooperation across Asia, Europe, Africa, and beyond. The BRI involves the construction of roads, railways, ports, and other infrastructure projects, with the goal of fostering economic integration and promoting trade.

However, the BRI is not without controversy. Some countries have raised concerns about excessive debt burdens, lack of transparency, and the geopolitical implications of China's expanding influence. It is crucial to understand the potential opportunities and challenges associated with the BRI in order to assess its impact on China's economic rise and global relations.

Conclusion:

The rise of China as an economic superpower has been a transformative event in contemporary history. Through ambitious economic reforms, infrastructure investments, and technological advancements, China has achieved remarkable economic growth. However, it also faces challenges such as income inequality, environmental concerns, and geopolitical tensions. The implications of China's ascent are profound, impacting global economic power dynamics, international relations, and the future of global governance. As China continues to navigate these opportunities and challenges, understanding its rise is essential for comprehending the complexities of the modern world.

Subsection: The Impact of Technology and Automation on the Job Market

The rapid advancement of technology and automation has had a profound impact on the job market. While technology has undoubtedly brought about numerous benefits, such as increased productivity and efficiency, it has also displaced certain jobs and raised concerns about the future of work. In this section, we will explore the various ways in which technology and automation have shaped the job market, the challenges they pose, and the potential opportunities they offer.

The Rise of Automation

Automation, driven by advancements in artificial intelligence (AI) and robotics, has led to significant changes in the job market. Jobs that involve repetitive and routine tasks, such as assembly line work, data entry, and customer service, are increasingly

SECTION 2: ECONOMIC DEVELOPMENTS

being automated. This has resulted in the displacement of many workers in these sectors, as machines can often perform these tasks faster, more accurately, and at a lower cost.

However, it is important to note that automation does not necessarily lead to job loss on a large scale. While certain jobs may become obsolete, new job opportunities are also created. Automation tends to eliminate low-skilled and routine jobs, but it also creates demand for highly skilled workers who can design, operate, and maintain the automated systems. Additionally, automation can lead to the emergence of entirely new industries and job categories that were previously unimaginable.

Challenges and Displacement

The displacement of workers due to automation poses significant challenges. Many individuals who lose their jobs to automation may find it difficult to transition into new employment, especially if they lack the necessary skills and training for the emerging job market. This can lead to unemployment, income inequality, and social unrest.

Certain industries are more vulnerable to automation than others. For example, industries like manufacturing, transportation, and retail are at a higher risk of job displacement. Jobs that involve routine physical or cognitive tasks are particularly susceptible to automation. It is crucial for policymakers, educators, and employers to anticipate these changes and take proactive steps to reskill and retrain workers in order to mitigate the negative effects of automation.

Opportunities and Skill Development

While automation presents challenges, it also offers opportunities for economic growth and job creation. As technology automates routine tasks, workers can focus on higher-level tasks that require creativity, problem-solving, and critical thinking. This shift in job requirements necessitates a greater emphasis on developing these skills in the workforce.

Investing in education and lifelong learning is crucial to equip individuals with the skills needed in the digital age. This includes promoting science, technology, engineering, and mathematics (STEM) education, as well as fostering a culture of continuous learning and adaptability. By nurturing a well-rounded and highly skilled workforce, countries can position themselves to take advantage of the opportunities presented by technological advancements.

Addressing the Impact on Workers

To ensure that the benefits of technology and automation are shared widely, it is essential to implement policies that support workers during the transition. This includes providing access to affordable and quality education and training programs, as well as social safety nets that protect individuals during periods of unemployment or job displacement.

Additionally, fostering entrepreneurship and supporting the creation of new businesses can help generate job opportunities in emerging sectors driven by technology. Governments and organizations can provide support through funding, mentorship programs, and access to resources, encouraging individuals to start their own ventures and contribute to economic growth.

Ethical Considerations and Human-Centered Design

As technology continues to advance, it is crucial to prioritize ethical considerations and human-centered design. Ensuring that technology is developed and deployed in ways that benefit society as a whole, rather than exacerbating inequalities, is of paramount importance.

Issues such as data privacy, algorithmic bias, and the impact of AI on decision-making processes must be carefully addressed. Governments, corporations, and individuals all have a role to play in shaping the ethical framework that guides the use of technology and automation, ensuring that it aligns with societal values and respects individual rights.

Real-World Examples

The impact of technology and automation on the job market can be seen in various industries. For example, self-checkout kiosks in supermarkets have replaced traditional cashiers, reducing the need for human intervention in the checkout process. In the transportation sector, the rise of autonomous vehicles has the potential to disrupt the job market for professional drivers.

On the other hand, technology has also created new job opportunities. The growth of e-commerce has led to a surge in demand for logistics and fulfillment center workers. The rapid expansion of the tech industry has resulted in increased employment opportunities for software engineers, data analysts, and AI specialists.

Conclusion

The impact of technology and automation on the job market is a complex and multifaceted issue. While automation presents challenges in terms of job displacement, it also offers opportunities for economic growth and the creation of new jobs. By investing in education and reskilling programs, fostering entrepreneurship, and addressing ethical considerations, countries can navigate the changing landscape of work and ensure that the benefits of technology are widely shared.

Section 3: Social and Cultural Transformations

Subsection: The Civil Rights Movement and the Fight for Racial Equality

The Civil Rights Movement of the mid-20th century was a pivotal time in history, marked by a widespread struggle for racial equality and social justice. It emerged as a response to centuries of systemic racism, discrimination, and segregation endured by African Americans in the United States. This subsection explores the key events, figures, and ideas that shaped the Civil Rights Movement, highlighting its significance and lasting impact.

Background: Systemic Racism and Segregation

To understand the Civil Rights Movement, it is crucial to acknowledge the historical context of systemic racism and segregation that provided the impetus for change. After the abolition of slavery in the 19th century, new forms of racial discrimination emerged, including the Jim Crow laws in the Southern states. These laws enforced racial segregation, denied African Americans their fundamental rights, and perpetuated a climate of inequality and injustice.

The Early Pioneers of the Civil Rights Movement

The Civil Rights Movement was propelled by a host of courageous individuals who dedicated their lives to challenging discrimination and advocating for equal rights. Some key figures include:

1. Rosa Parks: In 1955, Rosa Parks, a civil rights activist, refused to give up her bus seat to a white passenger in Montgomery, Alabama. Her arrest ignited the Montgomery Bus Boycott, a year-long campaign that successfully ended racial segregation on public buses.

62 *CHAPTER 1: THE WORLD IN THE AFTERMATH OF WORLD WAR II*

2. Martin Luther King Jr.: Dr. Martin Luther King Jr., a prominent civil rights leader, emerged as a key figure in the struggle for racial equality. He advocated for nonviolent resistance and delivered his iconic "I Have a Dream" speech during the 1963 March on Washington. King's leadership and activism galvanized millions of individuals, transcending racial boundaries.

3. Thurgood Marshall: As an attorney and the first African American Supreme Court justice, Thurgood Marshall played a pivotal role in using the legal system to challenge racial segregation. He successfully argued the landmark case of Brown v. Board of Education, which declared racial segregation in schools unconstitutional.

Key Events and Strategies of the Civil Rights Movement

The Civil Rights Movement encompassed a series of significant events and strategies aimed at effecting social change. Some notable ones include:

1. Montgomery Bus Boycott (1955-1956): The Montgomery Bus Boycott, ignited by Rosa Parks' arrest, was a coordinated effort in which African Americans boycotted public buses in protest against segregation. This successful protest served as a model for future nonviolent resistance movements.

2. Sit-ins and Freedom Rides: Beginning in the early 1960s, sit-ins and freedom rides became popular forms of protest against segregation. African American activists, often college students, would peacefully occupy segregated spaces such as restaurants, bus terminals, and libraries to challenge discriminatory practices.

3. March on Washington (1963): The March on Washington for Jobs and Freedom brought together an estimated 250,000 participants, making it one of the largest peaceful demonstrations in U.S. history. It was during this march that Martin Luther King Jr. delivered his iconic "I Have a Dream" speech, calling for an end to racism and discrimination.

4. Voting Rights Act (1965): The Voting Rights Act of 1965 was a landmark piece of legislation that abolished voting discrimination, especially against African Americans in the Southern states. It aimed to ensure that all citizens, regardless of race, could exercise their right to vote.

Changing Public Opinion and Media Influence

The Civil Rights Movement leveraged the power of media and public opinion to shed light on racial injustice. Television played a crucial role in bringing the realities of racial violence and discrimination into the living rooms of Americans nationwide. The shocking images of police brutality against peaceful protesters,

SECTION 3: SOCIAL AND CULTURAL TRANSFORMATIONS 63

such as the brutality witnessed during the Selma to Montgomery marches, helped sway public opinion in favor of the Civil Rights Movement.

Legacy and Lasting Impact

The Civil Rights Movement achieved significant milestones and brought about lasting changes that continue to shape society today. Some of its key legacies include:

1. Civil Rights Act of 1964: The Civil Rights Act of 1964 outlawed discrimination based on race, color, religion, sex, or national origin. It laid the foundation for equal treatment and protection of civil rights for all citizens.

2. Desegregation of Schools: The landmark Supreme Court case Brown v. Board of Education (1954) led to the desegregation of public schools, challenging the doctrine of "separate but equal" established by the earlier Plessy v. Ferguson ruling.

3. Empowerment of African Americans: The Civil Rights Movement empowered African Americans to assert their rights and demand change, fostering a sense of pride in their cultural heritage and identity.

4. Inspiration for Global Movements: The success of the Civil Rights Movement inspired other social justice movements worldwide, including the anti-apartheid movement in South Africa and struggles against racism and discrimination in various countries.

Unconventional Example: The Power of Music as a Catalyst for Change

Music played a significant role in the Civil Rights Movement, serving as a platform for shared expression and a means of inspiring hope and unity. Artists such as Bob Dylan, Sam Cooke, and Nina Simone used their music to communicate messages of social justice and racial equality. For example, Sam Cooke's song "A Change Is Gonna Come" became an anthem for the movement, resonating with activists and the broader public alike. The emotional impact of music created solidarity and galvanized support for the cause.

Exercises

1. Research and discuss the role of nonviolent resistance in the Civil Rights Movement. How did this strategy contribute to its success?

2. Compare and contrast the methods and goals of different civil rights leaders during the movement, such as Martin Luther King Jr., Malcolm X, and Rosa Parks.

64 CHAPTER 1: THE WORLD IN THE AFTERMATH OF WORLD WAR II

3. Investigate contemporary social justice movements and draw parallels to the Civil Rights Movement. How do these modern movements build upon the legacy of the Civil Rights Movement?

Resources

1. Books: a. "The Eyes on the Prize: America's Civil Rights Years, 1954-1965" by Juan Williams b. "Parting the Waters: America in the King Years 1954-1963" by Taylor Branch

2. Documentaries: a. "Eyes on the Prize" (1987-1990) - A critically acclaimed documentary series chronicling the Civil Rights Movement. b. "Freedom Riders" (2010) - A PBS documentary highlighting the brave individuals who participated in the Freedom Rides.

3. Websites: a. African American Civil Rights Movement (1954-1968) - History.com b. The Martin Luther King Jr. Center for Nonviolent Social Change - TheKingCenter.org

By understanding the struggles, achievements, and impact of the Civil Rights Movement, we gain insight into the tireless pursuit of racial equality and justice. It serves as a reminder that change is possible when individuals unite against oppression and fight for a more inclusive and egalitarian society.

Subsection: The Women's Liberation Movement and the Fight for Gender Equality

The Women's Liberation Movement, also known as the feminist movement, emerged as a social and political campaign in the late 1960s and early 1970s. Its primary goal was to confront and challenge the traditional gender roles and societal norms that perpetuated women's inequality and discrimination. This section explores the key objectives, significant events, and lasting impacts of the Women's Liberation Movement.

Background

Before delving into the Women's Liberation Movement, it is crucial to understand the historical context that fueled its emergence. For centuries, women were relegated to domestic roles and denied equal access to education, employment, and political participation. Societal expectations limited their opportunities and subjected them to systemic sexism and gender-based discrimination.

In the early 20th century, the first wave of feminism fought for women's suffrage and basic rights. However, it was not until the 1960s that the second

SECTION 3: SOCIAL AND CULTURAL TRANSFORMATIONS 65

wave, characterized by the Women's Liberation Movement, gained momentum. This movement aimed to challenge deeply rooted cultural and social norms that perpetuated gender inequality.

Key Objectives

The Women's Liberation Movement had several key objectives, all aimed at achieving gender equality:

1. Political Empowerment: The movement sought to expand women's political rights and representation. Activists pushed for legislative reforms that would grant women equal rights in areas such as voting, employment, and reproductive health.

2. Economic Equality: The movement fought against workplace discrimination, advocating for equal pay, job opportunities, and career advancement for women. Activists emphasized the need to challenge wage gaps and break down occupational barriers.

3. Reproductive Rights: The Women's Liberation Movement focused on women's right to make decisions regarding their bodies, including access to contraception, abortion, and comprehensive reproductive healthcare. The movement aimed to challenge restrictive laws and societal stigmas surrounding reproductive choices.

4. Ending Gender-Based Violence: The movement aimed to address the issue of gender-based violence, including domestic violence, sexual assault, and harassment. Activists worked towards creating safe spaces for women and holding perpetrators accountable.

5. Challenging Patriarchy: The Women's Liberation Movement sought to dismantle patriarchal structures that perpetuated gender inequality. Activists aimed to challenge traditional gender roles and expectations, promoting gender equity and fluidity.

Significant Events

The Women's Liberation Movement was marked by numerous significant events that furthered the fight for gender equality:

1. The Publication of "The Feminine Mystique" (1963): Betty Friedan's groundbreaking book exposed the discontent and frustrations of suburban housewives, sparking discussions about women's roles in society and serving as a catalyst for the movement.

2. National Organization for Women (NOW) Founding (1966): NOW, the largest feminist organization in the United States, was founded to advocate for

66 CHAPTER 1: THE WORLD IN THE AFTERMATH OF WORLD WAR II

women's rights in areas such as employment, education, and legal protection against discrimination.

3. Women's Strike for Equality (1970): On the 50th anniversary of women's suffrage, thousands of women across the United States participated in demonstrations, demanding equal rights. The strike brought attention to gender disparities and highlighted the unity within the movement.

4. Roe v. Wade Supreme Court Decision (1973): This landmark ruling legalized abortion in the United States, granting women the right to reproductive choice. It was a significant victory for the Women's Liberation Movement's advocacy for women's reproductive rights.

5. Take Back the Night Marches (1970s): These marches aimed to raise awareness about gender-based violence, particularly sexual assault and domestic abuse. The marches provided a platform for survivors to share their stories and demand societal change.

Lasting Impacts

The Women's Liberation Movement had far-reaching and lasting impacts on society:

1. Legal Advancements: The movement's activism contributed to the enactment of laws protecting women's rights, such as the Equal Pay Act and the Title IX of the Education Amendments. These legal advancements aimed to address gender disparities in employment and education.

2. Cultural Shifts: The movement challenged societal norms and sparked conversations about gender equality, encouraging men and women to critically examine gender roles. This cultural shift led to increased awareness and acceptance of gender diversity.

3. Reproductive Rights: The Women's Liberation Movement played a crucial role in advocating for reproductive rights and access to comprehensive healthcare. The movement's efforts continue to shape discussions around reproductive justice and women's autonomy.

4. Increased Women's Representation: The movement's advocacy for women's political empowerment led to a significant increase in women's representation in governments and decision-making positions worldwide. However, full gender parity is yet to be achieved.

5. Continued Activism: The Women's Liberation Movement paved the way for future activism, inspiring subsequent generations of feminists to continue fighting for gender equality. Movements such as #MeToo and intersectional feminism build upon the legacy of the Women's Liberation Movement.

SECTION 3: SOCIAL AND CULTURAL TRANSFORMATIONS

A Real-World Example

To illustrate the Women's Liberation Movement's impact, let's consider the case of the glass ceiling in the corporate world. The movement's efforts to challenge discriminatory practices and advocate for equal opportunities led to significant changes in the workplace. Today, numerous women hold top executive positions in multinational companies, shattering the notion that certain roles are reserved for men. However, despite these advancements, gender disparities persist, highlighting the ongoing need for intersectional feminist activism.

Resources for Further Study

For individuals interested in further exploring the Women's Liberation Movement and gender equality, the following resources are recommended:

1. Book: "The Feminine Mystique" by Betty Friedan 2. Book: "The Second Sex" by Simone de Beauvoir 3. Documentary: "She's Beautiful When She's Angry" directed by Mary Dore 4. Organization: National Organization for Women (NOW) 5. Website: Stanford Encyclopedia of Philosophy - Feminist Perspectives on Power

In conclusion, the Women's Liberation Movement emerged as a powerful force in the fight for gender equality. By challenging societal norms and advocating for change, the movement laid the foundation for significant advancements in women's rights. However, the struggle for gender equality continues, and ongoing activism is necessary to achieve a truly equitable society.

Subsection: The Sexual Revolution and Changing Attitudes towards Sexuality

The sexual revolution of the 1960s and 1970s marked a significant shift in societal attitudes towards sexuality. It challenged traditional norms and values, bringing about profound changes in gender roles, relationships, and the understanding of human sexuality. This subsection explores the key factors that contributed to the sexual revolution and the lasting impact it had on society.

Background

Before delving into the sexual revolution, it is essential to understand the societal context in which it emerged. Prior to the 1960s, sexuality was largely associated with marriage and procreation, and discussions surrounding alternative sexual practices or non-heteronormative identities were heavily stigmatized. The dominant cultural

Challenging the Status Quo

The sexual revolution emerged as a response to these restrictive norms and sought to challenge the status quo. It was influenced by various socio-political movements, such as the feminist movement, the civil rights movement, and the counterculture movement. These movements called for equality, freedom, and autonomy, including sexual liberation.

Birth Control and Contraception

One of the essential factors that fueled the sexual revolution was the widespread availability of birth control and contraception. The development of the birth control pill in the 1960s gave women unprecedented control over their reproductive choices. This newfound reproductive autonomy allowed individuals to engage in sexual activities without the fear of unwanted pregnancies, empowering them to explore sexual experiences outside of marriage.

Changing Gender Roles

The sexual revolution was intimately linked to changing gender roles and the feminist movement. The fight for gender equality challenged traditional gender expectations, empowering women to assert their sexual desires and preferences. Women challenged the notion that sex was solely for marriage or procreation, advocating for sexual pleasure and agency.

Redefining Relationships

The sexual revolution brought about a redefinition of relationships, allowing for greater exploration of non-traditional relationship structures. It was during this period that open relationships, polyamory, and alternative forms of partnerships gained recognition and acceptance. The focus shifted from the institution of marriage to individual autonomy and emotional fulfillment.

LGBTQ+ Rights and Visibility

The sexual revolution also played a significant role in the advancement of LGBTQ+ rights and visibility. Through public demonstrations and protests,

SECTION 3: SOCIAL AND CULTURAL TRANSFORMATIONS

LGBTQ+ activists fought against systemic discrimination and repression. The visibility of LGBTQ+ individuals increased, challenging societal norms and fostering greater acceptance and inclusion.

Impacts on Society

The sexual revolution had profound and lasting impacts on society. It reshaped cultural attitudes towards sexuality, challenging taboos and reducing stigma surrounding various sexual practices. It paved the way for greater sexual freedom, promoting open discussions about sexual health, consent, and pleasure.

Challenges and Critiques

While the sexual revolution brought about significant progress, it also faced challenges and critiques. Some argue that it led to a degradation of moral values, increased levels of promiscuity, and the spread of sexually transmitted infections. Others criticized the revolution for overshadowing deeper societal issues and reinforcing inequalities, particularly for marginalized communities.

Navigating the Modern Context

In the digital age, the sexual revolution continues to evolve through online platforms, dating apps, and the accessibility of sexual education resources. However, navigating modern-day issues, such as consent, online harassment, and the objectification of bodies, presents new challenges. It is crucial to foster healthy attitudes towards sexuality, promote comprehensive sexual education, and advocate for consent and inclusivity.

Resources and Further Reading

1. "The Sexual Revolution: Toward a Self-Regulating Character Structure" by Wilhelm Reich. 2. "Sexual Politics" by Kate Millett. 3. "The Feminine Mystique" by Betty Friedan. 4. "The Joy of Sex" by Alex Comfort. 5. "The Second Sex" by Simone de Beauvoir.

Exercise

Reflect on your own understanding of sexuality and how it has been shaped by societal attitudes. Consider the impact of the sexual revolution on your own life and relationships. In a journal entry, write about any changes you have noticed in the societal acceptance and understanding of diverse sexual identities and practices.

70CHAPTER 1: THE WORLD IN THE AFTERMATH OF WORLD WAR II

Subsection: The Hippie Counterculture and the Anti-Vietnam War Movement

During the 1960s, a wave of social and cultural transformations swept through American society. The Hippie Counterculture and the Anti-Vietnam War Movement emerged as powerful expressions of dissent against the status quo. This subsection explores the origins, principles, and impact of these movements, shedding light on their significant role in shaping contemporary history.

Origins of the Hippie Counterculture

The Hippie Counterculture emerged in the mid-1960s, largely as a reaction to the conformity and consumerism that characterized American society at the time. The movement drew inspiration from various sources, including Eastern philosophy, Civil Rights activism, and the Beat Generation. The Beat Generation, a group of writers and poets who rejected mainstream culture, laid the foundation for the countercultural movements that followed.

Principles of the Hippie Counterculture

The Hippie Counterculture embraced ideals of peace, love, and personal freedom. Its followers rejected materialism, advocating for a simpler, more communal way of life. They questioned established norms and values, promoting a broader acceptance of alternative lifestyles, including communal living, free love, and experimentation with drugs such as LSD. The Hippies also championed environmental consciousness and ecological sustainability.

Impact of the Hippie Counterculture

The Hippie Counterculture had a profound impact on American society. It challenged traditional social and gender roles, sparking a wave of feminism and LGBTQ+ activism. It also influenced popular culture, music, and fashion, giving rise to the Woodstock music festival and psychedelic art. Moreover, the counterculture's focus on ecological issues and sustainable living laid the groundwork for the modern environmental movement.

Origins of the Anti-Vietnam War Movement

Concurrent with the Hippie Counterculture, the Anti-Vietnam War Movement gained momentum as opposition to the Vietnam War escalated. The movement

SECTION 3: SOCIAL AND CULTURAL TRANSFORMATIONS 71

was inspired by pacifist beliefs, concern for human rights, and a rejection of U.S. foreign policy. It drew support from diverse groups, including students, intellectuals, civil rights activists, and veterans who questioned the legitimacy and morality of the war.

Principles of the Anti-Vietnam War Movement

The Anti-Vietnam War Movement called for an immediate end to the war and the withdrawal of U.S. troops from Vietnam. Its principles included non-violent protests, civil disobedience, and public demonstrations. Activists organized teach-ins, marches, and sit-ins to raise awareness and challenge the government's policies. The movement was also characterized by a broad anti-establishment sentiment and a demand for greater accountability and transparency in governance.

Impact of the Anti-Vietnam War Movement

The Anti-Vietnam War Movement played a significant role in bringing about a shift in public opinion regarding the war. It exposed the harsh realities of combat and the government's misrepresentations, contributing to a growing anti-war sentiment. The movement also compelled policymakers to reconsider their approach, leading to a gradual de-escalation and eventual withdrawal of U.S. troops from Vietnam. Additionally, it inspired subsequent social justice movements, shaping a renewed sense of activism and political engagement in the United States.

Unconventional Example: The Catonsville Nine

An unconventional yet relevant example of resistance within the Anti-Vietnam War Movement is the Catonsville Nine action. In May 1968, a group of nine activists, including priests, nuns, and laity, broke into the Selective Service office in Catonsville, Maryland, and burned draft files with homemade napalm. Their direct action, based on moral and religious grounds, aimed to symbolically disrupt the machinery of war and challenge the legality and morality of the Vietnam War. The Catonsville Nine sparked a nationwide debate about the role of civil disobedience and conscience in times of war.

Conclusion

The Hippie Counterculture and the Anti-Vietnam War Movement were transformative social and cultural phenomena of the 1960s and beyond. Their influence continues to resonate in contemporary society, shaping attitudes toward

72 CHAPTER 1: THE WORLD IN THE AFTERMATH OF WORLD WAR II

civil rights, social justice, and activism. Understanding the origins, principles, and impact of these movements provides valuable insights into the power of collective action and the capacity for individuals to effect change.

Subsection: The Environmental Movement and the Rise of Green Politics

The environmental movement and the rise of green politics have been instrumental in shaping the contemporary world. As the world has become more aware of the impact of human activities on the environment, there has been a growing concern for the protection of the planet and the implementation of sustainable practices. This section explores the history, principles, challenges, and opportunities of the environmental movement and its influence on the emergence of green politics.

History of the Environmental Movement

The environmental movement as we know it today can be traced back to the mid-20th century when concerns regarding pollution, deforestation, and other environmental issues began to gain public attention. A series of high-profile events, such as the publication of Rachel Carson's book "Silent Spring" in 1962, which highlighted the detrimental effects of pesticides, and the Santa Barbara oil spill in 1969, which caused extensive damage to the marine ecosystem, sparked public outrage and mobilized individuals to take action.

One of the key milestones in the environmental movement was the establishment of Earth Day on April 22, 1970. This annual event, which brings together millions of people around the world, serves as a platform to raise awareness about environmental issues and advocate for sustainable practices. It has played a crucial role in galvanizing support for environmental protection and creating a global network of activists.

Principles of the Environmental Movement

The environmental movement is guided by several key principles that form the basis for its advocacy and activism. These principles include:

1. Conservation: The belief in the responsible use and preservation of natural resources to ensure their availability for future generations.

2. Sustainability: The promotion of practices that meet the needs of the present without compromising the ability of future generations to meet their own needs.

SECTION 3: SOCIAL AND CULTURAL TRANSFORMATIONS   73

3. Environmental justice: The recognition that environmental issues disproportionately affect marginalized communities and the pursuit of fair and equitable solutions for all.

4. Pollution prevention: The emphasis on reducing or eliminating the release of pollutants into the environment through the adoption of cleaner technologies and practices.

5. Biodiversity conservation: The protection of the diversity of species and ecosystems, recognizing their intrinsic value and the services they provide.

6. Climate change mitigation and adaptation: The recognition of the urgent need to mitigate greenhouse gas emissions and adapt to the impacts of climate change.

Challenges Faced by the Environmental Movement

Despite significant progress made by the environmental movement, it continues to face several challenges that hinder the achievement of its goals. These challenges include:

1. Political resistance: The environmental movement often faces opposition from industries and politicians who prioritize short-term economic gain over long-term environmental sustainability.

2. Lack of awareness and education: Many people still lack awareness and understanding of the urgency and importance of environmental issues, making it challenging to mobilize broad-based support.

3. Global cooperation: Environmental issues transcend national boundaries, making international cooperation imperative. However, achieving consensus and collective action at a global scale can be complex.

4. Interests conflicts: Environmental protection initiatives can sometimes conflict with economic interests, leading to resistance and tension between different stakeholders.

5. Technological limitations: The development and implementation of sustainable technologies and solutions are often constrained by technological and economic barriers.

Green Politics: A Response to Environmental Concerns

The rise of the environmental movement has given birth to a new political ideology known as green politics. Green politics emphasizes the importance of ecological sustainability, social justice, grassroots democracy, and non-violence. It seeks to integrate environmental concerns into all areas of policy-making and governance.

74 CHAPTER 1: THE WORLD IN THE AFTERMATH OF WORLD WAR II

Green political parties have emerged around the world, advocating for environmental protection, renewable energy, sustainable agriculture, and social equity. These parties often prioritize long-term environmental sustainability over short-term economic gains and propose policies that promote ecological balance and the well-being of both humans and the natural world.

Examples of Green Politics in Action

Several countries have embraced green politics and implemented policies that prioritize environmental concerns. For instance, Germany has made significant investments in renewable energy, leading to a significant reduction in greenhouse gas emissions. The country's Energiewende (energy transition) initiative aims to shift to a more sustainable and decentralized energy system.

Costa Rica is another example of a country that has embraced green politics. It has set ambitious goals for achieving renewable energy production and has been able to generate almost all of its electricity from clean sources. Furthermore, the country has implemented policies to protect its rich biodiversity and has become a leader in sustainable tourism.

Opportunities and Solutions

The environmental movement and green politics present numerous opportunities and solutions for addressing environmental challenges. These include:

1. Renewable energy transition: Investing in renewable energy sources, such as solar and wind power, can help reduce dependence on fossil fuels and promote sustainable development.

2. Sustainable agriculture: Adopting sustainable farming practices, such as organic farming and agroecology, can protect soil health, minimize pesticide use, and promote biodiversity.

3. Conservation and restoration: Protecting and restoring natural habitats, such as forests and wetlands, can help preserve biodiversity and mitigate climate change.

4. Circular economy: Moving towards a circular economy model, where resources are reused and waste is minimized, can reduce environmental impact and promote sustainable consumption.

5. Environmental education and awareness: Investing in environmental education programs can help raise awareness and foster a sense of responsibility towards the environment from an early age.

Conclusion

The environmental movement and the rise of green politics have played a crucial role in raising awareness about environmental issues and advocating for sustainable practices. As the world faces increasing environmental challenges, it is imperative to continue supporting the environmental movement and embracing green politics to pave the way towards a more sustainable and resilient future. By prioritizing environmental conservation, sustainable development, and social justice, we can create a world where humans and nature coexist harmoniously.

Subsection: The LGBTQ+ Rights Movement and the Fight for Equality

The LGBTQ+ (Lesbian, Gay, Bisexual, Transgender, Queer/Questioning, and others) rights movement has been a pivotal force in shaping contemporary history. This subsection delves into the struggles, triumphs, and ongoing fight for equality faced by the LGBTQ+ community. We will explore the historical context, legal developments, social changes, and current challenges encountered by LGBTQ+ individuals.

Historical Context and Challenges

The LGBTQ+ community has faced significant persecution throughout history. Societal attitudes, influenced by cultural, religious, and political factors, have often marginalized and oppressed individuals who deviate from traditional gender and sexual identities. Homosexuality was considered a mental disorder by many medical professionals until the 1970s, and same-sex relationships were criminalized and subjected to severe punishment in various countries.

The section will highlight some of the key historical milestones and challenges faced by the LGBTQ+ community, including:

- The Stonewall Riots: The 1969 riots in New York City, sparked by police raids on a gay bar called the Stonewall Inn, marked a turning point in the LGBTQ+ rights movement. It galvanized the community and led to increased visibility and activism.

- LGBT Rights as Human Rights: The United Nations' Universal Declaration of Human Rights, adopted in 1948, laid the foundation for recognizing LGBTQ+ rights as fundamental human rights. This recognition has provided a framework for advocating for equality on a global scale.

76 CHAPTER 1: THE WORLD IN THE AFTERMATH OF WORLD WAR II

+ Legal Decriminalization and Declassification: Many countries have gradually decriminalized same-sex relationships and removed homosexuality from the list of mental disorders. The process has been marked by legal battles, activism, and changing public attitudes.

Legal Developments and Progress

The fight for LGBTQ+ rights has gained significant ground in recent decades, with legal developments playing a crucial role. This subsection highlights key legal milestones and progress made towards achieving equality for LGBTQ+ individuals.

+ Decriminalization and Anti-Discrimination Laws: Many countries have repealed laws criminalizing homosexuality and enacted legislation to protect LGBTQ+ individuals from discrimination in various areas of life, including employment, housing, and public accommodations.

+ Marriage Equality: The legalization of same-sex marriage has been a landmark achievement for the LGBTQ+ rights movement. This subsection explores the legal battles and social transformations that led to the recognition of same-sex marriage in several countries.

+ Adoption and Parental Rights: Legal recognition of LGBTQ+ individuals' rights to adopt and parent has been a significant battleground. We will delve into the challenges faced and progress made in ensuring equal rights for LGBTQ+ families.

Social Changes and Cultural Shifts

While legal developments have been instrumental, societal changes and cultural shifts have also played a crucial role in advancing LGBTQ+ rights. This subsection examines the groundbreaking social transformations and cultural milestones that have contributed to increased acceptance, inclusion, and visibility of LGBTQ+ individuals.

+ Coming Out and Personal Narratives: The act of coming out, often a deeply personal and courageous journey, has played a vital role in challenging stereotypes and increasing understanding and empathy. This subsection explores the power of personal narratives and their impact on society.

SECTION 3: SOCIAL AND CULTURAL TRANSFORMATIONS

- LGBTQ+ Representation in Media and Entertainment: The increased representation of LGBTQ+ individuals and stories in various forms of media has helped shape public opinion, challenge stereotypes, and promote acceptance. We will discuss the significance of positive LGBTQ+ representation in fostering social change.

- LGBTQ+ Allies and Advocacy: The support of allies, individuals who may not identify as LGBTQ+ but actively work towards advancing LGBTQ+ rights, has been instrumental. This subsection examines the role of allies and advocacy organizations in achieving equality.

Current Challenges and Ongoing Struggles

Despite significant progress, the LGBTQ+ community continues to face numerous challenges and ongoing struggles. This subsection addresses some of the current issues and hurdles that need to be addressed to ensure full equality and protection for LGBTQ+ individuals.

- Transgender Rights: Transgender individuals still face significant legal and societal obstacles, including barriers to gender-affirming healthcare, discrimination in employment, and violence. This subsection explores the specific challenges faced by the transgender community and highlights efforts to address them.

- Global Disparities and Human Rights Violations: LGBTQ+ individuals worldwide face varying degrees of legal and social acceptance. We will discuss the global disparities in LGBTQ+ rights and highlight efforts to address human rights violations and discrimination on an international scale.

- Intersectionality: The experiences of LGBTQ+ individuals cannot be viewed in isolation from other marginalized identities, including race, ethnicity, socioeconomic status, and disability. This subsection explores the concept of intersectionality and its importance in addressing the diverse needs of the LGBTQ+ community.

Resources, Support, and Activism

This subsection aims to provide resources, support networks, and avenues for advocacy that are available to LGBTQ+ individuals and their allies. It will

CHAPTER 1: THE WORLD IN THE AFTERMATH OF WORLD WAR II

highlight organizations, online platforms, and initiatives that offer assistance, information, and opportunities for activism.

- ◆ LGBTQ+ Support Organizations: We will provide an overview of national and international organizations that offer support, resources, and advocacy for LGBTQ+ individuals, including helplines, community centers, and legal support services.

- ◆ LGBTQ+ Education and Awareness Initiatives: Education and awareness are key to dismantling prejudice and promoting acceptance. This subsection will explore educational initiatives, training programs, and campaigns aimed at educating the public and fostering LGBTQ+ inclusivity.

- ◆ Online Communities and Safe Spaces: The internet has provided a vital platform for LGBTQ+ individuals to connect, seek support, and mobilize. We will highlight online communities, forums, and social media platforms that offer safe spaces for sharing experiences and receiving support.

Conclusion

The LGBTQ+ rights movement has achieved significant milestones, fostering greater acceptance and equality. However, there are still significant challenges to overcome. By understanding the historical context, legal developments, social changes, and current struggles, we can actively contribute to the fight for LGBTQ+ rights and create a more inclusive and equitable society.

Exercises:

1. Research a landmark legal case related to LGBTQ+ rights and present an argument highlighting its significance in advancing equality.

2. Design a social media campaign aimed at promoting LGBTQ+ acceptance and inclusivity. Create engaging content and strategies to reach a wide audience.

3. Write an essay exploring the intersectional experiences of LGBTQ+ individuals from different cultural backgrounds and identities. Discuss the unique challenges they face and propose strategies for creating more inclusive spaces.

Subsection: The Impact of Mass Media and Pop Culture on Society

The impact of mass media and pop culture on society is undeniable. In this section, we will explore how these forces have shaped and influenced various aspects of our lives, from shaping our beliefs and attitudes to influencing our behaviors and values.

SECTION 3: SOCIAL AND CULTURAL TRANSFORMATIONS 79

The Power of Mass Media

Mass media, including newspapers, radio, television, and the internet, has the power to reach a large audience and shape public opinion. It plays a significant role in disseminating information, shaping public discourse, and influencing public policy. The media has the power to create or destroy reputations, expose corruption, and rally public support for important causes.

One way mass media influences society is through agenda-setting, where it decides what issues and topics are deemed newsworthy and worthy of public attention. By choosing what to cover, media outlets can influence public opinion on specific issues and shape the public's understanding of events.

Furthermore, the media plays a critical role in framing how events and issues are presented to the public. The way a story is framed can influence how individuals perceive and interpret the information, leading to different opinions and attitudes.

Influence on Values and Beliefs

Mass media and pop culture have a profound influence on shaping our values, beliefs, and attitudes. Through television shows, movies, music, and advertising, we are constantly exposed to messages and narratives that shape our understanding of the world and our place in it.

For example, television shows and movies often portray certain lifestyles, relationships, and societal norms as desirable or worthy of aspiration. These depictions can shape our perceptions and values, influencing our choices and behaviors. Advertisements also play a significant role in shaping consumer behavior by creating desires, promoting certain products, and shaping our ideas of what is considered attractive or desirable.

Moreover, mass media and pop culture have the power to challenge societal norms and promote alternative perspectives. Through the representation of diverse characters, ideas, and narratives, media can challenge traditional stereotypes and foster inclusivity and acceptance.

Impact on Behavior and Identity

Mass media and pop culture can also significantly influence our behaviors and identities. They provide role models, create trends, and shape our sense of self.

For instance, celebrities and influencers often serve as role models for many individuals, especially young people. Their behaviors, choices, and lifestyles are often emulated and admired. This can influence how people choose to dress, behave, and even pursue certain careers.

80 CHAPTER 1: THE WORLD IN THE AFTERMATH OF WORLD WAR II

Furthermore, through social media platforms, individuals can curate and present their identities to the world. This can lead to the formation of online communities, where individuals with similar interests, beliefs, or identities can connect and share ideas. These online communities can have a significant impact on an individual's sense of identity and belonging.

Critiques and Challenges

While mass media and pop culture have undoubtedly had a significant impact on society, they are not without their critiques and challenges.

One criticism is the potential for media bias and misinformation. The media can sometimes prioritize certain narratives or viewpoints, leading to biased reporting and the spread of misinformation. This can significantly impact public understanding and decision-making.

Moreover, the constant exposure to unrealistic beauty standards and lifestyles portrayed in media can negatively impact individuals' self-esteem and body image. This can lead to the development of mental health issues and contribute to the perpetuation of harmful stereotypes.

Additionally, the rise of social media and the 24/7 news cycle have led to information overload and the spread of "fake news." It has become increasingly challenging to distinguish between reliable and unreliable sources of information, leading to public confusion and the erosion of trust in media.

Examples and Applications

To illustrate the impact of mass media and pop culture on society, let's consider a few examples:

1. The #MeToo Movement: The movement gained momentum through social media platforms, with individuals sharing their stories of sexual harassment and assault. This online campaign helped shed light on the pervasiveness of such issues and sparked a global conversation on consent, gender equality, and accountability.

2. Advertising and Consumer Behavior: Advertisements play a significant role in shaping consumer behavior. For example, the use of celebrity endorsements can influence consumers' purchasing decisions and perceptions of a brand's value and quality.

3. Representation in Media: The increased representation of diverse characters and storylines in television shows and movies has helped challenge stereotypes, promote inclusivity, and empower underrepresented communities.

SECTION 3: SOCIAL AND CULTURAL TRANSFORMATIONS　　81

Resources and Further Reading

To delve deeper into the impact of mass media and pop culture on society, the following resources and readings can provide valuable insights:

1. McLuhan, M. (1964). "Understanding Media: The Extensions of Man." This classic work explores the role of media in shaping society and its impact on human perception and interaction.

2. Fiske, J. (1987). "Television Culture." This book provides a critical analysis of television's influence on popular culture and society, examining its role in shaping identity, values, and social interaction.

3. Manovich, L. (2002). "The Language of New Media." This text explores the impact of digital media and the internet on culture and society, examining how it has transformed various aspects of our lives.

4. Jenkins, H. (2006). "Convergence Culture: Where Old and New Media Collide." This book explores the changing landscape of media and popular culture, highlighting the role of participatory culture and media convergence.

Through a comprehensive understanding of the impact of mass media and pop culture on society, we can critically engage with these forces and navigate their influence to shape a more inclusive, informed, and empowered society.

Subsection: The Rise of Consumerism and Materialism

Consumerism and materialism have become defining features of the modern world. In this subsection, we will explore the origins, impact, and consequences of the rise of consumerism and materialism, examining the factors that have contributed to their growth and the implications for individuals and society as a whole.

Understanding Consumerism

Consumerism can be defined as the culture of excessive consumption and the pursuit of material possessions. It is driven by the belief that acquiring more goods and services leads to greater personal satisfaction and happiness. Consumerism encourages individuals to prioritize their wants over their needs, leading to a constant desire for new products and experiences.

The roots of consumerism can be traced back to the Industrial Revolution, which brought about significant advancements in manufacturing and mass production. The availability of a wide range of affordable products, coupled with improved transportation and communication, fueled the desire for consumption. This desire was further perpetuated by the rise of advertising and marketing strategies that create a sense of need and desire for products.

82 CHAPTER 1: THE WORLD IN THE AFTERMATH OF WORLD WAR II

The Impact of Consumerism

The rise of consumerism has had far-reaching implications for individuals, society, and the environment. While it has contributed to economic growth and prosperity, it has also given rise to several challenges and concerns.

One of the primary impacts of consumerism is the effect on personal well-being. Consumerism encourages individuals to place their self-worth and identity in material possessions, leading to a never-ending pursuit of happiness through consumption. However, research has shown that the pursuit of material wealth often fails to provide lasting satisfaction and can lead to increased stress, anxiety, and a sense of emptiness.

Additionally, consumerism has led to a culture of overconsumption, which has significant environmental consequences. The production, use, and disposal of goods contribute to resource depletion, pollution, and climate change. The constant demand for new products also leads to excessive waste generation, contributing to the global waste crisis.

Consumerism and Social Issues

Consumerism has also been linked to various social issues. The relentless pursuit of material possessions can exacerbate economic inequality, as those with greater purchasing power have access to a wider range of goods and services. This inequality can lead to social divisions and a sense of dissatisfaction among those who are unable to keep up with the demands of consumer culture.

Furthermore, consumerism perpetuates a culture of comparison and competition. The pressure to conform to societal norms and acquire the latest trends can lead to social comparison and feelings of inadequacy. This can have detrimental effects on mental health and interpersonal relationships.

Addressing the Challenges

Addressing the challenges posed by consumerism and materialism requires a multidimensional approach. It involves a shift in individuals' values and behaviors, as well as changes in societal structures and policies.

On an individual level, cultivating a more mindful and conscious approach to consumption is crucial. This involves redefining personal values, seeking alternative sources of happiness, and practicing gratitude for what one already has. Adopting sustainable consumption practices, such as buying second-hand or locally produced goods, can also contribute to reducing the environmental impact of consumerism.

SECTION 3: SOCIAL AND CULTURAL TRANSFORMATIONS 83

At the societal level, it is essential to promote policies and initiatives that encourage responsible consumption. This could include measures such as promoting ethical and sustainable products, regulating advertising practices, and implementing policies that promote a circular economy and reduce waste generation. Education and awareness campaigns can also play a significant role in challenging the dominant consumerist narrative and promoting alternative perspectives on well-being and happiness.

Conclusion

The rise of consumerism and materialism has shaped the modern world in profound ways, influencing individuals, societies, and the environment. While consumerism offers the promise of happiness and fulfillment through material possessions, its negative impact on personal well-being, social cohesion, and the environment cannot be ignored.

By adopting a more mindful and sustainable approach to consumption and promoting policies that prioritize well-being over excessive materialism, it is possible to build a more balanced and equitable society. It is up to individuals and society as a whole to navigate the challenges posed by consumerism and embrace alternative paths to personal fulfillment and collective well-being.

Subsection: The Digital Revolution and the Transformation of Communication

The advent of the digital revolution has brought about a profound transformation in the way we communicate. The rapid development and widespread adoption of digital technologies have revolutionized the way we exchange information, connect with others, and participate in global conversations. In this subsection, we will explore the key aspects of this digital revolution and its impact on communication.

The Rise of the Internet

The Internet, conceived as a military project in the 1960s, has become the cornerstone of the digital revolution. It has fundamentally changed the way we communicate, breaking down geographical barriers and enabling instant access to information on a global scale. The Internet has democratized communication by giving individuals a platform to express their thoughts, opinions, and ideas, challenging traditional gatekeepers of information.

84 CHAPTER 1: THE WORLD IN THE AFTERMATH OF WORLD WAR II

The Democratization of Information

One of the most significant effects of the digital revolution is the democratization of information. With the proliferation of online platforms, anyone with an internet connection can now access vast amounts of information on virtually any topic. This has empowered people to become active participants in the creation and dissemination of knowledge, leading to a more inclusive and diverse global conversation.

However, the abundance of information on the internet has also given rise to challenges such as information overload and the spread of misinformation. Thus, digital citizens must develop critical thinking skills and information literacy to discern reliable sources from unreliable ones.

The Power of Social Media

Social media platforms have emerged as influential tools in the digital age, transforming the way we interact and communicate with others. Platforms like Facebook, Twitter, and Instagram have provided new avenues for connection, collaboration, and self-expression. They have also played pivotal roles in mobilizing social and political movements, amplifying marginalized voices, and facilitating global conversations.

However, social media has also given rise to concerns about privacy, online harassment, and the spread of hate speech. It is crucial for individuals to be mindful of their digital footprint and navigate social media spaces responsibly and ethically.

The Evolution of Online Communication

The digital revolution has not only transformed the way we communicate but has also introduced new modes of communication. Email, instant messaging, video conferencing, and voice over IP (VoIP) services have become commonplace, facilitating quick and efficient communication across vast distances.

Furthermore, the emergence of web-based communication tools like blogs, podcasts, and vlogs has provided avenues for individuals to share their stories and expertise with a global audience. These platforms have empowered individuals to create their own online communities and engage in meaningful dialogue.

SECTION 3: SOCIAL AND CULTURAL TRANSFORMATIONS   85

The Challenges of Digital Communication

While the digital revolution has undoubtedly enhanced communication in numerous ways, it has also posed challenges. Digital communication can be prone to misinterpretation and misunderstandings due to the absence of nonverbal cues. Additionally, the rapid pace of online communication can contribute to information overload and a decreased attention span.

Moreover, the digital divide remains a significant challenge, with disparities in access to digital technologies and internet connectivity limiting certain individuals and communities' ability to participate fully in the digital revolution.

The Future of Communication

As technology continues to evolve, the future of communication holds both exciting opportunities and potential challenges. Emerging technologies like virtual reality, augmented reality, and artificial intelligence are likely to shape the way we communicate in the years to come.

Virtual reality (VR) and augmented reality (AR) have the potential to revolutionize communication by creating immersive and interactive experiences. These technologies can enable individuals to participate in virtual meetings, collaborate in shared virtual spaces, and experience communication in entirely new ways.

Artificial intelligence (AI) is another technology that will have a profound impact on communication. AI-powered chatbots and virtual assistants are already transforming customer service and information retrieval. In the future, AI may become more integrated into communication processes, offering personalized and context-aware communication experiences.

In conclusion, the digital revolution has brought about a transformation in communication that is unprecedented in human history. The rise of the internet, the democratization of information, the power of social media, and the evolution of online communication have revolutionized the way we connect, collaborate, and share information. While there are challenges and concerns associated with digital communication, the future holds immense potential for further innovation and advancement in how we communicate. It is essential for individuals to adapt, remain digitally literate, and embrace the opportunities presented by the digital revolution.

8CHAPTER 1: THE WORLD IN THE AFTERMATH OF WORLD WAR II

Subsection: The Globalization of Popular Culture and the Homogenization of Society

The globalization of popular culture has been a significant phenomenon in the contemporary world, leading to the homogenization of society to some extent. It refers to the spread and integration of cultural products, practices, and values across national boundaries, facilitated by advancements in communication technology, transportation, and globalization in general.

Background

Popular culture encompasses various forms of media, entertainment, and consumer products that are predominantly enjoyed and consumed by the masses. It includes music, films, television shows, fashion trends, sports, video games, and other forms of entertainment that capture the interest and attention of people worldwide.

Historically, popular culture was shaped by local and regional influences, reflecting the distinct characteristics and traditions of different societies. However, in recent decades, technological advancements and the ease of global communication have accelerated the spread of popular culture around the world.

Principles of Globalization and Cultural Homogenization

The globalization of popular culture and the subsequent homogenization of society stem from several underlying principles:

1. Accessibility: The internet, satellite television, and affordable travel have made it easier for people from different countries to access and consume popular cultural products from around the world. This accessibility has led to a greater exposure to diverse cultural expressions.

2. Cultural Imperialism: Globalization has been criticized for fostering cultural imperialism, where dominant cultures, primarily those of Western societies, exert significant influence over other cultures. This influence can shape cultural preferences and result in the diffusion of Western cultural values and norms.

3. Media Convergence: Technological advancements have facilitated the convergence of various forms of media, enabling the seamless integration of content across different platforms. This convergence has resulted in the globalization of media, making popular culture more readily available and easily shared among diverse audiences.

4. Homogenization vs. Hybridization: While popular culture has become more globally accessible, cultural homogenization is not the only outcome.

SECTION 3: SOCIAL AND CULTURAL TRANSFORMATIONS   87

Hybridization also occurs, where elements from different cultures merge to create new and distinct cultural expressions. This phenomenon challenges the notion of complete homogenization.

Effects and Implications

The globalization of popular culture and the homogenization of society have several effects and implications:

1. Standardization of Taste: As popular culture spreads worldwide, certain trends and preferences become more dominant, leading to a standardization of taste. For example, global franchises like McDonald's and Starbucks offer similar experiences and products, catering to a universal consumer base.

2. Loss of Cultural Diversity: The dominance of certain cultural expressions can overshadow or marginalize local traditions and practices, leading to a loss of cultural diversity. Traditional forms of music, dance, and art may be overshadowed by mainstream international popular culture.

3. Changing Gender Roles and Identity: The globalization of popular culture has influenced perceptions of gender roles and identities. It has the potential to challenge traditional gender norms by promoting alternative representations and narratives. However, it can also perpetuate stereotypes and reinforce existing gender hierarchies.

4. Influence on Language: The globalization of popular culture has contributed to the diffusion of certain languages as global lingua francas. English, for example, has become widely used in music, films, and internet content, influencing language preferences and communication patterns.

5. Cultural Appropriation: Globalization has increased cultural exchange but has also sparked debates around cultural appropriation. The borrowing and adoption of elements from marginalized cultures by dominant cultures can lead to the commodification and exploitation of cultural artifacts.

Real-world Examples

1. K-pop: The rise of Korean popular music, or K-pop, has demonstrated the power of globalization in shaping popular culture. K-pop has gained significant international popularity, reaching audiences beyond South Korea. Its success highlights the global reach of popular culture and its ability to transcend national boundaries.

2. Americanization: The spread of American popular culture, such as Hollywood movies, American music, and fast-food chains, has been perceived as a

88 CHAPTER 1: THE WORLD IN THE AFTERMATH OF WORLD WAR II

form of cultural imperialism. The influence of American popular culture can be seen in various parts of the world, often leading to the adaptation and adoption of American cultural values and practices.

3. Social Media Influencers: Social media platforms have provided a platform for individuals to become global influencers, shaping popular culture and influencing trends worldwide. Influencers from different countries can reach a global audience, demonstrating the power of technology in disseminating popular culture.

Caveats and Criticisms

While the globalization of popular culture has its merits, it is not without criticisms and caveats:

1. Western Domination: Critics argue that the globalization of popular culture has primarily resulted in the domination of Western cultural values and norms. This dominance can lead to cultural imperialism and the marginalization of local and indigenous cultures.

2. Cultural Hegemony: The spread of popular culture can perpetuate unequal power dynamics, where dominant cultures maintain control over cultural production and dissemination. This can limit the representation of diverse voices and create a sense of cultural hegemony.

3. Resistance and Localism: There is also a resistance to the homogenization of popular culture, with calls for the preservation and revitalization of local cultural expressions. Local communities often strive to maintain their unique traditions and resist the influence of mainstream global popular culture.

Conclusion

The globalization of popular culture has undoubtedly contributed to the homogenization of society. However, it is essential to recognize that the impact of popular culture is complex and multifaceted. Cultural homogenization should not be viewed as a monolithic process, as there is room for cultural hybridization and resistance. By understanding the dynamics of globalization and popular culture, we can critically analyze its effects and implications on society and promote cultural diversity and inclusivity.

Chapter 2: The Information Age and Digital Revolution

Section 1: The Birth of the Internet

Subsection: The Origins of the Internet: ARPANET and Packet Switching

The origins of the internet trace back to the development of ARPANET (Advanced Research Projects Agency Network) and the concept of packet switching. In this subsection, we will explore the key milestones and principles behind the creation of ARPANET and the revolutionary idea of packet switching.

Background

In the late 1960s, the United States Department of Defense's Advanced Research Projects Agency (ARPA) initiated a program to support scientific research and development in various fields, including computer networking. At that time, the existing communication systems relied on dedicated circuits, which were expensive and inefficient for transmitting data between remote computers.

ARPANET: The Birth of the Internet

In 1969, ARPANET became the world's first operational packet-switched network. Its purpose was to interconnect various research institutions and universities to facilitate the sharing of resources and information. Instead of using traditional circuit-switched networks, ARPANET used packet switching, which allowed data to be broken down into small packets and sent independently across the network.

90 CHAPTER 2: THE INFORMATION AGE AND DIGITAL REVOLUTION

The design of ARPANET was based on a decentralized architecture, wherein multiple computers, called hosts, were interconnected using specialized network devices called Interface Message Processors (IMPs). These IMPs acted as the gateways between hosts and were responsible for routing packets to their destination.

ARPANET adopted the Transmission Control Protocol (TCP) as its primary communications protocol, which allowed reliable and error-free transmission of data over long distances. The development of TCP was a significant milestone as it formed the foundation for future internet protocols.

Packet Switching: The Revolutionary Idea

At the heart of ARPANET lies the concept of packet switching. Before packet switching, data transmission relied on circuit-switching, where a dedicated connection was established between two communicating parties. However, this approach was inefficient and impractical for transmitting data in a networked environment.

Packet switching introduced a new paradigm where data was divided into small packets, each with its own destination address. These packets were then independently routed through the network, hopping from one node to another until they reached their destination. This approach allowed for efficient utilization of network resources and improved scalability.

One of the key advantages of packet switching is its ability to handle network congestion. In a packet-switched network, if a particular route is congested, packets can be dynamically rerouted to other available paths. This dynamic routing mechanism ensures that data flows smoothly, even under heavy network load.

Principles of Packet Switching

Packet switching is built on several principles that define its functionality and efficiency. These principles include:

1. **Packetization:** The process of breaking data into smaller packets. Each packet contains a header that includes information about the source, destination, and sequence number.

2. **Routing:** The process of determining the most efficient path for each packet to reach its destination. This is achieved through routing algorithms and protocols.

SECTION 1: THE BIRTH OF THE INTERNET

3. **Store-and-Forward:** Upon receiving a packet, each node in the network stores it temporarily before forwarding it to the next node. This ensures that packets are transmitted reliably and without errors.

4. **Multiplexing:** Multiple packets from different sources can be multiplexed together and transmitted over the same network link. This allows for efficient utilization of network capacity.

5. **Error Control:** Packet switching includes mechanisms to detect and correct errors that may occur during transmission. These mechanisms ensure data integrity and reliability.

The Impact of ARPANET and Packet Switching

The development of ARPANET and the concept of packet switching laid the foundation for the modern internet. The introduction of a decentralized network architecture and the use of packet switching revolutionized the way information was transmitted and shared.

Over the years, ARPANET expanded and evolved into what we now know as the internet. The principles of packet switching continued to shape the development of new protocols, such as IP (Internet Protocol) and TCP/IP, which form the backbone of today's internet infrastructure.

The internet's growth and global reach have changed the way we communicate, work, and interact with information. It has opened up endless possibilities for collaboration, innovation, and the exchange of knowledge across boundaries.

Resources and Further Reading

If you're interested in diving deeper into the origins of the internet, here are some recommended resources:

- *Tubes: A Journey to the Center of the Internet* by Andrew Blum

- *Where Wizards Stay Up Late: The Origins of the Internet* by Katie Hafner and Matthew Lyon

- *The Innovators: How a Group of Hackers, Geniuses, and Geeks Created the Digital Revolution* by Walter Isaacson

These books provide fascinating insights into the history, technology, and visionaries behind the development of the internet.

96 *CHAPTER 2: THE INFORMATION AGE AND DIGITAL REVOLUTION*

Exercises

To test your understanding of ARPANET and packet switching, here are a few exercises:

1. Explain the differences between packet switching and circuit switching. Provide examples of applications that can benefit from each approach.

2. Discuss the advantages and disadvantages of a decentralized network architecture, as exemplified by ARPANET.

3. Research and describe the current state of the internet backbone infrastructure. How has it evolved since the days of ARPANET?

4. Investigate the challenges and solutions related to network congestion in packet-switched networks. How do modern protocols deal with this issue?

5. Explore the concept of Quality of Service (QoS) in relation to packet switching. How can QoS mechanisms ensure the efficient transmission of different types of data?

Feel free to research, discuss with your peers, and use additional resources to answer these exercises.

Subsection: The World Wide Web and the Democratization of Information

The advent of the World Wide Web (WWW) has revolutionized the way we access and share information, contributing to the democratization of knowledge. The WWW is an interconnected system of documents and resources, accessible via the internet, that has transformed the way we communicate, conduct business, and access information. In this subsection, we will explore the origins of the WWW, its impact on information accessibility, and its role in empowering individuals and communities.

Origins of the World Wide Web

The World Wide Web was developed by Sir Tim Berners-Lee in the late 1980s and early 1990s. Berners-Lee, a British computer scientist, envisioned a system that would allow people to share information and collaborate across different computers and networks. He developed the Hypertext Transfer Protocol (HTTP) and Hypertext Markup Language (HTML), the fundamental protocols and markup language that underpin the functioning of the WWW.

The WWW was built on the concept of hypertext, which allows the user to navigate between different pieces of information through hyperlinks. This

SECTION 1: THE BIRTH OF THE INTERNET 93

revolutionary concept enabled users to seamlessly navigate from one webpage to another, making it easy to browse and retrieve information.

Impact on Information Accessibility

One of the most significant contributions of the WWW is its democratization of information. Prior to the WWW, access to information was often limited to libraries, books, or specialized databases, which were not easily accessible to the general public. The WWW changed this by making vast amounts of information available to anyone with an internet connection.

The WWW allows individuals to access a wide range of information on various topics, including news, research articles, educational resources, and entertainment. This accessibility has empowered people to educate themselves, stay informed, and participate in public discourse.

Moreover, the WWW has leveled the playing field, enabling individuals and small organizations to share information and ideas on a global scale. Blogs, social media platforms, and online forums have provided a platform for diverse voices and perspectives to be heard. This has fostered the exchange of ideas, facilitated collaboration, and challenged traditional sources of authority.

Empowering Individuals and Communities

The democratization of information through the WWW has empowered individuals and communities in several ways. Firstly, it has provided individuals with the tools to research and learn independently. With access to a vast array of online educational resources, individuals can acquire knowledge on virtually any subject, sparking intellectual curiosity and personal growth.

Secondly, the WWW has facilitated the sharing of experiences and knowledge within communities. Online platforms have allowed people with shared interests, such as hobby groups or professional communities, to connect and share information, tips, and best practices. This has accelerated learning and innovation within these communities, benefiting their members and society as a whole.

Additionally, the WWW has played a crucial role in promoting transparency and accountability. Online platforms have become important tools for citizen journalism, enabling individuals to document and share information about social, political, and environmental issues. This has led to greater awareness and the mobilization of public opinion, creating pressure for positive change.

Despite its transformative impact, the WWW is not without its challenges. For instance, the sheer volume and diversity of information available online can make

94 CHAPTER 2: THE INFORMATION AGE AND DIGITAL REVOLUTION

it difficult to discern reliable and accurate sources. Misinformation and fake news have become significant issues, requiring critical thinking skills and digital literacy to navigate the online landscape responsibly.

In conclusion, the World Wide Web has revolutionized the way we access and share information, playing a pivotal role in the democratization of knowledge. By providing unprecedented access to information, the WWW has empowered individuals and communities, fostering learning, collaboration, and positive societal change. However, the challenges of information overload and misinformation necessitate the development of critical thinking skills and digital literacy to harness the full potential of the WWW.

Subsection: Internet Service Providers and the Expansion of Online Connectivity

In this subsection, we will explore the role of Internet Service Providers (ISPs) in the expansion of online connectivity. ISPs play a crucial role in connecting individuals and businesses to the internet, enabling access to various online services and resources. We will discuss the function of ISPs, their role in establishing connectivity, the different types of internet connections, and the challenges and opportunities they face in the ever-evolving digital landscape.

Function of Internet Service Providers

Internet Service Providers are companies or organizations that provide individuals, businesses, and other entities with access to the internet. Their primary function is to establish and maintain the infrastructure required for online connectivity. ISPs connect their users to the internet through various technologies, such as dial-up, DSL (Digital Subscriber Line), cable, fiber-optic, satellite, and wireless connections.

ISPs not only deliver internet access but also offer additional services such as email accounts, web hosting, virtual private networks (VPNs), and domain name registration. They act as intermediaries between users and the vast network of interconnected devices, delivering data packets across the internet.

Types of Internet Connections

There are different types of internet connections offered by ISPs, each with its own advantages and limitations. Let's explore some of these connections:

1. **Dial-up:** Dial-up was one of the earliest forms of internet connections and is still available in some remote areas. It uses existing telephone lines to establish

SECTION 1: THE BIRTH OF THE INTERNET 95

a connection, but it is slow and has limited bandwidth. Dial-up connections are gradually being replaced by more advanced technologies.

2. **DSL (Digital Subscriber Line):** DSL uses existing telephone lines but provides faster connection speeds compared to dial-up. It enables simultaneous internet access and phone communication, as it utilizes different frequencies for data and voice transmission. However, DSL speeds can vary depending on the distance from the user's location to the provider's central office.

3. **Cable:** Cable internet connections use cable television infrastructure to deliver high-speed internet access. It offers faster speeds than dial-up and DSL and is widely available in urban and suburban areas. Cable connections are shared among multiple users in a neighborhood, which can result in reduced speeds during peak usage times.

4. **Fiber-optic:** Fiber-optic connections use thin strands of glass or plastic fibers to transmit data using light signals. This technology provides incredibly high speeds and is more reliable compared to other connections. Fiber-optic networks are expanding, but their availability is limited to certain areas.

5. **Satellite:** Satellite internet connections use satellites in orbit to establish connectivity, making it available in remote and rural locations where other options may not be feasible. Satellite connections can experience latency due to the long distance data needs to travel to and from the satellite.

6. **Wireless:** Wireless internet connections, such as Wi-Fi and mobile networks, enable users to access the internet without the need for physical cables. Wi-Fi networks are commonly used in homes, businesses, and public spaces. Mobile networks, on the other hand, provide internet access to devices such as smartphones and tablets using cellular technology.

Challenges and Opportunities

As technology advances and the demand for internet connectivity grows, ISPs face various challenges and opportunities. Let's explore some of these:

1. **Quality of Service (QoS):** ISPs strive to offer high-quality internet service to their customers. They need to manage network congestion, ensure reliable connections, and provide sufficient bandwidth for their users' needs.

CHAPTER 2: THE INFORMATION AGE AND DIGITAL REVOLUTION

QoS techniques such as traffic shaping and prioritization are used to optimize network performance.

2. **Net Neutrality:** Net neutrality is the principle that all internet traffic should be treated equally, without discrimination or preferential treatment by ISPs. The debate around net neutrality has significant implications for ISPs, as it influences how they can prioritize or regulate internet traffic.

3. **Digital Divide:** The digital divide refers to the gap between those who have access to the internet and those who do not. ISPs play a crucial role in bridging this gap by expanding connectivity to underserved areas and promoting initiatives to provide affordable internet access to disadvantaged communities.

4. **Data Privacy and Security:** ISPs are responsible for safeguarding user data and ensuring the security of their internet connections. They need to implement robust cybersecurity measures to protect against data breaches, hacking attempts, and other online threats.

5. **Bandwidth Demands:** The increasing demand for bandwidth-intensive applications such as video streaming, online gaming, and cloud services poses a challenge for ISPs. They need to continually invest in network infrastructure and upgrade their technology to meet the growing bandwidth demands of their users.

6. **Emerging Technologies:** The expansion of online connectivity opens up opportunities for ISPs to embrace emerging technologies. For example, the deployment of 5G networks and the Internet of Things (IoT) presents new possibilities for ISPs to connect a wide range of devices and enable innovative services.

Overall, Internet Service Providers play a crucial role in expanding online connectivity and enabling individuals and businesses to access the internet. They face challenges in ensuring reliable and secure connections, managing increasing bandwidth demands, and addressing issues of net neutrality and the digital divide. As technology continues to evolve, ISPs have opportunities to explore new technologies and innovative solutions to meet the growing needs of their users.

Subsection: E-commerce and the Rise of Online Shopping

In this subsection, we will explore the emergence of e-commerce and its impact on the retail industry. We will discuss the advantages and disadvantages of online

SECTION 1: THE BIRTH OF THE INTERNET

shopping, as well as the challenges and opportunities it presents for both consumers and businesses. Additionally, we will delve into the technology behind e-commerce platforms and the future trends in online shopping.

The Evolution of E-commerce

The advent of the internet and the widespread availability of computers and mobile devices have revolutionized the way people shop. E-commerce, or electronic commerce, refers to the buying and selling of goods and services over the internet. It has grown exponentially over the past few decades, transforming the retail landscape and offering consumers unparalleled convenience and choice.

The roots of e-commerce can be traced back to the 1960s when businesses started using Electronic Data Interchange (EDI) to exchange business documents electronically. However, it was not until the 1990s that e-commerce gained mainstream popularity with the rise of the World Wide Web. With the introduction of secure payment systems and the establishment of online marketplaces, consumers could now shop from the comfort of their homes.

Advantages of Online Shopping

The rise of e-commerce has brought about numerous advantages for both consumers and businesses. Let's examine some of the key benefits of online shopping:

1. Convenience: One of the primary reasons for the popularity of online shopping is convenience. Consumers can browse and purchase products or services anytime, anywhere, without the need to visit physical stores. This accessibility has significantly reduced time and effort spent on shopping.

2. Wide Product Variety: Online shopping offers an extensive range of products and services, often surpassing what is available in brick-and-mortar stores. Consumers can browse through multiple brands and compare prices effortlessly, enabling them to make informed purchasing decisions.

3. Competitive Pricing: Due to increased competition among online retailers, consumers can often find better deals and discounts compared to traditional stores. Additionally, online platforms enable consumers to easily compare prices across different sellers, ensuring they get the best value for their money.

4. Personalization and Customization: E-commerce platforms leverage data analytics and customer profiling to provide personalized recommendations and tailored shopping experiences. This level of customization allows consumers to discover relevant products and make purchases based on their preferences.

98 CHAPTER 2: THE INFORMATION AGE AND DIGITAL REVOLUTION

5. Seamless Transaction Process: Online shopping offers a streamlined transaction process, with secure payment options and convenient delivery methods. Customers can choose from a variety of payment methods, including credit cards, digital wallets, and cash on delivery. Furthermore, efficient logistics and delivery services ensure prompt and hassle-free product delivery.

Disadvantages and Challenges

While online shopping has its advantages, there are also some drawbacks and challenges that need to be addressed:

1. Lack of Physical Interaction: Unlike traditional retail stores, online shopping lacks personal interaction with salespeople. This limitation makes it difficult for consumers to physically examine products before making a purchase. To mitigate this, e-commerce platforms provide detailed product descriptions, images, and customer reviews to help customers make informed choices.

2. Security and Privacy Concerns: Online shopping involves sharing personal and financial information, raising concerns about data security and privacy. Cybercriminals can exploit vulnerabilities in e-commerce platforms to access sensitive information. To address this issue, reputable online retailers implement robust security measures, such as data encryption and secure payment gateways.

3. Delivery Challenges: Timely and reliable product delivery is crucial in online shopping. However, logistical challenges such as delayed deliveries, damaged products, or incorrect shipments can occur. E-commerce companies need to invest in efficient supply chain management and reliable delivery partners to ensure customer satisfaction.

4. Returns and Exchanges: Returning or exchanging products purchased online can be more challenging compared to physical stores. Consumers may face difficulties in the return process, including shipping costs, restocking fees, or complicated return policies. Online retailers need to offer hassle-free return and exchange policies to enhance customer trust and satisfaction.

Technological Infrastructure

Behind the scenes, e-commerce platforms rely on a robust technological infrastructure to facilitate online transactions. Key features and technologies of e-commerce platforms include:

1. Website Development: E-commerce websites serve as the virtual storefronts for online retailers. They need to be user-friendly, visually appealing, and capable of

SECTION 1: THE BIRTH OF THE INTERNET 99

handling high traffic volumes. Web technologies such as HTML, CSS, and JavaScript are used to create dynamic and interactive online shopping experiences.

2. Secure Payment Systems: Online payment systems ensure the security and integrity of financial transactions. Encryption protocols, such as Secure Sockets Layer (SSL) and Transport Layer Security (TLS), protect sensitive information during data transmission. Payment gateways, like PayPal or Stripe, enable secure online transactions.

3. Inventory Management Systems: E-commerce platforms require efficient inventory management systems to keep track of product availability, handle stockouts, and automate order fulfillment. These systems integrate with the website and logistics infrastructure to ensure seamless order processing.

4. Customer Relationship Management (CRM): CRM systems help retailers manage customer interactions and provide personalized experiences. They store customer data, order history, and preferences, enabling targeted marketing campaigns and customer support.

5. Analytics and Data Insights: E-commerce platforms capture large volumes of data related to customer behavior, purchase patterns, and website performance. Analytical tools and techniques help retailers make data-driven decisions, optimize marketing strategies, and improve the overall customer experience.

Future Trends

As e-commerce continues to evolve, several trends are shaping the future of online shopping:

1. Mobile Commerce: With the proliferation of smartphones and tablets, mobile commerce (m-commerce) is gaining momentum. Retailers are optimizing their websites for mobile devices and developing dedicated mobile apps to provide seamless shopping experiences on smaller screens.

2. Augmented Reality (AR) and Virtual Reality (VR): AR and VR technologies have the potential to revolutionize online shopping by offering immersive and interactive experiences. Customers can virtually try on clothes, visualize furniture in their homes, or experience products in a virtual environment before making a purchase.

3. Voice Commerce: Voice assistants such as Amazon's Alexa and Apple's Siri are increasingly integrated into e-commerce platforms, allowing users to make purchases through voice commands. Voice commerce offers a hands-free and convenient way of shopping, providing a more natural and personalized experience.

4. Sustainability and Ethical Consumerism: Consumers are becoming more conscious of the environmental and ethical impact of their purchases. E-commerce

CHAPTER 2: THE INFORMATION AGE AND DIGITAL REVOLUTION

platforms are responding to this trend by promoting sustainable products, transparent supply chains, and eco-friendly packaging options.

5. Artificial Intelligence (AI) and Machine Learning (ML): AI and ML technologies are playing a vital role in improving customer experiences in e-commerce. Chatbots and virtual assistants provide instant customer support, while recommendation systems offer personalized product suggestions based on customer preferences and browsing history.

To embrace these trends and remain competitive, online retailers must continuously innovate and adapt their strategies to meet evolving consumer needs and technology advancements.

Conclusion

The rise of e-commerce and online shopping has transformed the retail landscape, offering consumers unparalleled convenience, choice, and personalized experiences. While online shopping offers numerous advantages, there are also challenges such as security concerns, logistical issues, and the absence of physical interaction. However, with ongoing technological advancements and evolving consumer preferences, e-commerce continues to evolve and shape the future of retail. As we move forward, it is crucial for businesses to embrace these changes and leverage the opportunities presented by the digital revolution to thrive in the interconnected world.

Subsection: Social Media and the Transformation of Online Communication

Social media platforms have revolutionized the way we communicate and interact with others online. With the rise of Facebook, Twitter, Instagram, and other popular social networking sites, individuals from all over the world can easily connect, share information, and engage in conversations. This subsection explores the transformative impact of social media on online communication.

The Power of Social Media

Social media has transformed the landscape of online communication, giving individuals the power to disseminate information and express their opinions on a global scale. Through platforms like Twitter, news spreads rapidly, and ideas can gain traction quickly. Hashtags and trending topics bring attention to important issues, amplifying the voices of marginalized communities and providing a platform for social and political activism.

The Democratization of Information

Social media has democratized the access to information, allowing users to share news, articles, and blogs with a wide audience. Traditional gatekeepers, such as newspapers and television networks, no longer have a monopoly on news dissemination. This has led to a more diverse range of perspectives and increased citizen journalism, empowering individuals to shape public discourse and challenge mainstream narratives.

Evolving Modes of Communication

Social media has expanded the possibilities of online communication beyond traditional email and instant messaging. Platforms like Facebook Messenger and WhatsApp allow individuals to connect with friends and family in real-time, irrespective of geographical boundaries. We can now participate in video calls, share photos and videos, and send voice messages effortlessly.

Implications for Relationships

The advent of social media has significantly impacted the dynamics of personal relationships. It has made it easier to maintain connections with distant friends and family members, bridging the gap created by physical distance. However, it has also been associated with increased feelings of loneliness and dependence on virtual interactions. Online interactions sometimes lack the depth and intimacy of face-to-face communication.

Fake News and Misinformation

One of the biggest challenges brought about by social media is the spread of fake news and misinformation. Because anyone can share information online, it can be challenging to discern reliable sources from falsehoods. This phenomenon has significant implications for public opinion, political discourse, and trust in institutions. Battling fake news requires media literacy skills and critical thinking.

Privacy and Security Concerns

Social media platforms collect vast amounts of personal information, raising concerns about privacy and data security. Users need to be aware of the risks associated with sharing personal details and should utilize privacy settings to protect their data. Additionally, social engineering and cyber threats are prevalent on social media, making it important for users to exercise caution and stay vigilant.

Online Harassment and Cyberbullying

While social media has provided a means for connecting people, it has also given rise to online harassment and cyberbullying. Individuals can face abusive comments, hate speech, and targeted campaigns. It is crucial for social media platforms to create and enforce policies that prioritize user safety and address these issues effectively. Users should also be educated on responsible online behavior.

The Influence of Social Media on Politics

Social media has emerged as a powerful tool in shaping political narratives and mobilizing support for various causes. It has enabled political candidates to reach and engage with a broader audience, leading to new campaign strategies. However, it has also raised concerns about the influence of misinformation, echo chambers, and algorithmic bias on the democratic process.

Social Media Marketing and Influencer Culture

Social media platforms have become an essential medium for marketing and advertising. Influencers with substantial online followings have transformed into powerful brand ambassadors, using their influence to endorse products and services. This has led to the emergence of influencer culture, where individuals can build lucrative careers solely through their online presence.

The Future of Social Media

As technology continues to advance rapidly, the future of social media is likely to bring further transformations to online communication. Emerging trends such as augmented reality, virtual reality, and artificial intelligence will shape the way we interact and engage with social media platforms. It is essential for users and policymakers to anticipate and adapt to these changes responsibly.

In conclusion, social media has fundamentally transformed the way we communicate, connect, and share information online. While it has brought about numerous positive changes, such as democratizing access to information and empowering marginalized communities, it also presents various challenges, including the spread of fake news and privacy concerns. Understanding the impact of social media is crucial for navigating the digital landscape responsibly and harnessing its potential for positive change.

SECTION 1: THE BIRTH OF THE INTERNET 103

Subsection: Search Engines and the Age of Information Accessibility

In this subsection, we will explore the emergence of search engines and their impact on information accessibility in the digital age. We will discuss the principles behind search engine technologies, their evolution over time, and the challenges and opportunities they present.

Background

The development of the World Wide Web in the late 20th century led to an explosion of digital information, making it increasingly challenging for users to find the information they needed. Search engines emerged as a solution to this problem, providing a structured and efficient way to navigate the vast amount of information available online.

Principles of Search Engines

Search engines are sophisticated software systems designed to retrieve and organize information from the web. They use complex algorithms to analyze web pages, index their content, and rank them based on their relevance to user queries. The principles that underlie search engine functionality can be summarized as follows:

1. **Crawling and Indexing:** Search engines deploy automated programs called "web crawlers" that systematically browse the web, discovering and storing web pages in a vast database known as the index. These crawlers follow hyperlinks, collecting information about the content, structure, and relationships between web pages.

2. **Query Processing:** When a user enters a query into a search engine, the system matches the query against the indexed web pages. This process involves several steps, including tokenization (splitting the query into individual terms), stemming (reducing words to their root form), and ranking (determining the most relevant web pages based on various factors such as keyword frequency and link popularity).

3. **Presentation of Results:** Once the relevant web pages are identified, search engines display a list of results to the user. The results are typically ordered based on their ranking, with the most relevant pages appearing at the top. Search engines also provide additional features like snippets (short excerpts from web pages), image or video previews, and suggestions for related queries.

CHAPTER 2: THE INFORMATION AGE AND DIGITAL REVOLUTION

Evolution of Search Engines

Search engines have undergone significant evolution since their inception. Early search engines such as Yahoo and AltaVista relied on manual indexing and categorization of web pages. However, as the web grew exponentially, these methods proved inadequate in keeping up with the sheer volume of information.

In the late 1990s, Google revolutionized the search engine landscape with its PageRank algorithm. PageRank used the linkage structure of the web to assess the importance of web pages. By considering the number and quality of links pointing to a page, Google was able to rank pages in a more meaningful way, providing users with highly relevant search results.

Today, Google remains the dominant search engine, continually refining its algorithms to provide more accurate and personalized results. Other search engines like Bing and Baidu have also gained prominence in specific regions, offering competition and alternative search experiences.

Challenges and Opportunities

While search engines have transformed the accessibility of information, they also face several challenges and present new opportunities.

One significant challenge is the issue of **information overload**. With billions of web pages indexed and constantly growing, search engines must continually improve their algorithms to surface the most relevant and useful information. There is also a need to combat **spam** and **disinformation**, ensuring that search results are reliable and trustworthy.

Another challenge is **privacy and data security**. Search engines collect a vast amount of user data to personalize search results and improve the search experience. However, this data collection raises concerns about privacy breaches and unauthorized access to personal information.

On the other hand, search engines also present exciting opportunities. They have facilitated the democratization of knowledge, enabling users around the world to access information that was previously unavailable or difficult to find. Search engines have also become a critical tool for businesses, as **search engine optimization** (SEO) techniques help websites improve their visibility and reach.

Example: Search Engine Advertising

An essential aspect of search engines is their advertising model, which plays a significant role in their revenue generation. Google's advertising platform, Google

SECTION 1: THE BIRTH OF THE INTERNET 105

Ads, provides businesses with the opportunity to display targeted ads alongside search results.

For example, suppose a user searches for "best budget smartphone." The search engine would display both organic search results and sponsored ads related to budget smartphones. These sponsored ads are usually placed at the top or bottom of the search results page and are tailored to match the user's query and browsing history.

This advertising model benefits businesses by allowing them to reach a highly targeted audience actively searching for products or services. At the same time, search engine users can discover relevant products and services that meet their needs.

Resources for Further Learning

If you're interested in delving deeper into search engine technology and its impact on information accessibility, here are some recommended resources:

- *The Search: How Google and Its Rivals Rewrote the Rules of Business and Transformed Our Culture* by John Battelle provides an in-depth exploration of the history, impact, and challenges of search engines.

- *Search Engine Optimization All-in-One For Dummies* by Bruce Clay offers a comprehensive guide to understanding SEO techniques and optimizing websites for search engines.

- *The Filter Bubble: How the New Personalized Web Is Changing What We Read and How We Think* by Eli Pariser discusses the potential consequences of personalized search results and their impact on information diversity.

Conclusion

Search engines have revolutionized the way we access and navigate information in the digital age. Through the process of crawling, indexing, and advanced ranking algorithms, search engines provide users with fast and efficient access to relevant web pages. While there are challenges such as information overload and privacy concerns, the opportunities and benefits of search engines are undeniable. Understanding the principles and evolution of search engines can help us navigate and leverage the vast sea of information available online.

CHAPTER 2: THE INFORMATION AGE AND DIGITAL REVOLUTION

Subsection: Online Privacy and Security Concerns

In this subsection, we will explore the pressing issue of online privacy and security concerns that have become increasingly relevant in today's interconnected world. As technology continues to advance, the digital age has brought about a multitude of benefits and opportunities. However, it has also opened the door to various threats and risks, particularly in the realm of privacy and security.

Understanding Online Privacy

Privacy is a fundamental human right that is essential for maintaining autonomy, personal freedom, and dignity. In the digital realm, online privacy refers to an individual's ability to control the collection, use, and dissemination of their personal information in the online environment. It involves protecting sensitive data, such as personal details, financial information, and browsing habits from unauthorized access, exploitation, or surveillance.

However, maintaining online privacy can be particularly challenging, given the vast amount of data that is generated, collected, and stored by numerous online platforms, websites, and applications. This data includes personal identifiers, browsing history, social media interactions, and online transactions, among others. The continuous tracking and profiling of individuals for targeted marketing, surveillance, and data monetization purposes have raised significant concerns regarding the erosion of privacy.

Threats to Online Privacy

There are several threats to online privacy that individuals must be aware of to protect themselves effectively. These threats include:

1. **Data Breaches and Cyberattacks:** With the increasing reliance on online services and cloud storage, data breaches have become a pervasive risk. Cybercriminals target organizations to gain unauthorized access to sensitive data, including personal information, financial records, and login credentials. These breaches can result in identity theft, financial loss, and serious privacy violations.

2. **Tracking and Profiling:** Online platforms and service providers often employ various tracking technologies to collect data on individuals' online activities. This includes tracking cookies, browser fingerprinting, and device identifiers. Such practices enable the creation of detailed user profiles that can be used for targeted

SECTION 1: THE BIRTH OF THE INTERNET

advertising, content personalization, and even manipulation of individuals' opinions and behaviors.

3. Government Surveillance: Governments around the world engage in mass surveillance programs to monitor and collect citizens' online communications. While governments argue that surveillance is necessary for national security purposes, it raises concerns about privacy infringement and the potential abuse of power.

4. Social Engineering and Phishing Attacks: Social engineering techniques, such as phishing emails or fake websites, attempt to manipulate individuals into divulging personal information, passwords, or financial details. These attacks exploit human vulnerabilities and can lead to identity theft or unauthorized access to personal accounts.

Best Practices for Online Privacy

To safeguard online privacy, individuals can adopt various best practices to mitigate the risks and protect their personal information. These practices include:

1. Strong and Unique Passwords: Using strong and unique passwords for online accounts significantly reduces the risk of unauthorized access. Password managers can help create and store complex passwords for multiple accounts securely.

2. Two-Factor Authentication (2FA): Enabling 2FA adds an extra layer of security to online accounts by requiring a second form of verification, such as a temporary code sent to a smartphone, in addition to the password.

3. Encryption and Security Tools: Utilizing encryption technologies, virtual private networks (VPNs), and secure browsing tools can protect online activities from surveillance and monitoring. Encryption ensures that data transmitted between devices remains confidential and secure.

4. Privacy Settings and Consent: Carefully reviewing and adjusting privacy settings on social media platforms, mobile applications, and web browsers can limit the amount of personal data shared with third parties. Additionally, being cautious when granting consent for data collection and sharing can help protect privacy.

108 CHAPTER 2: THE INFORMATION AGE AND DIGITAL REVOLUTION

5. Regular Software Updates and Patches: Keeping software, operating systems, and applications updated with the latest security patches is crucial to protect against known vulnerabilities that hackers can exploit.

6. Cybersecurity Awareness and Education: Staying informed about the latest online threats and practicing good cybersecurity habits, such as being vigilant against phishing attempts and understanding the risks associated with sharing personal information online, are essential for maintaining online privacy.

Legislation and Regulations

Governments and regulatory bodies have recognized the importance of online privacy and have enacted legislation and regulations to protect individuals' personal information. These include:

1. **General Data Protection Regulation (GDPR):** The GDPR is a comprehensive privacy framework implemented by the European Union to regulate how personal data is collected, processed, and stored by organizations operating within the EU. It provides individuals with rights regarding their personal data, such as the right to access, rectify, and erase their information.

2. **California Consumer Privacy Act (CCPA):** The CCPA is a state-level privacy law enacted in California, USA, aimed at providing individuals with enhanced control over their personal information collected by businesses. It grants California residents specific rights, including the right to know what personal information is collected and the right to opt-out of the sale of their data.

3. **Children's Online Privacy Protection Act (COPPA):** COPPA is a US federal law that imposes certain requirements on websites and online services directed towards children under the age of 13. It aims to protect children's privacy by placing restrictions on the collection, use, and disclosure of personal information from minors.

Conclusion

Online privacy and security concerns are critical considerations in today's digitally interconnected world. Individuals must understand the threats they face and take proactive measures to protect their personal information. By implementing best practices, staying informed, and advocating for robust legislation and regulations,

SECTION 1: THE BIRTH OF THE INTERNET 109

we can strive to maintain a balance between the benefits of the digital age and the preservation of privacy and security.

Resources for Further Reading

- Greenwald, G. (2014). *No place to hide: Edward Snowden, the NSA, and the U.S. surveillance state.* Metropolitan Books.
    - Harris, S. (2014). *Data privacy and security.* Oxford University Press.
    - Solove, D. J. (2008). *Understanding privacy.* Harvard University Press.
    - Tene, O., & Polonetsky, J. (2013). *Privacy in the modern age: The search for solutions.* New Press.

Subsection: The Digital Divide and Global Technology Inequality

In today's interconnected world, the digital divide has become a significant issue, representing the gap between those who have access to digital technology and the internet and those who do not. This divide not only affects individuals but also entire communities and countries, perpetuating inequality on a global scale. In this subsection, we will explore the concept of the digital divide, its causes and consequences, and potential solutions to bridge this gap.

Understanding the Digital Divide

The digital divide refers to the gap that exists between individuals, communities, and countries in terms of access to and use of digital technology and the internet. It encompasses not only the physical access to devices and connectivity but also the skills and knowledge required to effectively utilize these resources.

According to statistics from the International Telecommunication Union (ITU), as of 2020, more than half of the world's population still does not have access to the internet. This divide is more prevalent in developing regions, rural areas, and disadvantaged communities where infrastructure, resources, and affordability are major barriers.

Causes of the Digital Divide

Several factors contribute to the digital divide and global technology inequality:

1. **Infrastructure:** Limited or inadequate internet infrastructure, such as a lack of broadband connectivity, particularly in rural or remote areas, hinders access to the internet for many individuals and communities.

CHAPTER 2: THE INFORMATION AGE AND DIGITAL REVOLUTION

2. **Affordability:** The cost of digital devices, internet services, and data plans can be prohibitive for individuals with limited financial means, making them unable to afford these resources.

3. **Education and Skills:** Insufficient education and digital literacy skills prevent individuals from utilizing digital technologies effectively. This includes the ability to navigate the internet, understand online safety, and utilize online resources.

4. **Gender and Socioeconomic Factors:** Gender disparities and socioeconomic inequalities exacerbate the digital divide. Women, rural populations, individuals with disabilities, and marginalized communities often face additional barriers to accessing and using digital technology.

Consequences of the Digital Divide

The digital divide has wide-reaching implications for individuals, communities, and countries. Some of the key consequences include:

- **Education:** Limited access to digital technology and the internet hampers educational opportunities, particularly in remote areas. Students without internet access may struggle to access educational resources, complete online assignments, or participate in digital learning platforms, further deepening educational disparities.

- **Employment and Economic Opportunities:** The digital divide creates employment and economic inequalities. With limited or no access to technology, individuals are unable to acquire digital skills and take advantage of online job opportunities or entrepreneurial ventures. This further widens the income gap between those who can harness digital technology and those who cannot.

- **Healthcare:** Access to digital health services, telemedicine, and online health education is essential, especially in underserved areas. The digital divide limits individuals' access to these services, hindering their ability to receive timely medical assistance and information.

- **Democratic Participation:** The digital divide can limit access to information, online platforms for social and political engagement, and the ability to exercise democratic rights. This can marginalize certain groups and hinder their ability to voice their concerns and participate fully in public discourse.

Addressing the Digital Divide

Addressing the digital divide requires concerted efforts from governments, private organizations, and civil society. Here are some potential strategies to bridge the gap:

1. **Infrastructure Development:** Governments and organizations can invest in expanding and improving internet infrastructure, particularly in remote and underserved areas. This includes the deployment of broadband networks and the establishment of public Wi-Fi hotspots.

2. **Affordability Initiatives:** Governments and service providers can introduce policies and initiatives to make digital devices, internet services, and data plans more affordable. This can involve subsidizing costs, providing low-cost options, or offering discounted rates for specific demographic groups.

3. **Digital Skills Training:** Investing in digital literacy programs is crucial to empower individuals with the skills needed to utilize digital technology effectively. These programs should focus on providing training in basic digital skills, internet safety, online navigation, and critical thinking.

4. **Partnerships and Collaborations:** Public-private partnerships can play a significant role in bridging the digital divide. Collaborations between governments, tech companies, and non-profit organizations can help share resources, expertise, and funding to expand digital access and provide training opportunities.

5. **Community Empowerment:** Engaging local communities and involving them in the decision-making process is vital for sustainable solutions. Community centers or libraries can serve as hubs for digital access, offering resources, training, and support to bridge the divide.

Case Study: One Laptop per Child (OLPC)

One notable initiative that aimed to bridge the digital divide is the One Laptop per Child (OLPC) project. Started in 2005, this non-profit organization focused on providing low-cost, rugged laptops to students in developing countries.

The OLPC project recognized the importance of digital literacy and aimed to empower children with access to technology and educational resources. The laptops were designed to withstand harsh conditions and showcased a simple, intuitive interface suitable for young learners.

CHAPTER 2: THE INFORMATION AGE AND DIGITAL REVOLUTION

Although the OLPC project faced challenges and criticism, it demonstrated the potential of technology to bridge educational gaps and empower disadvantaged communities.

Conclusion

The digital divide and global technology inequality pose significant challenges in today's interconnected world. As access to digital technology becomes increasingly essential for education, employment, healthcare, and democratic participation, bridging this divide is crucial for fostering inclusivity, equality, and sustainable development.

To address the digital divide, governments, organizations, and individuals must work together to invest in infrastructure, reduce costs, provide digital skills training, and empower communities. By ensuring universal access to technology and promoting digital literacy, we can create a more equitable and interconnected global society.

SECTION 1: THE BIRTH OF THE INTERNET 113

Subsection: Internet Censorship and the Threat to Free Speech

In today's interconnected world, the internet plays a crucial role in facilitating communication and the free exchange of ideas. However, with the increasing reliance on online platforms for information sharing, the issue of internet censorship has become a significant concern. Internet censorship refers to the control or suppression of online content, limiting access to certain websites, blocking specific information, or monitoring online activities. This form of censorship poses a serious threat to free speech and raises important questions about the balance between protecting individuals and maintaining an open and inclusive digital space.

Internet censorship is often implemented by governments or other authorities, claiming various justifications such as national security, protecting public morals, or preventing the spread of misinformation. While these concerns are valid, the methods used to censor the internet can result in the infringement of individuals' rights to free expression and access to information. It is essential to critically examine the impact of internet censorship on society, democracy, and the free flow of information.

The Implications of Internet Censorship

Internet censorship has far-reaching implications on different aspects of society. Firstly, it limits the ability of individuals to express their opinions freely and engage in open dialogue. Censorship can stifle dissenting voices and restrict the diversity of viewpoints available to the public. By controlling access to information, authorities can manipulate public perception, suppress political opposition, and maintain their power unchecked. This undermines the principles of democracy and transparency that are essential for a functioning society.

Secondly, internet censorship hinders the development of knowledge and intellectual growth. The internet serves as a vast repository of information, allowing individuals to access a breadth of knowledge on various subjects. Censorship obstructs this flow of information, preventing individuals from exploring different perspectives, conducting research, and expanding their understanding of the world. It hampers educational growth, innovation, and critical thinking.

Thirdly, internet censorship poses challenges to privacy and data security. In their efforts to control online content, governments and authorities may engage in surveillance activities, monitoring citizens' online activities, and collecting personal data. This invasion of privacy raises concerns about the protection of individuals'

CHAPTER 2: THE INFORMATION AGE AND DIGITAL REVOLUTION

rights and the misuse of collected data. Moreover, it can have a chilling effect on individuals, deterring them from freely expressing their opinions online.

Examples of Internet Censorship

Numerous countries around the world implement internet censorship to varying degrees. China, for instance, operates one of the most extensive censorship systems globally, known as the Great Firewall. It blocks access to international websites and services, such as Google, Facebook, and Twitter, replacing them with state-controlled alternatives. China's internet censorship primarily aims to control the flow of information and prevent the spread of dissenting viewpoints.

In Turkey, internet censorship has been used to suppress political opposition and control online discourse. Authorities in Turkey frequently block access to social media platforms and news websites critical of the government. Similarly, in Russia, online platforms are regulated and restricted to maintain state control over information dissemination.

Furthermore, some censorship efforts extend beyond national borders. In recent years, several countries have passed legislation requiring online platforms to remove or block content deemed illegal or offensive. These measures have raised concerns about the potential restriction of free speech on a global scale and the enforcement of laws that may violate established human rights standards.

Navigating the Threats

Protecting free speech and combating internet censorship requires a multi-faceted approach that involves various stakeholders, including governments, civil society organizations, and individuals. Here are some strategies to navigate the threats posed by internet censorship:

Advocacy and Awareness: Raising awareness about the importance of free speech and the impact of internet censorship is crucial. Civil society organizations, human rights activists, and individuals can play an essential role in advocating for freedom of expression and informing the public about the consequences of censorship.

Technological Solutions: Advancements in technology have enabled the development of tools and software that can circumvent internet censorship. Virtual Private Networks (VPNs), decentralized networks, and encryption technologies can provide individuals with alternative means to access information

SECTION 1: THE BIRTH OF THE INTERNET 115

and protect their privacy. Promoting the use of such tools can help individuals bypass censorship and maintain access to uncensored information.

International Pressure: Engaging in international dialogue and exerting diplomatic pressure on governments that engage in internet censorship can be effective. International bodies and organizations can advocate for the protection of free speech, monitor human rights violations, and apply pressure to ensure compliance with international standards.

Promoting Digital Literacy: Educating individuals about the importance of critical thinking, media literacy, and responsible internet use is paramount in navigating the threats of internet censorship. By fostering digital literacy, individuals can identify and evaluate biased or misleading information, reducing the impact of censorship on their ability to access diverse viewpoints.

Conclusion

Internet censorship presents a significant threat to free speech and access to information in the digital age. Governments and authorities must strike a balance between safeguarding societal values and upholding individuals' rights to express themselves freely. It is crucial to continue challenging internet censorship, fostering open dialogue, and advocating for the protection of free speech to ensure a vibrant and inclusive digital landscape for generations to come.

Subsection: The Future of the Internet: Artificial Intelligence and Virtual Reality

The future of the internet holds the promise of transformative technologies that will reshape our lives in ways we can only begin to imagine. Two such technologies that are expected to play a significant role in this future are Artificial Intelligence (AI) and Virtual Reality (VR). In this subsection, we will explore the potential of both AI and VR and their implications for the internet.

Artificial Intelligence (AI)

AI refers to the ability of machines to mimic human intelligence and perform tasks that would typically require human intelligence. The field of AI encompasses a wide range of techniques and approaches, including machine learning, natural language processing, computer vision, and robotics.

CHAPTER 2: THE INFORMATION AGE AND DIGITAL REVOLUTION

The future of the internet will be greatly influenced by the advancements in AI. Here are some key areas where AI is expected to have a significant impact:

1. **Personalization:** AI algorithms can analyze vast amounts of user data to understand individual preferences and provide personalized recommendations. This can enhance the user experience by tailoring content, products, and services to the specific needs and interests of each user.

2. **Automation:** AI-powered automation has the potential to revolutionize industries by replacing repetitive and manual tasks with intelligent machines. From customer service chatbots to self-driving cars, AI can streamline processes and increase efficiency.

3. **Data Analysis:** AI algorithms can analyze large datasets, identify patterns, and extract valuable insights. This has significant implications for fields such as healthcare, finance, and marketing, where AI can help in making data-driven decisions and predictions.

4. **Cybersecurity:** As the internet evolves, the complexity and scale of cybersecurity threats also increase. AI can play a crucial role in detecting and preventing cyber attacks by continuously monitoring network traffic, identifying anomalies, and responding in real-time.

5. **Healthcare:** AI has the potential to transform healthcare by improving diagnosis and treatment outcomes. From early disease detection to personalized medicine, AI-powered systems can assist doctors in making more accurate decisions and providing better patient care.

While AI offers immense opportunities, it also raises ethical concerns, such as privacy, bias, and job displacement. It is crucial to develop AI systems that are transparent, accountable, and unbiased, and to ensure that the benefits of AI are accessible to all.

Virtual Reality (VR)

Virtual Reality (VR) refers to the immersive digital experience that simulates real or imaginary environments. It typically involves the use of a head-mounted display and other input devices to create a sense of presence in a virtual world.

The future of the internet will see VR revolutionize various industries and offer new possibilities for communication, entertainment, education, and more. Here are some key areas where VR is expected to make a significant impact:

1. **Communication and Collaboration:** VR can enable people to communicate and collaborate in virtual environments, transcending physical boundaries. From virtual meetings and conferences to immersive social experiences, VR has the potential to redefine how we connect and interact with others.

SECTION 1: THE BIRTH OF THE INTERNET

2. **Education and Training**: VR can create realistic and interactive learning experiences, allowing students to explore virtual environments and interact with virtual objects. From virtual field trips to medical simulations, VR can enhance education and training across various disciplines.

3. **Entertainment and Gaming**: VR has already made a significant impact on the entertainment and gaming industries, offering immersive experiences and new forms of storytelling. From virtual concerts to fully immersive gaming worlds, VR pushes the boundaries of entertainment.

4. **Therapy and Rehabilitation**: VR has shown promise in therapeutic applications, such as treating phobias, anxiety disorders, and post-traumatic stress disorder. By creating controlled virtual environments, VR can provide a safe space for exposure therapy and rehabilitation.

5. **Architecture and Design**: VR can revolutionize the way architects and designers visualize and present their ideas. By immersing clients in virtual environments, VR allows them to experience spaces before they are built and make informed decisions.

Despite its potential, VR faces challenges such as high costs, technical limitations, and motion sickness. However, as technology advances and becomes more accessible, VR is expected to become a mainstream medium with widespread adoption.

The Intersection of AI and VR

The convergence of AI and VR has the potential to unlock even more transformative possibilities. By combining AI's ability to analyze data and understand user behavior with VR's immersive experiences, we can create highly personalized and interactive virtual worlds.

Some potential applications of the intersection of AI and VR include:

1. **Smart Virtual Assistants**: AI-powered virtual assistants, similar to Siri or Alexa but in a VR environment, can provide personalized assistance, answer questions, and perform tasks in a more natural and engaging way.

2. **AI-driven NPCs**: Non-playable characters (NPCs) in virtual reality games can be enhanced with AI algorithms to create more realistic and intelligent interactions, making the virtual world feel more lifelike.

3. **Virtual AI Companions**: AI companions in VR can provide emotional support and companionship, offering personalized conversations and adaptive behaviors based on user preferences and interactions.

122 CHAPTER 2: THE INFORMATION AGE AND DIGITAL REVOLUTION

4. **Real-time Translation and Interpretation:** AI and VR can come together to break language barriers by providing real-time translation and interpretation services in virtual meetings and interactions.

5. **Immersive Data Visualization:** AI can transform complex datasets into immersive visualizations in VR, allowing users to explore and interact with data in a more intuitive and immersive way.

These are just a few examples of how AI and VR can complement each other to create unique and transformative experiences. As AI and VR continue to evolve, we can expect further innovations and advancements in this intersection.

Conclusion

The future of the internet holds immense potential with the integration of Artificial Intelligence (AI) and Virtual Reality (VR). AI's ability to mimic human intelligence and VR's immersive experiences will reshape industries, communication, education, and entertainment.

However, as with any emerging technology, it is essential to address the ethical and societal implications of AI and VR. Privacy, bias, accessibility, and job displacement are among the concerns that need careful consideration.

By leveraging the strengths of AI and VR and addressing the challenges, we can create a future where the internet becomes an even more immersive, personalized, and intelligent space, transforming the way we live, work, and interact.

Section 2: The Impact of Technology on Society

Subsection: Automation and the Future of Work

Automation, the use of technology and machines to perform tasks previously done by humans, has been transforming various industries and reshaping the future of work. In this subsection, we will explore the impact of automation on employment, skills required in the digital era, and the challenges and opportunities that arise in this rapidly changing landscape.

1. **Automation and Job Displacement:** The advent of automation has raised concerns about job loss and the displacement of workers. As machines and algorithms become increasingly capable of performing both routine and non-routine tasks, certain jobs become obsolete or reduced in demand. For example, manufacturing assembly lines have been automated, leading to a decline in employment for manual laborers. While some jobs may disappear, automation also creates new opportunities and shifts the nature of work.

SECTION 2: THE IMPACT OF TECHNOLOGY ON SOCIETY

Case Study: The rise of autonomous vehicles brings forth the potential for job displacement among truck drivers. However, this technology also creates a demand for engineers, technicians, and data analysts specializing in autonomous systems.

2. **Skills for the Digital Era:** Automation drives the need for a shift in workforce skills. As routine tasks are automated, there is an increasing demand for skills that complement machines rather than duplicate their abilities. These skills include creativity, problem-solving, critical thinking, complex communication, and adaptability.

Example: While machines can analyze vast amounts of data, they often rely on humans to interpret the results and make strategic decisions. Therefore, data analytics skills coupled with the ability to derive actionable insights are crucial in leveraging automation effectively.

3. **The Rise of Augmentation:** Automation does not necessarily eliminate jobs entirely; rather, it often augments human capabilities. The collaboration between humans and machines can enhance productivity, efficiency, and innovation. This integration emphasizes the importance of skill development and lifelong learning to ensure workers can adapt and thrive in the evolving workforce.

Case Study: In healthcare, robotic surgical systems assist surgeons during intricate procedures, enabling more precise and minimally invasive operations. Surgeons must develop expertise in utilizing these technologies effectively and understanding their limitations.

4. **New Job Opportunities:** Although automation may displace some jobs, it also creates new roles and industries. Occupations that rely on advanced technological skills, such as data scientists, cybersecurity experts, and AI engineers, have emerged and are in high demand. Additionally, jobs related to maintaining and developing automation technologies also have substantial growth potential.

Example: The growing field of robotic process automation (RPA) requires specialists who can design, implement, and maintain automated systems, ensuring their smooth operation and continuous improvement.

5. **The Human Element:** While automation can perform repetitive and mundane tasks, it often falls short in areas requiring human emotional intelligence, creativity, and interpersonal skills. Jobs that involve empathy, leadership, negotiation, and complex decision-making are less susceptible to automation.

Case Study: Customer service representatives, despite advancements in chatbots and automated responses, continue to be essential for handling complex customer inquiries, offering personalized support, and building strong customer relationships.

6. **Preparing for the Future:** To thrive in the age of automation, individuals and societies need to adapt and prepare effectively. This includes investing in education

CHAPTER 2: THE INFORMATION AGE AND DIGITAL REVOLUTION

and training programs that foster technological literacy, digital skills, and critical thinking. Reskilling and upskilling initiatives play a crucial role in providing workers with the tools to navigate the changing job market.

Example: Governments and educational institutions have introduced coding and robotics programs in schools to equip students with foundational skills needed to understand automation technology and stimulate interest in related fields.

7. **Ethical Considerations:** Automation raises important ethical questions regarding data privacy, algorithmic bias, and the potential for job polarization. As machines increasingly make decisions that impact individuals and society, addressing these concerns becomes paramount to ensure fair and accountable automation practices.

Case Study: Facial recognition technology, when used in automated surveillance systems, raises concerns about privacy invasion and potential misuse. Striking a balance between security and individual liberties becomes a pertinent ethical challenge.

8. **Collaboration between Humans and Machines:** To harness the full potential of automation, it is crucial to design human-machine collaboration frameworks that promote shared responsibilities and strengths. Establishing effective human-machine interfaces, trust, and transparent decision-making processes are key considerations in achieving successful collaboration.

Example: Cobots (collaborative robots) are designed to work alongside humans, leveraging their strength and precision while allowing workers to focus on more high-level tasks that require cognitive abilities and fine motor skills.

In conclusion, the advent of automation presents both challenges and opportunities for the future of work. While some jobs may be displaced, automation also creates new roles and demands a shift in skills. Effective collaboration between humans and machines, investment in skill development, and addressing ethical considerations are crucial in reimagining work in the age of automation. By embracing innovation, individuals and societies can navigate the changing landscape and capitalize on the benefits that automation brings.

Subsection: The Gig Economy and the Rise of Freelancing

In the digital age, the nature of work has undergone a significant transformation. Traditional employment models are being challenged by the emergence of the gig economy and the rise of freelancing. This subsection explores the gig economy, its impact on the labor market, and the reasons behind the increasing popularity of freelancing.

SECTION 2: THE IMPACT OF TECHNOLOGY ON SOCIETY

Understanding the Gig Economy

The gig economy refers to a labor market characterized by the prevalence of short-term contracts, freelance work, and independent contractors. It is a departure from the traditional model of long-term, stable employment. In the gig economy, individuals are hired for specific projects or tasks on a temporary basis. They are often referred to as "gig workers" or "gigsters."

Factors Driving the Growth of the Gig Economy

There are several key factors that have contributed to the growth of the gig economy and the rise of freelancing:

Technological Advancements - The advent of digital platforms and technological advancements has made it easier for individuals to connect with employers or clients worldwide. Online platforms such as Upwork, Fiverr, and TaskRabbit have created marketplaces where gig workers can offer their skills and services.

Flexibility and Autonomy - Many freelancers are attracted to the flexibility and autonomy that gig work provides. They have the freedom to choose when and where they work, and can often set their own rates. This flexibility is particularly appealing to individuals who value work-life balance or have other commitments.

Skills and Expertise - Many gig workers possess specialized skills or expertise in specific areas. Companies and employers often seek out freelancers to access niche talent and avoid long-term commitments. This demand for specialized skills has contributed to the growth of the gig economy.

Cost Savings for Businesses - Hiring gig workers can be cost-effective for businesses. Instead of paying for full-time employees with benefits, they can engage freelancers as needed for specific projects. This allows businesses to reduce overhead costs and scale their workforce according to demand.

Challenges and Opportunities in the Gig Economy

While the gig economy offers opportunities for both workers and businesses, it also presents unique challenges. The following are some of the key challenges and opportunities associated with the gig economy:

126CHAPTER 2: THE INFORMATION AGE AND DIGITAL REVOLUTION

Income Instability - Gig workers often face income instability due to the unpredictable nature of freelance work. They may experience fluctuations in income and may struggle during periods of low demand. Building a stable income stream requires careful financial planning and diversification of clients.

Lack of Benefits and Protections - Unlike traditional employees, gig workers typically do not receive benefits such as health insurance, retirement plans, or paid leave. They are also not entitled to the same level of legal protections and employment rights. This lack of benefits and protections can leave gig workers vulnerable in times of need.

Career Development and Upskilling - Freelancers must continuously invest in their professional development and upskill to stay competitive in the gig economy. They must adapt to changing market demands, acquire new skills, and build a strong personal brand to attract clients. This emphasis on continuous learning presents opportunities for personal growth and career advancement.

Work-Life Balance and Flexibility - One of the significant advantages of the gig economy is the flexibility it offers. Gig workers have the freedom to design their work schedule and prioritize their personal life. They can choose projects that align with their passions and create a better work-life balance.

Building a Reputation and Networking - Reputation and networking play a crucial role in the success of gig workers. Building a positive reputation and expanding professional networks can lead to more opportunities and higher-paying projects. Leveraging online platforms, social media, and professional communities can help freelancers showcase their skills and connect with potential clients.

Real-World Example: Uber and the Transportation Industry

One of the most prominent examples of the gig economy's impact is Uber, the ride-sharing platform. Uber has revolutionized the transportation industry by allowing individuals to use their own vehicles to provide transportation services. Drivers have the flexibility to work whenever they want, and users can easily book rides through the Uber app. This example highlights how the gig economy can disrupt traditional industries and create new opportunities for individuals to generate income on their own terms.

SECTION 2: THE IMPACT OF TECHNOLOGY ON SOCIETY 123

Resources for Freelancers

For individuals considering a career in the gig economy or looking to enhance their freelancing skills, there are several valuable resources available:

Freelance Platforms - Online platforms such as Upwork, Freelancer, and Toptal provide opportunities for freelancers to find clients and showcase their skills. These platforms offer a range of projects across various industries and act as intermediaries between freelancers and clients.

Professional Communities and Associations - Joining professional communities and associations can provide freelancers with access to networking opportunities, mentorship, and industry insights. Examples include the Freelancers Union, the International Freelancers Academy, and local Meetup groups focused on freelancing.

Online Learning Platforms - Platforms like Udemy, Coursera, and LinkedIn Learning offer a vast array of courses and resources to help freelancers develop new skills or enhance existing ones. These platforms often provide certifications that can boost a freelancer's credibility and marketability.

Financial Management Tools - Freelancers need to manage their finances effectively. Tools such as QuickBooks, FreshBooks, or Wave can assist freelancers in invoicing clients, tracking expenses, and managing cash flow. These tools can streamline financial processes and provide insights into the financial health of a freelancer's business.

Conclusion

The gig economy and the rise of freelancing are transforming the way we work. Technology, flexibility, and demand for specialized skills are driving the growth of gig work. While there are challenges, such as income instability and lack of benefits, there are also opportunities for career growth and a better work-life balance. As the gig economy continues to evolve, it is important for freelancers to adapt, continuously learn, and leverage available resources to thrive in this changing work landscape.

CHAPTER 2: THE INFORMATION AGE AND DIGITAL REVOLUTION

Subsection: Telecommunications and the Transformation of Communication

In today's interconnected world, telecommunications plays a crucial role in transforming the way we communicate. The advent of telecommunication technologies has revolutionized various aspects of our lives, from personal interactions to business operations. In this subsection, we will explore the impact of telecommunications on communication and its broader implications for society.

The Evolution of Telecommunications

Telecommunication systems have come a long way since the invention of the telegraph in the 19th century. Over time, we have witnessed the emergence of various technologies that have shaped the landscape of communication.

One significant milestone in the history of telecommunications is the development of the telephone. Alexander Graham Bell's invention revolutionized long-distance communication by allowing individuals to talk to each other in real-time, regardless of the distance between them. Telephone networks enabled global connectivity, transforming communication into a more immediate and interactive experience.

With the rapid advancement of technology, the internet emerged as a game-changer in the telecommunications industry. The internet provides a platform for various communication services, such as email, instant messaging, voice and video calls, and social media. The widespread adoption of the internet has facilitated seamless communication, breaking down the barriers of time and distance.

Impact on Personal Communication

Telecommunications has had a profound impact on personal communication. It has brought people closer together, allowing instant communication across vast distances. Friends and family can stay connected through voice and video calls, bridging the gap between continents and time zones. Telecommunication technologies have made it possible to share memories and experiences in real-time, enhancing the quality of personal relationships.

Social media platforms have become pervasive in the world of telecommunications, enabling individuals to connect and interact on a global scale. People can share photographs, videos, and updates with their network of friends and followers, fostering a sense of community and belonging. Moreover, social

SECTION 2: THE IMPACT OF TECHNOLOGY ON SOCIETY 125

media has emerged as a powerful tool for social activism, allowing individuals to voice their opinions and mobilize for causes they care about.

However, the digital age has also raised concerns about the impact of telecommunications on interpersonal relationships. The constant availability of communication can lead to addiction and a decrease in face-to-face interactions. It is essential to strike a balance between the convenience of virtual communication and the richness of in-person connections.

Impact on Business Communication

The transformation of communication through telecommunications has had a significant impact on business operations. It has revolutionized the way organizations operate, collaborate, and reach out to customers.

Telecommunication technologies have enabled remote work, breaking down the barriers of physical location. Employees can communicate and collaborate with colleagues from different parts of the world, facilitating global teams and decentralized workforces. This has led to increased productivity, reduced costs, and a more diverse and inclusive work environment.

Additionally, telecommunications has transformed customer interactions. Businesses can now provide real-time customer support through various channels, such as phone calls, live chats, and social media platforms. Customer relationship management systems enable organizations to manage customer data effectively, tailor their communication strategies, and provide personalized experiences.

Challenges and Ethical Considerations

While telecommunications has brought significant benefits, it also comes with its own set of challenges and ethical considerations.

One of the primary concerns is the issue of privacy and data security. With the increasing exchange of information through telecommunications, protecting sensitive data has become crucial. Cybersecurity threats, such as hacking and data breaches, pose a significant risk to individuals and organizations. It is imperative to implement robust security measures to safeguard personal and confidential information.

Another challenge is the digital divide, which refers to the gap in access to telecommunications technologies. Not everyone has equal access to reliable internet connections or affordable communication devices, creating inequalities in information access, education, and economic opportunities. Bridging the digital

CHAPTER 2: THE INFORMATION AGE AND DIGITAL REVOLUTION

divide requires efforts to ensure universal access to telecommunications infrastructure and promoting digital literacy.

Furthermore, the rapid advancement of telecommunications technologies raises ethical questions. For instance, the collection and utilization of personal data for targeted advertising purposes raise concerns about privacy and informed consent. It is essential to establish ethical frameworks and regulations to protect individuals' rights and promote responsible use of telecommunications technologies.

Conclusion

Telecommunications has transformed communication, bringing people together and revolutionizing the way we interact with one another. From personal relationships to business operations, telecommunications has enabled instantaneous and global connectivity. However, it is essential to navigate the challenges and ethical considerations associated with telecommunications to ensure a secure and inclusive digital future.

Further Reading: - Castells, M. (2010). The Information Age: Economy, Society and Culture. John Wiley & Sons. - Jenkins, H. (2006). Convergence Culture: Where Old and New Media Collide. NYU Press. - Rheingold, H. (2014). Net Smart: How to Thrive Online. MIT Press. - Turkle, S. (2012). Alone Together: Why We Expect More from Technology and Less from Each Other. Basic Books.

Exercises: 1. Reflect on your personal communication habits and discuss the ways in which telecommunications technologies have influenced your interactions with others. 2. Research the digital divide in a specific region or country and discuss the challenges it poses to education and economic development. 3. Analyze a recent case of a data breach or cybersecurity incident and discuss its implications for personal privacy and organizational security.

Subsection: Cloud Computing and the Shift towards Data Storage

Cloud computing has revolutionized the way individuals and organizations store and access data. In this subsection, we will explore the concept of cloud computing and its impact on data storage. We will discuss the benefits of cloud storage, the challenges that come with it, and the trends shaping the future of data storage.

Understanding Cloud Computing

Cloud computing refers to the delivery of computing resources and services over the internet. It allows users to store and access data, run applications, and utilize

SECTION 2: THE IMPACT OF TECHNOLOGY ON SOCIETY

computational power without the need for on-premises infrastructure. Cloud computing providers, such as Amazon Web Services (AWS), Microsoft Azure, and Google Cloud Platform, offer scalable and flexible solutions to meet the evolving needs of individuals and businesses.

Cloud computing operates on a pay-as-you-go model, providing cost-effectiveness and scalability. It eliminates the need for investing in expensive hardware and software infrastructure, and instead, users can access resources on-demand, as required. This model allows for quick deployment of applications and efficient utilization of resources.

The Benefits of Cloud Storage

Cloud storage has several advantages over traditional local storage methods. Here are some key benefits:

- **Scalability:** Cloud storage allows users to scale their data storage needs easily. Whether you need a few gigabytes or several petabytes, cloud providers can accommodate your requirements without significant upfront investment.

- **Accessibility:** Cloud storage provides ubiquitous access to data from any location with an internet connection. This accessibility enables collaboration among geographically dispersed teams and facilitates remote work.

- **Data protection and redundancy:** Cloud providers often offer built-in data redundancy and backup mechanisms. This redundancy ensures that data remains accessible even in the event of hardware failures or natural disasters.

- **Cost-effectiveness:** With cloud storage, organizations can avoid the costs associated with maintaining their own physical data centers. Cloud providers handle hardware maintenance, security, and software updates, reducing the burden on IT departments.

- **Flexibility:** Cloud storage allows users to choose from a variety of storage options based on specific needs. Whether it's object storage for unstructured data, block storage for databases, or file storage for file sharing, cloud providers offer a range of choices.

Challenges and Risks

While cloud storage offers numerous benefits, it also comes with its own set of challenges and risks that need to be addressed:

CHAPTER 2: THE INFORMATION AGE AND DIGITAL REVOLUTION

- **Data security:** Storing data in the cloud raises concerns about its security and privacy. Organizations need to ensure that appropriate security measures, such as encryption, access controls, and data backup strategies, are implemented to protect sensitive information.

- **Data governance and compliance:** Cloud storage may introduce challenges related to data governance and compliance with industry regulations. Organizations must ensure that their cloud storage solutions meet regulatory requirements and adhere to data privacy standards.

- **Dependency on internet connectivity:** Accessing data stored in the cloud requires a stable internet connection. Any disruptions in connectivity can limit or restrict access to critical data, impacting business operations.

- **Vendor lock-in:** Migrating data between different cloud providers can be challenging and costly. Organizations should carefully consider the compatibility and portability of their data when selecting a cloud storage provider.

Trends in Data Storage

The field of data storage is constantly evolving to meet the growing needs of businesses. Here are some trends shaping the future of data storage:

- **Hybrid cloud storage:** Organizations are increasingly adopting hybrid cloud storage models, combining public cloud services with on-premises storage infrastructure. This approach allows for greater flexibility, control, and cost optimization.

- **Edge computing and edge storage:** With the proliferation of Internet of Things (IoT) devices, edge computing and edge storage are gaining prominence. Edge storage brings computing and data storage closer to the source, reducing latency and bandwidth requirements.

- **Software-defined storage (SDS):** SDS abstracts the underlying hardware and provides a layer of software-defined intelligence to manage storage resources. It enables organizations to scale storage independently from hardware, simplifies management, and improves resource utilization.

- **Object storage for unstructured data:** Unstructured data, such as multimedia files and documents, is growing rapidly. Object storage, which

SECTION 2: THE IMPACT OF TECHNOLOGY ON SOCIETY 129

organizes data into discrete units called objects, offers scalability and cost-effectiveness for managing large volumes of unstructured data.

- **Data deduplication and compression:** Data deduplication and compression techniques help optimize storage resources by eliminating duplicate or redundant data and reducing storage space requirements. These techniques improve efficiency and reduce costs.

- **Quantum storage:** Quantum storage, based on the principles of quantum mechanics, has the potential to revolutionize data storage by offering higher capacity, longer data retention, and greater security. Although still in its early stages, quantum storage research holds promise for the future.

Real-World Example: Dropbox

Dropbox is a popular cloud storage service that exemplifies the shift towards data storage in the cloud. It allows users to store and synchronize files across multiple devices, making them accessible from anywhere. Dropbox's data storage infrastructure is distributed across various data centers globally, ensuring both data availability and redundancy.

Users can easily upload and share files with others, making collaboration seamless. Dropbox offers different storage plans to cater to individual and business needs, providing scalable storage options.

To address data security concerns, Dropbox encrypts data at rest and in transit, providing robust protection against unauthorized access. It also offers features like two-factor authentication and granular access controls to enhance the security of the stored data.

Conclusion

Cloud computing has transformed data storage by offering scalable, accessible, and cost-effective solutions. While it brings numerous benefits, organizations need to address challenges related to data security, governance, and connectivity. By staying updated on emerging trends and adapting to new technologies, businesses can harness the power of cloud storage to drive innovation and efficiency in their operations.

CHAPTER 2: THE INFORMATION AGE AND DIGITAL REVOLUTION

Exercises

1. **Discussion:** Discuss the advantages and disadvantages of using cloud storage for personal data backup.

2. **Case Study:** Research and analyze a real-world example of a company that experienced a data breach in the cloud. Identify the security vulnerabilities and propose measures to prevent future breaches.

3. **Exploration:** Investigate the current state of quantum storage research and its potential implications for future data storage technologies. Present your findings to the class.

4. **Hands-on Activity:** Sign up for a free trial account with a cloud storage provider such as AWS, Azure, or Google Cloud. Explore the features and functionalities of the platform and create a simple storage project.

Additional Resources

- Dikaiakos, M. D., Katsaros, D., Mehra, P., Pallis, G., & Vakali, A. (2009). Cloud Computing: Distributed Internet Computing for IT and Scientific Research. IEEE Internet Computing, 13(5), 10-13.

- Mell, P., & Grance, T. (2011). The NIST Definition of Cloud Computing. National Institute of Standards and Technology.

- Armbrust, M., Fox, A., Griffith, R., Joseph, A. D.", Katz, R., Konwinski, A., ... & Zaharia, M. (2010). A View of Cloud Computing. Communications of the ACM, 53(4), 50-58.

Key Terms

- Cloud computing

- Scalability

- Accessibility

- Data protection and redundancy

- Cost-effectiveness

- Flexibility

SECTION 2: THE IMPACT OF TECHNOLOGY ON SOCIETY

- Data security

- Data governance and compliance

- Dependency on internet connectivity

- Vendor lock-in

- Hybrid cloud storage

- Edge computing and edge storage

- Software-defined storage (SDS)

- Object storage for unstructured data

- Data deduplication and compression

- Quantum storage

Subsection: Robotics and the Potential for Technological Unemployment

Robots and automation have become increasingly prevalent in modern society, revolutionizing various industries and sectors. While this technological advancement brings great benefits in terms of efficiency, productivity, and cost reduction, there are concerns about the potential impact on employment and job displacement. This subsection explores the concept of technological unemployment in the context of robotics and provides an analysis of the challenges and opportunities this phenomenon presents.

Understanding Technological Unemployment

Technological unemployment refers to the displacement of workers by automation and advanced technologies. It occurs when machines and robots are capable of performing tasks that were previously done by human workers, leading to a decrease in demand for human labor. This displacement can affect workers from various industries and skill levels, ranging from manual laborers to highly skilled professionals.

The fear of technological unemployment is not new. Throughout history, technological advancements have caused disruption and changes in the labor market. However, the current wave of automation, driven by robotics and artificial

136 CHAPTER 2: THE INFORMATION AGE AND DIGITAL REVOLUTION

intelligence, is more significant and widespread than ever before. Robots are becoming increasingly capable of performing complex tasks, leading to concerns about the potential loss of jobs and the impact on society.

Factors Contributing to Technological Unemployment

Several factors contribute to the potential for technological unemployment in the context of robotics:

1. **Automation of Routine Tasks:** Robots excel at performing repetitive and predictable tasks with speed and precision. As technology advances, robots can increasingly handle tasks that were once exclusive to humans, leading to potential job displacement in industries such as manufacturing, logistics, and agriculture.

2. **Advancements in Artificial Intelligence:** The integration of artificial intelligence (AI) with robotics enables machines to perform cognitive tasks that were previously thought to be the preserve of human intelligence. This includes tasks involving decision-making, problem-solving, and pattern recognition. As AI capabilities improve, the potential for job displacement in industries like customer service, data analysis, and even professions like law and finance increases.

3. **Economic Incentives:** Businesses often adopt automation technologies to reduce labor costs and improve efficiency. While this can lead to higher profits and productivity gains, it can also result in workforce reductions. The economic incentives of automation can make companies more inclined to invest in robotics, potentially leading to higher unemployment rates.

4. **Evolving Robotics Technology:** Robotics technology continues to advance rapidly, with robots becoming more versatile, dexterous, and capable of performing complex tasks. This progress increases the feasibility of robots replacing human workers, particularly in physically demanding or dangerous occupations.

5. **Socioeconomic Factors:** Technological unemployment is influenced by various socioeconomic factors, including government policies, education systems, and income distribution. These factors can exacerbate or mitigate the impact of automation on employment. Adequate measures need to be in place to ensure the benefits of automation are shared equitably across society.

SECTION 2: THE IMPACT OF TECHNOLOGY ON SOCIETY 133

It is important to note that while technological unemployment may lead to short-term job displacement, it can also create opportunities for new jobs and industries to emerge. As technology evolves, new occupations and tasks that complement automation can be developed.

Addressing the Challenges

Addressing the challenges posed by technological unemployment requires a comprehensive approach that considers both short-term and long-term solutions. Here are some strategies to mitigate the potential negative impacts:

1. **Education and Skill Development:** Investing in education and skill development is crucial to equip individuals with the necessary skills for the changing job market. Emphasis should be placed on cultivating creativity, critical thinking, and adaptability, which are difficult for automation to replicate. Lifelong learning programs and vocational training can help workers transition into new occupations and industries.

2. **Promoting Entrepreneurship and Innovation:** Encouraging entrepreneurship and innovation can lead to the creation of new job opportunities and industries. Governments and organizations can provide support and resources to individuals and startups to foster innovation and entrepreneurship.

3. **Social Safety Nets:** As automation disrupts the job market, social safety nets need to be strengthened to provide support for workers who face job displacement. This can include unemployment benefits, job placement assistance, and reskilling programs to facilitate their transition into new employment.

4. **Collaboration between Humans and Robots:** Rather than perceiving robots as direct competitors, efforts should be made to integrate robots into workplaces to augment human capabilities. This collaborative approach, known as "cobots," allows humans and robots to work together, with humans focusing on tasks that require creativity, empathy, and complex decision-making.

5. **Ethical Considerations:** As robotics and AI continue to advance, it is essential to address ethical considerations, such as the impact on privacy, security, and social inequality. Developing ethical guidelines and regulations

CHAPTER 2: THE INFORMATION AGE AND DIGITAL REVOLUTION

can ensure the responsible deployment of robots and minimize potential negative consequences.

Real-world Examples

The potential for technological unemployment can be observed in various industries today. For instance:

- **Manufacturing:** Industrial robots have significantly transformed the manufacturing sector, leading to increased automation and reduced demand for human workers in assembly lines and production processes.

- **Transportation:** The emergence of self-driving vehicles threatens to disrupt the transportation industry, potentially displacing millions of truck drivers, taxi drivers, and delivery personnel.

- **Customer Service:** Chatbots and virtual assistants are being increasingly deployed in customer service roles, potentially reducing the need for human customer support agents.

- **Healthcare:** Surgical robots are increasingly utilized in the healthcare industry, allowing for more precise and efficient surgeries. While this improves patient outcomes, it may impact employment opportunities for certain surgical specialties.

These examples highlight the need for proactive measures to navigate the challenges brought about by technological unemployment while harnessing the benefits of robotics and automation.

Conclusion

The rise of robotics and automation brings immense opportunities for increased efficiency and productivity. However, it also raises concerns about job displacement and technological unemployment. Understanding the factors contributing to technological unemployment and implementing strategies to address these challenges are crucial for a smooth and inclusive transition into a future where humans and robots collaborate. By investing in education, promoting innovation, and developing ethical frameworks, society can adapt to the changing dynamics of the labor market and ensure a prosperous future for all.

SECTION 2: THE IMPACT OF TECHNOLOGY ON SOCIETY

Subsection: Biotechnology and the Ethics of Genetic Engineering

Biotechnology is a rapidly advancing field that involves the application of scientific knowledge and techniques to manipulate living organisms for practical purposes. One of the most controversial and ethically challenging areas of biotechnology is genetic engineering, which involves modifying an organism's genetic material to achieve desired traits or characteristics. The potential benefits of genetic engineering are vast, ranging from improved crop yields and disease resistance to the development of new medicines. However, it also raises profound ethical questions and concerns about the impact on the environment and human society.

Overview of Genetic Engineering

Genetic engineering involves the manipulation of an organism's DNA, the hereditary material that determines its traits. This can be done by inserting, deleting, or modifying specific genes to alter the organism's characteristics. The tools used in genetic engineering include restriction enzymes, which cut DNA at specific sequences, and DNA ligases, which join DNA fragments together. The development of recombinant DNA technology has allowed scientists to transfer genes between different organisms, including those that would not naturally breed or exchange genetic material.

The potential applications of genetic engineering are diverse. In agriculture, genetically modified crops (GM crops) have been developed to improve yield, reduce susceptibility to pests and diseases, and enhance nutritional value. In medicine, genetic engineering holds promise for developing new treatments for genetic disorders and producing therapeutic proteins such as insulin and growth hormones. It also has applications in environmental remediation, bioremediation, and the production of biofuels.

Ethical Considerations

Genetic engineering raises several ethical considerations, as it involves making deliberate changes to the genetic makeup of organisms. These considerations can be broadly classified into three categories: environmental, health and safety, and social and ethical.

Environmental Considerations: One of the major concerns regarding genetic engineering is its potential impact on the environment. The introduction of genetically modified organisms (GMOs) into ecosystems can have unintended consequences, such as the transfer of modified genes to wild populations or the

CHAPTER 2: THE INFORMATION AGE AND DIGITAL REVOLUTION

disruption of natural ecosystems. The release of genetically modified organisms must be carefully controlled and regulated to prevent ecological harm.

Health and Safety Considerations: Genetic engineering also raises concerns about the safety of genetically modified products for human consumption. The long-term effects of consuming genetically modified foods are still not fully understood, and there is a need for rigorous testing and regulation to ensure their safety. Additionally, there is a risk that genetically modified organisms could become invasive or create new diseases, necessitating careful risk assessment and management.

Social and Ethical Considerations: Genetic engineering raises profound ethical questions about the boundaries of human intervention in nature. Some argue that genetic engineering is an unnatural manipulation of life and violates the sanctity of nature. Others raise concerns about the potential for genetic discrimination or inequality if certain genetic enhancements become available only to the wealthy. There is also a need to ensure transparency and public engagement in decision-making processes related to genetic engineering.

Regulatory Framework

Given the ethical and safety concerns associated with genetic engineering, many countries have established regulatory frameworks to govern its use. These frameworks typically include risk assessment procedures, labeling requirements for genetically modified products, and mechanisms for public consultation and engagement. However, the regulatory landscape varies between countries, leading to different levels of oversight and public acceptance of genetically modified organisms.

Internationally, the Cartagena Protocol on Biosafety, an international treaty adopted under the Convention on Biological Diversity, provides a framework for the safe transfer, handling, and use of genetically modified organisms. The protocol aims to ensure the protection of biodiversity and human health in the context of biotechnology.

Case Study: Genetically Modified Crops

One of the most controversial applications of genetic engineering is the development and cultivation of genetically modified crops. Advocates argue that these crops can help address food security challenges by increasing yields, improving nutritional content, and reducing the need for pesticides. Critics, on the

SECTION 2: THE IMPACT OF TECHNOLOGY ON SOCIETY 137

other hand, raise concerns about potential environmental impacts, monopolistic control of the seed market, and potential health risks.

An example of a genetically modified crop is Golden Rice, which has been engineered to produce beta-carotene, a precursor of vitamin A. Vitamin A deficiency is a significant health problem in many developing countries, leading to blindness and other adverse health effects. Golden Rice has the potential to address this issue by providing a dietary source of vitamin A. However, its commercialization has faced significant regulatory and public acceptance challenges.

The Need for Ethical Consideration

As genetic engineering continues to advance, it is essential to ensure that ethical considerations play a central role in decision-making processes. Ethics committees, composed of experts from various fields, can provide guidance and oversight to ensure that the potential benefits of genetic engineering are balanced with the ethical, environmental, and societal implications.

Furthermore, public engagement and dialogue are crucial to fostering informed decision-making and societal acceptance of genetic engineering. Open and transparent communication about the risks, benefits, and uncertainties associated with genetic engineering is essential to build trust and facilitate meaningful participation in decision-making processes.

Conclusion

The field of biotechnology, particularly genetic engineering, offers immense potential for innovation and advancement in various sectors. However, the ethical considerations associated with genetic engineering cannot be overlooked or brushed aside. It is crucial to strike a balance between scientific progress and responsible application, taking into account environmental impacts, health and safety concerns, and social and ethical considerations. By promoting transparency, public engagement, and rigorous regulation, we can navigate the complex ethical landscape inherent to genetic engineering and ensure its responsible and sustainable use in shaping our future.

Subsection: Virtual Reality and the Augmentation of Reality

Virtual Reality (VR) and Augmented Reality (AR) are cutting-edge technologies that have revolutionized the way we perceive and interact with the world around us.

CHAPTER 2: THE INFORMATION AGE AND DIGITAL REVOLUTION

In this subsection, we will explore the concepts of VR and AR, their applications, and their impact on various fields.

Definition and Principles of Virtual Reality

Virtual Reality refers to a computer-generated environment that simulates a real or imaginary world. It immerses users in a 3D environment, providing a sense of presence and allowing them to interact with objects and characters in the virtual space. The key principles of VR include immersion, which involves creating a sense of being physically present in the virtual world, and interactivity, which allows users to manipulate and control their virtual surroundings.

Hardware and Software for Virtual Reality

To experience VR, users typically need a combination of hardware and software. The hardware includes a high-resolution display, often in the form of a headset, which covers the user's field of view and tracks their head movements. It also includes motion-tracking devices, such as controllers or sensors, which allow users to interact with the virtual environment. The software consists of the virtual world itself, which can be created using specialized software development tools and platforms.

Applications of Virtual Reality

Virtual Reality has found applications in various fields, including gaming, education, healthcare, and architecture. In the gaming industry, VR has brought a new level of immersion, allowing players to step into the virtual world and interact with characters and objects in a more realistic and engaging way. In education, VR provides immersive learning experiences, allowing students to explore historical sites, conduct scientific experiments, or practice real-life scenarios in a safe and controlled environment.

In healthcare, VR is used for training medical professionals, simulating surgical procedures, and treating patients with phobias or anxiety disorders. It enables medical students to practice complex surgeries without the risk associated with real patients. Moreover, VR therapy has proven effective in treating post-traumatic stress disorder (PTSD) and other mental health conditions.

Architects and designers also use VR to visualize and present their projects. They can create virtual walkthroughs of buildings, allowing clients to experience the space before it is constructed. By manipulating virtual objects and environments, architects can make real-time design changes and test different configurations.

SECTION 2: THE IMPACT OF TECHNOLOGY ON SOCIETY 139

Definition and Principles of Augmented Reality

Augmented Reality, on the other hand, overlays digital information onto the real world, enhancing the user's perception and adding virtual elements to their environment. Unlike VR, AR does not completely immerse users in a virtual world but rather supplements their real-world experience. AR can be experienced through various devices, including smartphones, tablets, and AR glasses.

Hardware and Software for Augmented Reality

To experience AR, users need a device with a camera and a screen, such as a smartphone or a tablet. The camera captures the real-world view, and the AR software overlays virtual elements onto it. The software utilizes computer vision and image recognition algorithms to identify objects and surfaces in the real world, allowing precise placement of virtual objects. Additionally, AR glasses, such as Microsoft HoloLens or Google Glass, provide a hands-free AR experience, allowing users to see virtual objects in their field of view.

Applications of Augmented Reality

Augmented Reality has a wide range of applications across industries. In the field of entertainment, AR is used in mobile games, bringing virtual characters and objects into the real world. It enables users to interact with virtual creatures or solve puzzles in their own environment. AR is also used in marketing and advertising, allowing brands to create immersive and interactive experiences for their customers.

In the field of education, AR enhances traditional learning methods by providing additional information and context. Students can use AR apps to scan textbooks and access supplementary multimedia content, such as videos or 3D models, to deepen their understanding of the subject matter. AR also has applications in the workplace, where it can provide real-time assistance and guidance, such as overlaying repair instructions onto machinery or displaying information during complex tasks.

In design and architecture, AR allows designers to visualize their creations in the real world, helping them make informed decisions and communicate their ideas effectively. Additionally, AR has practical applications in fields like medicine, where it can assist surgeons during procedures by displaying vital patient information or guiding them with step-by-step instructions.

144 CHAPTER 2: THE INFORMATION AGE AND DIGITAL REVOLUTION

Challenges and Future Directions

While VR and AR offer exciting possibilities, there are still challenges that need to be addressed. One of the main challenges is the need for more advanced hardware to improve the overall immersive experience. This includes higher-resolution displays, lightweight and comfortable headsets, and better motion-tracking capabilities.

Another challenge is the development of compelling and engaging content for VR and AR experiences. Creating realistic and immersive virtual environments requires skilled designers and developers. Additionally, ensuring compatibility across different platforms and devices is essential for widespread adoption.

In the future, we can expect further advancements in VR and AR technology. For VR, advancements in haptic feedback and motion tracking will enhance the sense of immersion. AR will likely evolve to provide more seamless integration of virtual and real-world elements, with advancements in wearable AR devices and improved object recognition capabilities.

Moreover, the potential of VR and AR in fields like medicine, education, and entertainment is vast. As the technology continues to evolve, it will become more accessible, affordable, and integrated into our everyday lives, creating new opportunities for innovation and transformation.

In conclusion, Virtual Reality and Augmented Reality are transformative technologies that have the potential to reshape our perception of reality. They offer novel ways to interact with information, objects, and environments, opening up new possibilities across various domains. As the technology continues to advance, VR and AR will play an increasingly significant role in shaping the future of how we learn, work, and experience the world around us.

Subsection: Cybersecurity and the Battle against Hacking

In our interconnected world, where technology plays a central role in our daily lives, the importance of cybersecurity cannot be overstated. With the rise of the digital age, the battle against hacking has become an ongoing challenge for individuals, businesses, governments, and organizations alike. In this subsection, we will explore the concept of cybersecurity, the various types of hacking, and the strategies employed to protect against cyber threats.

Understanding Cybersecurity

Cybersecurity is the practice of protecting computer systems, networks, and data from unauthorized access, theft, or damage. It involves a range of measures,

SECTION 2: THE IMPACT OF TECHNOLOGY ON SOCIETY 141

including the use of hardware and software technologies, as well as the implementation of policies and procedures to safeguard information.

At its core, cybersecurity addresses three key objectives: confidentiality, integrity, and availability. Confidentiality ensures that sensitive information remains private and is accessible only to authorized individuals. Integrity ensures that data is accurate and has not been tampered with. Availability ensures that information and systems are accessible and usable when needed.

Types of Hacking

Hacking refers to unauthorized attempts to exploit vulnerabilities in computer systems and networks for personal gain or malicious purposes. It is essential to understand the different types of hacking to develop effective defensive strategies. Some common forms of hacking include:

1. **Malware Attacks:** Malware, short for malicious software, refers to programs designed to infiltrate and damage computer systems. Examples of malware include viruses, worms, ransomware, and spyware.

2. **Phishing Attacks:** Phishing involves tricking individuals into revealing sensitive information, such as usernames, passwords, or credit card details, through deceptive emails, messages, or websites.

3. **Denial of Service (DoS) Attacks:** DoS attacks overload a system or network with traffic, making it unavailable to legitimate users. Distributed Denial of Service (DDoS) attacks involve multiple sources, making them even more difficult to defend against.

4. **Social Engineering:** Social engineering exploits human psychology to manipulate individuals into divulging confidential information or granting unauthorized access. Techniques include impersonation, baiting, and pretexting.

5. **Zero-Day Exploits:** Zero-day exploits take advantage of previously unknown vulnerabilities in software or hardware before a patch is available. They are particularly challenging to defend against because there is no existing defense mechanism.

Protecting Against Cyber Threats

To combat hacking and enhance cybersecurity, various strategies and best practices can be employed. Some essential measures include:

1. **Strong Passwords:** Creating complex passwords and regularly updating them is crucial. Password managers can help generate and store unique passwords securely.

CHAPTER 2: THE INFORMATION AGE AND DIGITAL REVOLUTION

2. **Multi-Factor Authentication (MFA)**: MFA adds an extra layer of security by requiring additional verification steps, such as a fingerprint scan or SMS code, along with passwords.

3. **Encryption**: Encrypting sensitive data ensures that even if it is intercepted, it remains unreadable to unauthorized users. Encryption algorithms like Advanced Encryption Standard (AES) are commonly used.

4. **Regular Updates and Patches**: Keeping software and operating systems up to date is vital. Updates often include bug fixes and security patches that address known vulnerabilities.

5. **Firewalls and Intrusion Detection Systems**: Firewalls monitor and control incoming and outgoing network traffic, while intrusion detection systems detect and respond to suspicious activities.

6. **Employee Education and Awareness**: Training employees on cybersecurity best practices and the risks associated with hacking can prevent many cyber attacks.

7. **Monitoring and Incident Response**: Implementing security monitoring tools and incident response plans enables swift detection and mitigation of cyber threats.

Case Study: The Equifax Data Breach

To emphasize the real-world impact of cyber threats, let's examine the Equifax data breach that occurred in 2017. Equifax, a consumer credit reporting agency, experienced a massive cyber attack that exposed the personal information of approximately 147 million people. The breach was a result of unpatched software and poor security practices.

The significance of this breach cannot be overstated, as it led to widespread identity theft and financial fraud. It serves as a stark reminder of the importance of robust cybersecurity measures and the catastrophic consequences that can result from negligence.

Resources for Further Learning

For those interested in delving deeper into the world of cybersecurity, a wealth of resources is available. Some recommended books include:

- "The Art of Intrusion: The Real Stories Behind the Exploits of Hackers, Intruders, and Deceivers" by Kevin Mitnick and William L. Simon.

- "Metasploit: The Penetration Tester's Guide" by David Kennedy, Jim O'Gorman, Devon Kearns, and Mati Aharoni.

SECTION 2: THE IMPACT OF TECHNOLOGY ON SOCIETY 143

- "Hacking: The Art of Exploitation" by Jon Erickson.

Additionally, numerous online courses and certifications can help individuals build their cybersecurity skills and knowledge. Some prominent platforms that offer cybersecurity training include:

- Coursera (www.coursera.org)

- Udemy (www.udemy.com)

- SANS Institute (www.sans.org)

- (ISC)² (www.isc2.org)

Remember, the battle against hacking is ongoing, and staying informed and proactive is key to maintaining cybersecurity in our interconnected world.

Key Takeaways

- Cybersecurity is crucial for protecting computer systems, networks, and data from unauthorized access or damage.

- Hacking encompasses various forms, including malware attacks, phishing, DoS attacks, social engineering, and zero-day exploits.

- Effective cybersecurity measures include using strong passwords, adopting multi-factor authentication, encrypting sensitive data, regular updates and patches, and employee education.

- The Equifax data breach serves as a reminder of the real-world consequences of poor cybersecurity practices.

- Further learning resources, such as books and online courses, are available for individuals interested in expanding their cybersecurity knowledge.

Now that we have explored the critical topic of cybersecurity and the battle against hacking, we can move on to the next section in our comprehensive textbook.

CHAPTER 2: THE INFORMATION AGE AND DIGITAL REVOLUTION

Subsection: The Internet of Things and the Connected World

The Internet of Things (IoT) refers to the network of physical devices, vehicles, appliances, and other objects that are embedded with sensors, software, and connectivity, enabling them to connect and exchange data. The IoT has transformed the way we interact with our surroundings, providing new opportunities and challenges in various sectors. In this subsection, we will explore the concept of IoT, its applications, and the implications it has on our interconnected world.

Introduction to the Internet of Things

The Internet of Things is a result of the convergence of various technologies, including wireless communication, cloud computing, and miniaturized sensors. These technologies have enabled everyday objects to become smart and interconnected, gathering and sharing data that can be used to enhance efficiency, enable automation, and improve decision-making processes.

At its core, the concept of IoT revolves around the ability of devices to communicate with one another through the internet. This connectivity enables devices to collect and exchange data, creating a vast interconnected network of physical objects. The data collected can range from simple measurements like temperature and humidity to more complex information like location, movement, and user behavior.

Applications of the Internet of Things

The applications of the Internet of Things are vast and have the potential to revolutionize many industries. Let's explore some of the key areas where IoT is making a significant impact:

Smart Home Technology: IoT has transformed the way we interact with our homes. From smart thermostats that can learn and adjust the temperature based on our preferences to voice-activated virtual assistants that can control various aspects of our homes, IoT has made our living spaces more convenient and energy-efficient.

Industrial IoT: IoT has revolutionized industries such as manufacturing, logistics, and agriculture. In manufacturing, IoT sensors can monitor equipment performance, detect faults, and enable predictive maintenance, minimizing downtime and optimizing production processes. In logistics, IoT-enabled tracking

SECTION 2: THE IMPACT OF TECHNOLOGY ON SOCIETY   145

devices can provide real-time visibility into the movement of goods, improving supply chain efficiency. In agriculture, IoT sensors can monitor soil conditions, weather patterns, and crop health, enabling farmers to make data-driven decisions and optimize yield.

Healthcare and Wearable Devices: IoT has the potential to transform healthcare by enabling remote patient monitoring, personalized medicine, and efficient healthcare delivery. Wearable devices equipped with sensors can collect vital signs, track physical activity, and monitor chronic conditions, providing valuable data for both patients and healthcare providers. This enables early intervention, better management of chronic diseases, and improved overall patient outcomes.

Smart Cities: IoT is instrumental in creating smart cities that utilize technology to improve the quality of life for residents. Smart lighting systems can adjust the brightness based on traffic and weather conditions, optimizing energy consumption. Smart parking systems can help drivers find available parking spots, reducing congestion and emissions. IoT sensors can monitor air quality, waste management, and traffic patterns, enabling the implementation of efficient and sustainable city infrastructure.

Challenges and Considerations

While the Internet of Things brings numerous benefits and opportunities, it also poses several challenges and considerations that need to be addressed:

Privacy and Security: As more and more devices become interconnected, the potential for data breaches and privacy violations increases. It is crucial to ensure that proper security measures are in place to protect sensitive data and prevent unauthorized access. Additionally, user consent and transparency in data collection and usage should be emphasized to maintain user trust.

Data Management and Analysis: The massive volume of data generated by IoT devices poses challenges in terms of storage, processing, and analysis. It is essential to have robust data management systems in place to handle the influx of data and derive meaningful insights from it. Furthermore, data governance frameworks and standards should be established to ensure data quality, interoperability, and ethical use.

CHAPTER 2: THE INFORMATION AGE AND DIGITAL REVOLUTION

Interoperability and Standards: With a plethora of IoT devices and platforms available, interoperability and standardization become crucial to facilitate seamless communication and integration.   Common protocols and interfaces should be established to ensure compatibility and interoperability between different devices and systems.

Reliability and Resilience: IoT systems need to be reliable and resilient to function optimally in different environments.   Redundancy, backup systems, and failover mechanisms should be implemented to handle system failures or network disruptions effectively.   Additionally, ensuring the longevity of IoT devices and managing software updates are essential to avoid security vulnerabilities and obsolescence.

Real-world Example: Smart Grid

One example of the Internet of Things in action is the implementation of smart grids.   A smart grid is an electricity network that integrates advanced communication and automation technologies to monitor, control, and optimize the generation, transmission, and distribution of electricity.

IoT devices, such as smart meters and sensors, are deployed throughout the grid to collect real-time data on energy consumption, load demand, and grid conditions. This data is transmitted to utility companies, enabling them to make informed decisions regarding supply and demand management, load balancing, and energy distribution.

Smart grids offer several benefits, including improved energy efficiency, reduced costs, and increased grid reliability. The real-time data provided by IoT devices allows utility companies to identify areas of high energy consumption, implement demand response programs, and detect and respond to outage events more effectively.

Conclusion

The Internet of Things has transformed our world into an interconnected ecosystem of smart devices and systems.   Through its applications in various sectors, IoT has the potential to enhance efficiency, improve decision-making, and create more sustainable and connected communities.

However, it is essential to address the challenges and considerations associated with IoT, such as privacy and security, data management, interoperability, and

SECTION 2: THE IMPACT OF TECHNOLOGY ON SOCIETY   147

reliability. By doing so, we can fully harness the benefits of IoT while ensuring the responsible and ethical use of this technology.

The Internet of Things continues to evolve, and its impact will only grow more significant in the coming years. Embracing this interconnected world presents us with endless possibilities to create a smarter, more efficient, and sustainable future.

Subsection: The Future of Technology: Quantum Computing and Beyond

In this subsection, we will explore the exciting field of quantum computing and its potential to revolutionize technology as we know it. Quantum computing harnesses the principles of quantum mechanics to perform complex computations at an exponential speed compared to classical computers. In this section, we will delve into the fundamental concepts of quantum computing, discuss the challenges it faces, explore its potential applications, and envision what lies beyond quantum computing.

Fundamental Concepts of Quantum Computing

Before delving into the intricacies of quantum computing, let's first understand the foundational concepts that make it possible.

1. Superposition: In the quantum world, particles can exist in multiple states simultaneously. This concept is known as superposition. Unlike classical bits, which can be either 0 or 1, quantum bits, or qubits, can exist in a superposition of both 0 and 1 until measured.

2. Quantum Entanglement: Quantum entanglement is a phenomenon in which two or more qubits become correlated in such a way that the state of one qubit cannot be described independently of the state of the others. This property enables the transmission of information instantaneously over long distances, a process known as quantum teleportation.

3. Quantum Gates: Quantum gates are the building blocks of quantum circuits, which manipulate qubits' states. These gates, such as the Hadamard gate and the Pauli-X gate, allow for complex operations on qubits, enabling quantum algorithms to solve problems that are computationally intractable for classical computers.

Challenges in Quantum Computing

While the potential of quantum computing is immense, there are several challenges that need to be overcome before it becomes a practical reality. Let's explore some of these challenges:

148 CHAPTER 2: THE INFORMATION AGE AND DIGITAL REVOLUTION

1. **Quantum Decoherence:** Quantum systems are incredibly delicate and susceptible to environmental disturbances. The phenomenon known as quantum decoherence occurs when a qubit's fragile quantum state interacts with its surroundings, causing it to lose its quantum properties. This poses a significant challenge in maintaining qubits' coherence for a sufficiently long time to perform meaningful computations.

2. **Error Correction:** Quantum systems are prone to errors due to factors such as noise, interference, and imperfections in hardware. Developing error correction techniques is crucial for building reliable and fault-tolerant quantum computers.

3. **Scalability:** Currently, quantum computers have a limited number of qubits, typically in the range of tens to hundreds. To tackle complex problems, scalable quantum computers with thousands or even millions of qubits are required. Achieving scalability is a significant technical hurdle that researchers are actively working on.

Applications of Quantum Computing

Despite the challenges, quantum computing shows great promise in various fields. Here are some potential applications:

1. **Cryptography and Cybersecurity:** Quantum computers have the potential to break conventional encryption algorithms, which rely on the difficulty of factoring large numbers. Quantum-resistant encryption algorithms, based on the principles of quantum mechanics, can ensure secure communications in the face of quantum attacks.

2. **Optimization and Simulation:** Quantum computing can greatly enhance optimization problems, such as resource allocation, supply chain management, and route optimization. It can also simulate complex physical systems, leading to breakthroughs in material design, drug discovery, and climate modeling.

3. **Machine Learning and AI:** Quantum algorithms have the potential to accelerate machine learning tasks, enabling faster training and better models. Quantum machine learning algorithms can overcome the limitations of classical approaches, leading to advancements in areas such as image recognition, natural language processing, and recommendation systems.

Beyond Quantum Computing

As we explore the future of technology, it is crucial to look beyond quantum computing. Here are some emerging fields that are expected to have a significant impact:

SECTION 3: CHALLENGES AND OPPORTUNITIES IN THE
INFORMATION AGE

1. **Quantum Networking**: Quantum networking aims to establish secure, long-distance communication channels using quantum entanglement. This field has the potential to revolutionize secure communication, quantum teleportation, and quantum internet.

2. **Topological Quantum Computing**: Topological quantum computing is a fascinating approach that relies on particles with non-Abelian anyons, called Majorana fermions. These particles could provide a more robust platform for qubits, as they are less vulnerable to errors caused by environmental factors.

3. **Quantum Artificial Intelligence**: Quantum AI seeks to integrate quantum computing with artificial intelligence techniques. By leveraging the computational power of quantum computers, this field aims to unlock new possibilities in deep learning, optimization, and data analysis.

In conclusion, quantum computing holds tremendous potential to revolutionize technology, paving the way for unprecedented advancements in various fields. However, there are still significant challenges to overcome, such as quantum decoherence, error correction, and scalability. Despite these obstacles, quantum computing applications in cryptography, optimization, and machine learning are expected to bring about significant breakthroughs. Looking beyond quantum computing, fields such as quantum networking, topological quantum computing, and quantum AI show promise in shaping the future of technology. The journey towards realizing the full potential of quantum computing and exploring the possibilities beyond is an exciting and ongoing endeavor.

Section 3: Challenges and Opportunities in the Information Age

Subsection: The Impact of Fake News and Online Disinformation

Fake news and online disinformation have become a significant issue in the digital age. With the rise of the internet and social media, the spread of false information has reached unprecedented levels, affecting individuals, societies, and even democratic processes. In this subsection, we will explore the impact of fake news and online disinformation, the reasons behind their proliferation, and potential solutions to address this growing problem.

The Proliferation of Fake News

Fake news refers to false information presented as factual news. It is often intentionally created and disseminated to deceive the public or advance specific

CHAPTER 2: THE INFORMATION AGE AND DIGITAL REVOLUTION

agendas. The proliferation of fake news can be attributed to several factors:

- **Ease of Dissemination:** The internet and social media platforms have made it easy for anyone to create and spread news quickly. With just a few clicks, false information can reach millions of people within seconds.

- **Lack of Fact-checking:** In the digital era, information is abundant, but fact-checking is often neglected. Many individuals share news without verifying its authenticity, perpetuating the spread of fake news.

- **Confirmation Bias:** People tend to seek information that aligns with their existing beliefs and biases. Fake news creators exploit this by crafting stories that resonate with the target audience, making it more likely to be shared and believed.

- **Monetization:** Some individuals and organizations intentionally spread fake news to generate traffic and profit from online ads. This financial incentive encourages the creation and circulation of false information.

Consequences of Fake News

The impact of fake news and online disinformation reaches far and wide, affecting various aspects of society:

1. **Undermining Trust in Institutions:** Fake news erodes trust in institutions, including the media, government, and even scientific research. When false information is presented alongside legitimate news, it becomes challenging for the public to discern the truth.

2. **Manipulation of Public Opinion:** Fake news can be used as a tool to manipulate public opinion and sway elections. By spreading false narratives, political actors can shape public perceptions, leading to a polarized and fragmented society.

3. **Social Division and Conflict:** The circulation of fake news can exacerbate social divisions by promoting hate speech, stereotypes, and prejudice. It can amplify existing tensions within communities and contribute to the escalation of conflicts.

4. **Economic Consequences:** Fake news can have economic repercussions. For example, false information about a company's financial performance can cause stock prices to fluctuate, resulting in financial losses for investors.

SECTION 3: CHALLENGES AND OPPORTUNITIES IN THE INFORMATION AGE

5. **Health and Safety Risks:** Misinformation about health-related issues, such as vaccines or treatments, can have severe consequences. It can lead to the spread of preventable diseases and pose dangers to public health and safety.

Addressing the Issue

Tackling fake news and online disinformation requires a multifaceted approach involving various stakeholders:

1. **Promoting Media Literacy:** Education plays a vital role in combating fake news. Teaching critical thinking skills and media literacy can empower individuals to evaluate information critically and discern reliable sources.

2. **Fact-checking and Verification:** Fact-checking organizations and journalists play a crucial role in verifying information and debunking fake news. Collaborative efforts to identify and expose false information are essential in countering its influence.

3. **Transparency from Tech Companies:** Social media platforms and tech companies need to take responsibility for the content shared on their platforms. Implementing algorithms and policies to identify and flag misleading or false information can help curb the spread of fake news.

4. **Government Regulations:** Governments can play a role in regulating the dissemination of fake news while upholding freedom of speech. Legislation that promotes transparency, accountability, and consequences for spreading false information can act as a deterrent.

5. **Collaboration among Stakeholders:** Addressing the issue of fake news requires collaboration between governments, tech companies, civil society organizations, and individuals. Creating partnerships and sharing best practices can lead to more effective strategies.

Real-world Examples

The impact of fake news and online disinformation can be observed in various real-world examples:

- During the 2016 United States presidential election, fake news stories spread widely on social media platforms, influencing public opinion and shaping the political discourse.

156 CHAPTER 2: THE INFORMATION AGE AND DIGITAL REVOLUTION

+ False information about the safety of vaccines has led to decreased vaccination rates in some communities, resulting in outbreaks of preventable diseases.

+ The COVID-19 pandemic has seen a surge in misinformation and conspiracy theories, causing confusion and hindering public health efforts to combat the virus.

Conclusion

Fake news and online disinformation pose significant challenges in the digital age. Their impact on trust, public opinion, and societal harmony cannot be ignored. Addressing this issue requires a collective effort from individuals, governments, tech companies, and civil society organizations. By promoting media literacy, encouraging fact-checking, enhancing transparency, and fostering collaboration, we can mitigate the influence of fake news and foster a more informed and resilient society.

Subsection: Cybercrime and the Threat to Personal and National Security

Cybercrime has emerged as a major threat to personal and national security in the interconnected world of the information age. With the increasing reliance on technology and the internet, criminals have found new avenues to exploit vulnerabilities, steal data, and disrupt critical systems. This subsection explores the various dimensions of cybercrime, its impact on individuals and countries, and the measures taken to mitigate these threats.

Understanding Cybercrime

Cybercrime refers to criminal activities that are conducted over digital networks or targeted at digital devices. It encompasses a wide range of illegal activities, including unauthorized access to computer systems, theft of sensitive information, financial fraud, identity theft, malware attacks, and cyberterrorism. The motivation behind cybercrimes varies, ranging from financial gain to political or ideological objectives.

One of the most concerning aspects of cybercrime is its borderless nature. Criminals can operate from any part of the world, making it challenging for law enforcement agencies to track and apprehend them. Additionally, the rapid evolution of technology presents new opportunities for cybercriminals to exploit emerging vulnerabilities and launch sophisticated attacks.

SECTION 3: CHALLENGES AND OPPORTUNITIES IN THE INFORMATION AGE

Threats to Personal Security

Cybercrime poses significant threats to personal security, exposing individuals to financial losses, identity theft, and invasion of privacy. Some common types of cybercrimes that target individuals include:

- **Phishing Attacks:** Phishing emails or messages are designed to trick individuals into providing sensitive information, such as credit card details or login credentials, to malicious actors posing as legitimate entities. These attacks can result in financial losses and identity theft.

- **Identity Theft:** Cybercriminals may steal personal information, such as social security numbers, addresses, or birthdates, to assume someone's identity. This stolen identity can be used for various fraudulent activities, including opening bank accounts, obtaining loans, or committing tax fraud.

- **Ransomware:** Ransomware is a type of malware that encrypts files on the victim's device, rendering them inaccessible until a ransom is paid. This can lead to significant financial loss and disruption of personal and professional activities.

- **Cyberstalking:** Online harassment, stalking, and bullying have become prevalent in the digital age. Cyberstalkers can use various methods, such as tracking someone's online activities, sending threatening messages, or sharing personal information, to instill fear and manipulate their victims.

Threats to National Security

Cybercrime also poses significant threats to national security, affecting government institutions, critical infrastructure, and the overall functioning of a country. Some key examples of cyber threats to national security include:

- **Cyber Espionage:** Nation-states engage in cyber espionage to gain unauthorized access to sensitive government information, military secrets, or intellectual property. Such breaches can jeopardize national security, economic interests, and diplomatic relations.

- **Critical Infrastructure Attacks:** Cybercriminals may target critical infrastructure, such as power grids, transportation systems, or communication networks, aiming to disrupt essential services and cause chaos. These attacks can impact public safety, economic stability, and national defense capabilities.

CHAPTER 2: THE INFORMATION AGE AND DIGITAL REVOLUTION

- **Cyberterrorism:** Cyberterrorism involves launching cyber attacks with the intention of causing fear, panic, or social unrest. This can range from disrupting government websites and services to spreading propaganda or coordinating attacks on physical targets.

- **State-sponsored Hacking:** Governments may sponsor hackers or hacking groups to conduct offensive cyber operations against other countries. These operations can include stealing sensitive government documents, manipulating elections, or launching disruptive attacks on critical infrastructure.

Addressing the Threats

Addressing the threats posed by cybercrime requires a multi-faceted approach involving both individuals and governments. Some key strategies and measures to mitigate cybercrime risks include:

- **Awareness and Education:** Individuals need to be aware of the risks associated with cybercrime and educated about best practices for online safety and security. This includes recognizing phishing attempts, using strong and unique passwords, and regularly updating software and antivirus protections.

- **Collaboration and International Cooperation:** Cybercrime is a global phenomenon, and addressing it requires international cooperation. Governments, law enforcement agencies, and cybersecurity organizations need to collaborate, share information, and work together to investigate and prosecute cybercriminals.

- **Legislation and Regulation:** Governments play a crucial role in enacting legislation and regulations to combat cybercrime effectively. This includes criminalizing cyber activities, establishing robust data protection laws, and empowering law enforcement agencies with the necessary resources and legal frameworks to fight cybercrime.

- **Cybersecurity Measures:** Individuals and organizations need to implement robust cybersecurity measures to protect their digital infrastructure and data. This includes using up-to-date antivirus software, implementing firewalls, encrypting sensitive information, and regularly backing up data to prevent data loss.

SECTION 3: CHALLENGES AND OPPORTUNITIES IN THE
INFORMATION AGE 155

- **Public-Private Partnerships:** Collaboration between the public and private sectors is vital in combating cybercrime. Governments can work with tech companies, financial institutions, and other industries to share threat intelligence, develop best practices, and implement security measures to safeguard critical infrastructure and sensitive data.

Case Study: NotPetya Ransomware Attack

One notable example of the devastating impact of cybercrime is the NotPetya ransomware attack in 2017. This cyberattack targeted businesses and government organizations worldwide, primarily in Ukraine but also causing significant damage globally. The malware spread through a compromised update of a popular accounting software, encrypting files on infected systems and demanding ransom for their release.

The NotPetya attack disrupted critical infrastructure, including power grids, transportation systems, and banks, costing billions of dollars in damages. It highlighted the vulnerability of global networks and the potential for cybercriminals to exploit interconnected systems for financial and political gain.

This case study illustrates the need for robust cybersecurity measures, regular software updates, and international collaboration to prevent and mitigate the impact of cybercrime on personal and national security.

Conclusion

Cybercrime poses a significant threat to the personal and national security of individuals and countries alike. With the increasing reliance on technology and the internet, it is crucial to understand the different types of cyber threats and implement effective measures to mitigate the risks.

By raising awareness, promoting cybersecurity education, enacting appropriate legislation, and fostering international cooperation, we can combat cybercrime and safeguard personal information, critical infrastructure, and the overall stability of nations in an increasingly connected world.

Subsection: Digital Activism and the Power of Online Movements

Digital activism, also known as online activism or internet activism, refers to the use of digital technologies such as social media, websites, and other online platforms for the purpose of promoting social and political change. In recent years, digital activism has emerged as a powerful force in shaping public opinion, mobilizing communities, and challenging traditional power structures. This

CHAPTER 2: THE INFORMATION AGE AND DIGITAL REVOLUTION

subsection explores the principles, strategies, and impact of digital activism in today's interconnected world.

Introduction to Digital Activism

Digital activism harnesses the power of technology to facilitate and amplify activism efforts. It provides individuals and communities with a platform to raise awareness, organize protests, advocate for causes, and challenge oppressive systems. The widespread availability and accessibility of the internet have democratized the ability to engage in activism, enabling individuals from various backgrounds to participate in social and political movements.

Platforms and Tools for Digital Activism

Various platforms and tools have emerged to facilitate digital activism. Social media platforms such as Facebook, Twitter, and Instagram have become vital spaces for activists to share information, raise awareness, and mobilize supporters. Hashtags, trending topics, and viral campaigns have played a significant role in amplifying messages and creating online movements. Additionally, online petition platforms like Change.org have made it easier for activists to gather signatures and advocate for specific causes.

Strategies and Tactics of Digital Activism

Digital activism employs a range of strategies and tactics to achieve its goals. Here are some prominent examples:

- **Online campaigning:** Digital activists utilize online tools to launch campaigns, solicit support, and spread their message. This can involve creating compelling multimedia content, organizing virtual events, and using targeted advertising to reach larger audiences.

- **Crowdsourcing and collective intelligence:** Digital activism often leverages collective intelligence by crowdsourcing information, ideas, and resources from a vast online network. Collaborative platforms like Wikipedia enable the collective creation of knowledge, while crowdfunding platforms like Kickstarter and GoFundMe allow activists to raise funds for their causes.

- **Hacktivism:** Hacktivism refers to the use of hacking techniques and cyberattacks as a form of activism. While controversial, hacktivist groups

SECTION 3: CHALLENGES AND OPPORTUNITIES IN THE INFORMATION AGE

like Anonymous have used their technical skills to expose corruption, advocate for human rights, and challenge oppressive regimes.

- **Data visualization and storytelling:** Visualizing data through interactive charts, infographics, and maps helps digital activists communicate complex information in a compelling and accessible way. Storytelling techniques, including personal narratives and testimonials, can further engage audiences and generate empathy.

Case Studies: Impact and Examples

Digital activism has yielded significant impacts and successes in various contexts. Let's explore a few notable case studies:

1. **Arab Spring:** The Arab Spring movement, which emerged in 2010, demonstrated the power of digital activism in mobilizing mass protests and overthrowing authoritarian regimes. Activists used social media platforms like Twitter and Facebook to coordinate protests, share information, and expose human rights abuses.

2. **Black Lives Matter:** The Black Lives Matter movement, sparked by the killing of Trayvon Martin in 2012, gained widespread traction through the use of social media. Hashtags like #BlackLivesMatter brought attention to police brutality, racial injustice, and systemic racism, leading to nationwide protests and policy reforms.

3. **Me Too:** The Me Too movement, initiated by activist Tarana Burke in 2006 and popularized on social media platforms in 2017, shed light on the prevalence of sexual assault and harassment. Survivors and supporters shared personal stories using the hashtag #MeToo, sparking a global conversation and prompting changes in workplace policies and attitudes towards consent.

These case studies highlight how digital activism can transcend physical boundaries, amplify marginalized voices, and create widespread impact.

Challenges and Ethical Considerations

While digital activism offers immense potential, it also faces several challenges and raises ethical considerations:

CHAPTER 2: THE INFORMATION AGE AND DIGITAL REVOLUTION

- **Digital divide:** The digital divide, characterized by unequal access to technology and digital infrastructure, poses a significant barrier to effective digital activism. Limited internet connectivity and disparities in digital literacy can hinder the participation of marginalized communities.

- **Online harassment and trolling:** Digital activists often face online harassment, threats, and trolling from opponents. Online platforms need to address issues of safety and create mechanisms to protect activists from abuse.

- **Filter bubbles and echo chambers:** Online environments can reinforce existing beliefs and isolate activists within filter bubbles and echo chambers. This polarization can hinder constructive dialogue and limit the effectiveness of digital activism in reaching diverse audiences.

- **Data privacy and security:** The collection and dissemination of personal data in digital activism raise concerns about privacy and security. Activists need to be mindful of potential risks and take measures to protect sensitive information.

- **Accountability and misinformation:** With the ease of spreading information online, digital activists need to ensure the accuracy and accountability of their messaging. Misinformation and disinformation campaigns can undermine the credibility and impact of digital activism.

Navigating these challenges requires ongoing awareness, critical thinking, and responsible digital practices.

Conclusion

Digital activism has transformed the landscape of social and political activism, offering new avenues for mobilization, collaboration, and advocacy. It has played a critical role in shaping public opinion, challenging power dynamics, and driving social change. As technology continues to evolve, digital activists must adapt and navigate the complexities of the online world, while staying true to their values and goals. By harnessing the power of digital platforms, individuals and communities can come together to create a more just and equitable society.

Further Reading

- Castells, M. (2015). Networks of outrage and hope: Social movements in the internet age. John Wiley & Sons.

*SECTION 3: CHALLENGES AND OPPORTUNITIES IN THE
INFORMATION AGE* 159

⁺ Earl, J., and Kimport, K. (2011). Digitally enabled social change: Activism in the internet age. MIT Press.

⁺ Jenkins, H., Ford, S., and Green, J. (2013). Spreadable media: Creating value and meaning in a networked culture. New York University Press.

⁺ Shirky, C. (2010). Cognitive surplus: Creativity and generosity in a connected age. Penguin.

These resources provide deeper insights into the theories, strategies, and impact of digital activism in contemporary society.

Subsection: The Role of Social Media in Political Campaigns

In today's digital age, the influence of social media on various aspects of our lives cannot be overstated. One area where social media has had a significant impact is in political campaigns. Social media platforms such as Facebook, Twitter, Instagram, and YouTube have become powerful tools for political candidates to reach and engage with voters. In this subsection, we will explore the role of social media in political campaigns, discussing its advantages, challenges, and potential impact on electoral outcomes.

Social Media as a Platform for Political Communication

Social media has transformed the way political candidates communicate with the electorate. In the past, candidates relied heavily on traditional media outlets, such as television, radio, and newspapers, to disseminate their campaign messages. However, social media platforms have provided candidates with direct and immediate access to a vast audience. They can bypass traditional gatekeepers and communicate their messages in real-time, reaching millions of users with a single post.

One advantage of using social media as a platform for political communication is its potential for increased engagement and interaction. Candidates can not only share their policy positions and campaign promises but also directly engage with voters by responding to comments, addressing concerns, and participating in live Q&A sessions. This interaction fosters a sense of accessibility and transparency, allowing voters to feel more connected to the candidates and the political process.

Furthermore, social media allows political campaigns to target specific demographics and tailor their messages accordingly. Platforms like Facebook and Twitter collect vast amounts of data about their users, including their interests, demographics, and online behavior. Campaigns can leverage this data to create targeted advertisements and content that resonate with specific voter groups, maximizing the impact of their campaign efforts.

The Influence of Social Media on Political Opinions

Beyond facilitating communication between candidates and voters, social media also plays a role in shaping and influencing political opinions. One of the key ways this occurs is through the viral spread of information and the formation of online echo chambers.

Social media algorithms are designed to prioritize content that aligns with users' preferences and interests. As a result, users are more likely to encounter and engage with content that reinforces their existing beliefs and opinions. This phenomenon can create echo chambers, where individuals are exposed only to like-minded perspectives, reinforcing their existing biases and potentially polarizing political discourse.

Moreover, the viral nature of social media allows for the rapid spread of information, both accurate and misleading. False information and misinformation can quickly gain traction, leading to confusion and potentially distorting public perceptions. The challenge lies in distinguishing between reliable and unreliable sources, as the democratized nature of social media means that anyone can share information, regardless of its accuracy.

Challenges and Controversies

While social media presents numerous opportunities for political campaigns, it also poses challenges and controversies. One significant challenge is the issue of online disinformation and fake news. The viral nature of social media platforms makes them susceptible to the spread of false information, which can mislead voters and undermine the integrity of electoral processes. Addressing this challenge requires a multi-pronged approach, involving the platforms themselves, fact-checking organizations, and individual users being critical consumers of information.

Another challenge is the potential for manipulation and interference in the political process. Foreign actors or malicious individuals can exploit social media platforms to spread propaganda, sow discord, or even influence election outcomes. Ensuring the security and integrity of social media platforms, as well as promoting digital literacy among users, are crucial in addressing this challenge.

SECTION 3: CHALLENGES AND OPPORTUNITIES IN THE
INFORMATION AGE   161

Controversies surrounding privacy and data protection are also pertinent in the context of political campaigns on social media. Platforms collect vast amounts of user data, raising concerns about how campaigns use this data to target and influence voters. Striking a balance between leveraging data for effective campaigning and safeguarding user privacy is a complex issue that requires ongoing discussions and regulations.

Case Study: Social Media in the 2016 US Presidential Election

To illustrate the impact of social media in political campaigns, we will examine the case of the 2016 US presidential election. During this election, social media played a prominent role, particularly in the campaigns of Donald Trump and Hillary Clinton.

Donald Trump effectively utilized Twitter as his primary communication tool, bypassing traditional media outlets and directly connecting with his supporters. His unconventional and often controversial tweets garnered extensive media coverage, further amplifying his messages and keeping the focus on his campaign. Trump's social media strategy played a significant role in his ability to connect with disenchanted voters and create a sense of authenticity and rapport.

On the other hand, Hillary Clinton's campaign struggled to effectively utilize social media to connect with voters. While Clinton had a significant presence on platforms like Facebook and Twitter, her messaging often lacked the same resonance as Trump's. This case study highlights the importance of not only utilizing social media but also understanding the unique dynamics and preferences of each platform's user base.

Conclusion

Social media has revolutionized political campaigns, providing candidates with unprecedented access to voters and creating new avenues for political communication. However, it also presents challenges such as the spread of misinformation, the potential for manipulation, and concerns about privacy and data protection.

For political campaigns to harness the full potential of social media, responsible use, transparency, and authenticity are essential. Adequate regulation, digital literacy initiatives, and efforts to combat disinformation are crucial in maintaining the integrity of political campaigns in the evolving digital landscape.

In the next section, we will explore the implications of big data and the ethics of data collection and analysis in the context of social media and political campaigns.

166 CHAPTER 2: THE INFORMATION AGE AND DIGITAL REVOLUTION

Subsection: Big Data and the Ethics of Data Collection and Analysis

Big data has become a buzzword in recent years, referring to the vast amount of information that is generated every day. It encompasses data from a wide variety of sources, such as social media posts, online transactions, sensor readings, and more. This data is often collected, processed, and analyzed to extract valuable insights and patterns that can inform decision-making and drive innovation. However, the increasing use of big data raises important ethical considerations regarding data collection and analysis.

The Importance of Ethical Considerations

In the age of big data, it is crucial to carefully consider the ethical implications of data collection and analysis. Several key concerns arise when it comes to handling big data:

- **Privacy:** The collection of large amounts of data often involves the collection of personal information. This raises concerns about privacy, as individuals may not be aware of what data is being collected about them and how it is being used.

- **Fairness and Bias:** Big data analysis can uncover patterns and correlations that can have significant societal impact. However, if these analyses are biased or unfair, they can perpetuate existing social inequalities or create new ones.

- **Data Ownership:** Determining who owns the data collected in big data projects can be complicated. This is particularly relevant in cases where personal data is involved, as individuals may want control over how their data is used.

- **Transparency:** The algorithms and methods used to analyze big data are often complex and opaque. This lack of transparency can lead to a lack of trust and accountability for the results produced.

- **Data Security:** Big data repositories are attractive targets for hackers due to the potential value of the information contained within them. Ensuring the security of big data is essential to protect individuals and organizations from data breaches and other cyber threats.

Addressing these ethical concerns is essential to ensure that the benefits of big data analysis are realized while minimizing potential harms.

SECTION 3: CHALLENGES AND OPPORTUNITIES IN THE INFORMATION AGE 163

Ethical Frameworks for Big Data

To navigate the ethical complexities of big data, several frameworks have been proposed. These frameworks provide guidance and principles for responsible data collection and analysis. Here are some key ethical frameworks that are commonly used:

- **Informed Consent**: Obtaining informed consent from individuals before collecting their data is a fundamental ethical principle. This means ensuring that individuals are fully aware of what data is being collected, how it will be used, and who will have access to it.

- **Purpose Limitation**: Data collection should have a specific purpose, and data should only be used for that purpose. This principle helps prevent data misuse and ensures that individuals' privacy is respected.

- **Data Minimization**: Collecting only the necessary data minimizes the risk of privacy violations. The principle of data minimization encourages organizations to collect and retain only the minimal amount of data required to achieve their objectives.

- **Fairness and Unbiased Analysis**: Big data analysis should be conducted in a fair and unbiased manner. This involves being aware of potential biases in the data and taking steps to minimize their impact on the analysis.

- **Data Security and Anonymization**: Protecting the security of big data is essential to prevent unauthorized access and breaches. Anonymizing personal data, or removing identifying information, can help protect privacy and reduce the risk of re-identification.

- **Transparency and Accountability**: Organizations should be transparent about their data collection and analysis practices. This includes providing clear explanations of how data is used and ensuring that individuals have avenues to address any concerns or complaints.

Adopting these ethical frameworks can guide organizations in navigating the complex landscape of big data, ensuring that data is collected, stored, and analyzed in a responsible and ethical manner.

CHAPTER 2: THE INFORMATION AGE AND DIGITAL REVOLUTION

Case Study: Big Data in Healthcare

To illustrate the ethical considerations in big data, let's consider a case study in healthcare. In recent years, the use of big data in healthcare has shown tremendous potential in improving patient outcomes, optimizing healthcare delivery, and advancing medical research. However, the ethical challenges are also significant.

For example, the collection and analysis of large sets of patient health data can provide valuable insights into disease patterns, treatment effectiveness, and population health trends. But it also raises concerns about patient privacy, the security of sensitive medical data, and the potential for discrimination based on health information.

To address these concerns, ethical guidelines and regulations have been developed in the healthcare industry. These include strict data protection regulations, such as the Health Insurance Portability and Accountability Act (HIPAA) in the United States, which governs the use and disclosure of personal health information.

Additionally, healthcare organizations must implement rigorous data security measures, including encryption, access controls, and audit trails, to protect patient data from unauthorized access. They must also ensure that individuals have the right to access their own health information and have control over how it is shared.

Furthermore, healthcare providers and researchers must consider the potential biases in big data analysis, particularly in relation to underrepresented populations. Failure to account for these biases can lead to disparities in healthcare delivery and exacerbate existing health inequalities.

In conclusion, the ethical considerations surrounding big data and the analysis of large datasets are vital to ensure that the benefits of this technology are realized without compromising individual privacy, fairness, and the public good. Adhering to ethical frameworks and guidelines, such as informed consent, purpose limitation, fairness, transparency, and data security, can help organizations navigate the ethical complexities of big data while unlocking its tremendous potential for positive societal impact.

Subsection: The Role of Artificial Intelligence in Healthcare

Artificial Intelligence (AI) has become a prominent force in transforming various industries, and the field of healthcare is no exception. In recent years, AI has demonstrated its potential to revolutionize healthcare delivery, diagnosis, treatment, and overall patient care. This subsection explores the critical role of AI in healthcare and its implications for the future.

SECTION 3: CHALLENGES AND OPPORTUNITIES IN THE
INFORMATION AGE 165

The Advantages of AI in Healthcare

AI possesses several advantages that make it an invaluable tool in healthcare. Firstly, AI algorithms can rapidly process and analyze vast amounts of healthcare data, including medical records, patient histories, diagnostic images, and scientific literature. By leveraging machine learning techniques, AI can detect patterns, identify trends, and generate insights that can aid clinicians in making accurate diagnoses and treatment decisions. This ability to process large datasets quickly saves time and enables clinicians to provide more personalized and evidence-based care.

Furthermore, AI-driven predictive analytics can identify patients who are at a high risk of developing certain diseases or health complications. By analyzing various risk factors, such as genetics, lifestyle, and medical history, AI algorithms can generate risk scores and provide early warnings, allowing healthcare providers to intervene proactively and prevent or mitigate potential health problems.

AI-powered telemedicine systems also enable remote patient monitoring and virtual consultations. This technology facilitates access to healthcare services, especially for individuals in remote areas or with limited mobility. Patients can receive timely medical advice and monitoring from the comfort of their homes, reducing the burden on healthcare facilities and improving the overall patient experience.

Applications of AI in Healthcare

AI in healthcare has a wide range of applications, each with its unique benefits and potential to transform the field. Here are some notable examples:

1. **Medical Imaging Analysis:** AI algorithms can analyze medical images, such as X-rays, CT scans, and MRI scans, to assist radiologists in detecting abnormalities and diagnosing diseases. Deep learning techniques have shown promising results in accurately identifying tumors, fractures, and other conditions, improving diagnostic accuracy and efficiency.

2. **Drug Discovery and Development:** AI can significantly expedite the drug discovery and development process. By analyzing vast amounts of biological and chemical data, AI algorithms can identify potential drug targets, predict their efficacy, optimize drug candidates, and simulate drug interactions. This enables researchers to streamline the discovery process, discover novel therapeutics, and reduce time and cost.

CHAPTER 2: THE INFORMATION AGE AND DIGITAL REVOLUTION

3. **Genomic Medicine:** AI algorithms can analyze genomic data to identify genetic variants associated with specific diseases or drug responses. This information helps clinicians to personalize treatments and optimize patient outcomes. AI can also assist in genetic counseling, predicting disease risks, and identifying population-specific health patterns.

4. **Clinical Decision Support Systems:** AI-powered clinical decision support systems integrate patient data, medical knowledge, and treatment guidelines to provide evidence-based recommendations to healthcare providers. These systems can assist in diagnosing complex conditions, choosing appropriate treatment options, and predicting patient outcomes, leading to improved clinical decision-making.

5. **Healthcare Operations and Workflow Optimization:** AI algorithms can optimize healthcare operations by automating administrative tasks, streamlining patient triage, and predicting patient flow. This reduces the burden on healthcare staff, enhances resource allocation, and improves overall efficiency.

Challenges and Ethical Considerations

While AI holds great promise in transforming healthcare, it is not without its challenges and ethical considerations. Some key challenges include:

- **Data Quality and Bias:** The accuracy and reliability of AI systems heavily depend on the quality and representativeness of the data they are trained on. Biased or incomplete datasets can lead to biased algorithms, resulting in inaccurate predictions and potentially perpetuating health disparities.

- **Privacy and Security:** The use of AI in healthcare involves handling sensitive patient information. Ensuring the privacy and security of healthcare data is critical to maintain patient trust and comply with legal and ethical standards.

- **Regulatory and Legal Frameworks:** The rapid pace of AI advancements often outpaces regulatory and legal frameworks. Healthcare organizations must navigate complex regulatory landscapes to ensure compliance and mitigate potential risks.

- **Clinical Adoption and Interoperability:** Successfully integrating AI into existing healthcare systems requires overcoming technical and cultural barriers. Ensuring interoperability with electronic health records,

SECTION 3: CHALLENGES AND OPPORTUNITIES IN THE INFORMATION AGE

overcoming resistance to change, and providing adequate training to healthcare professionals are crucial for successful AI adoption.

Ethical considerations also arise concerning the responsibility and accountability of AI systems. Transparency, explainability, and accountability should be prioritized to ensure clinicians and patients can understand and trust AI-driven decisions. Additionally, ongoing monitoring, validation, and refinement of AI algorithms are essential to identify and rectify any biases or errors.

Case Study: AI in Early Cancer Detection

One compelling application of AI in healthcare is early cancer detection. Traditional cancer screening methods, such as mammography and colonoscopy, often have limitations in terms of sensitivity, specificity, and accessibility. AI algorithms can improve cancer detection rates by analyzing imaging data, identifying subtle patterns indicative of early-stage tumors, and assisting radiologists in their diagnosis.

For instance, a deep learning algorithm developed by Google Health demonstrated the ability to detect breast cancer in mammograms with greater accuracy than human radiologists. By analyzing thousands of mammograms, the algorithm achieved a reduction in false negatives and false positives, potentially improving early detection rates and patient outcomes.

The use of AI in early cancer detection has the potential to revolutionize cancer care by enabling earlier intervention, reducing unnecessary procedures, and improving survival rates. However, challenges related to data quality, bias, and regulatory frameworks must be addressed to ensure the safe and effective implementation of AI in this context.

Conclusion

The role of AI in healthcare is rapidly evolving, offering promising possibilities for improving diagnostics, treatment decisions, patient monitoring, and overall healthcare management. As AI continues to advance, it is essential to address the challenges and ethical considerations associated with its implementation. By embracing the potential of AI while prioritizing patients' well-being, privacy, and equity, we can harness the transformative power of AI to revolutionize healthcare and provide better outcomes for individuals worldwide.

168 CHAPTER 2: THE INFORMATION AGE AND DIGITAL REVOLUTION

Subsection: Virtual Education and the Transformation of Learning

Virtual education, also known as online education or e-learning, has emerged as a transformative approach to learning in the digital age. It refers to the delivery of educational content and instruction through digital platforms, allowing learners to access and engage with educational materials anytime and anywhere. This subsection explores the impact of virtual education on traditional learning methods, its benefits and challenges, and its potential to revolutionize education systems worldwide.

The Rise of Virtual Education

Virtual education has gained significant momentum over the past two decades due to the advancements in technology and the internet. It has become an increasingly popular choice for both traditional students and adult learners seeking flexible educational opportunities. Online courses, degree programs, and Massive Open Online Courses (MOOCs) have proliferated, offering a wide range of subjects and specializations.

The transformation of learning through virtual education can be attributed to several key factors. First, the internet has enabled the dissemination of knowledge to a global audience, breaking down geographic barriers to education. Second, advancements in multimedia technologies have enhanced the delivery of interactive and engaging educational content. Lastly, the increasing need for lifelong learning and upskilling in a rapidly changing job market has fueled the demand for flexible and accessible learning options.

Benefits of Virtual Education

Virtual education offers numerous benefits that traditional classroom-based learning often struggles to provide.

First and foremost, virtual education provides flexibility and convenience for learners. Students can access course materials, lectures, and assignments at their own pace and schedule, accommodating personal and professional commitments. This flexibility is particularly advantageous for working professionals, parents, or individuals with disabilities who may face time or physical constraints.

Second, virtual education promotes self-paced learning. Learners can review and revisit content as needed, allowing them to grasp complex concepts at their own pace. This personalized approach to learning caters to different learning styles and ensures a deeper understanding of the subject matter.

SECTION 3: CHALLENGES AND OPPORTUNITIES IN THE
INFORMATION AGE

Third, virtual education broadens access to education, especially for underserved populations. It eliminates physical and financial barriers, making education more accessible to those who may not have the means or opportunity to attend traditional brick-and-mortar institutions.

Furthermore, virtual education promotes collaborative learning. Online discussion boards, video conferencing, and group projects facilitate interaction among students, fostering the development of critical thinking and teamwork skills. This collaborative aspect of virtual education enhances the learning experience and prepares students for the interconnected work environment.

Challenges and Considerations

While virtual education offers numerous benefits, it also presents unique challenges and considerations.

One significant challenge is the need for self-discipline and motivation. Without the structure and accountability of traditional classroom settings, some learners may struggle to stay engaged and complete their coursework. Time management and self-motivation skills are essential for success in virtual education.

Another challenge is the potential for social isolation. Virtual education lacks the face-to-face interaction found in traditional classrooms, which can affect social connections and the development of interpersonal skills. To mitigate this, educational institutions should incorporate interactive elements, such as virtual group projects and discussion forums, to promote social interaction and collaboration among students.

Moreover, virtual education requires reliable access to technology and the internet, which may be a barrier in underserved areas or developing countries. Addressing the digital divide is crucial to ensure equal access to educational opportunities for all.

The Future of Virtual Education

As technology continues to advance, the future of virtual education holds immense potential. It is expected that virtual reality (VR) and augmented reality (AR) technologies will be increasingly integrated into virtual education platforms, providing immersive and interactive learning experiences.

Additionally, artificial intelligence (AI) and machine learning algorithms can be leveraged to personalize and optimize the learning process. AI-powered virtual tutors can adapt to individual learners' needs and provide tailored feedback and guidance. This personalized learning approach can enhance student outcomes and make education more efficient and effective.

Furthermore, the integration of virtual education with real-world applications and simulations can bridge the gap between theoretical knowledge and practical skills. Virtual laboratories, virtual field trips, and virtual internships can provide hands-on experiences that were previously limited to physical settings.

In conclusion, virtual education has emerged as a transformative approach to learning, offering flexibility, accessibility, and personalized learning experiences. While it presents challenges, the advancements in technology and the potential for innovation hold promise for the future of education. By embracing and harnessing the power of virtual education, we can transform the way we learn and equip individuals with the skills and knowledge needed in the modern world.

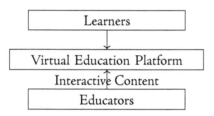

Figure 0.1: Illustration of the interaction between learners, educators, and a virtual education platform. The platform delivers interactive content to learners and facilitates communication and collaboration between learners and educators.

Further Readings and Resources

1. Bates, A. W. (2019). Teaching in a digital age: Guidelines for designing teaching and learning. Tony Bates Associates Ltd.

2. Siemens, G., & Baker, R. (2012). Learning analytics and educational data mining: Towards communication and collaboration. In Proceedings of the 2nd International Conference on Learning Analytics and Knowledge (pp. 252-254).

3. Khan Academy. (n.d.). Retrieved from https://www.khanacademy.org/

4. Coursera. (n.d.). Retrieved from https://www.coursera.org/

5. TED-Ed. (n.d.). Retrieved from https://ed.ted.com/

*SECTION 3: CHALLENGES AND OPPORTUNITIES IN THE
INFORMATION AGE*

Subsection: Online Entertainment and the Rise of Streaming Platforms

The advent of the internet and the digital revolution has revolutionized various aspects of our lives, including entertainment. In this subsection, we will explore the rise of online entertainment and the increasing popularity of streaming platforms. We will examine the impact of these platforms on traditional media, the benefits and challenges they present, and the future of online entertainment.

The Changing Landscape of Entertainment

The entertainment industry has undergone a significant transformation in recent years. Traditional forms of entertainment, such as television, movies, and music, have faced new challenges and opportunities with the rise of streaming platforms. These platforms, such as Netflix, Amazon Prime Video, and Spotify, provide users with convenient access to a vast library of content, allowing them to consume entertainment on-demand and across multiple devices.

Streaming platforms have disrupted traditional distribution channels and have created a global market for entertainment. They offer a diverse range of content, including movies, TV shows, documentaries, and music, catering to a wide variety of interests and preferences. This has led to a democratization of content creation, allowing independent filmmakers, musicians, and content creators to reach a global audience without the need for traditional gatekeepers.

Benefits of Streaming Platforms

Streaming platforms have brought numerous benefits to both consumers and creators.

For consumers, the rise of streaming platforms has increased accessibility to a wealth of entertainment options. Users can access a vast library of movies, TV shows, and music at their fingertips, eliminating the need for physical media or cable subscriptions. Additionally, these platforms often provide personalized recommendations based on user preferences, enhancing the discovery of new content.

For content creators, streaming platforms offer new avenues for distribution and monetization. Independent artists can reach a global audience without the need for a record label or production company. Moreover, these platforms employ algorithms and analytics to identify and promote content based on viewership data, increasing the visibility of lesser-known creators.

176 CHAPTER 2: THE INFORMATION AGE AND DIGITAL REVOLUTION

Challenges and Concerns

While streaming platforms have revolutionized the entertainment industry, they also present various challenges and concerns.

One concern is the issue of fair compensation for artists and creators. Streaming platforms often operate under complex royalty systems, where compensation is based on factors such as the number of streams and subscription fees. This has sparked debates about the adequacy of payment for artists and the sustainability of content creation in the digital age.

There are also concerns regarding the concentration of power in the hands of a few dominant platforms. As streaming services become increasingly popular, the competition between platforms intensifies, leading to exclusivity deals and fragmented content distribution. This can result in a more limited selection for consumers and challenges for smaller or niche content creators.

Furthermore, streaming platforms face challenges related to piracy and copyright infringement. The ease of digital distribution has made it easier for unauthorized copying and sharing of copyrighted material. This has raised questions about how to protect intellectual property rights and ensure fair compensation for content creators.

The Future of Online Entertainment

The future of online entertainment is likely to be shaped by several key trends and developments.

Firstly, we can expect further growth and expansion of streaming platforms. As internet connectivity improves and access to high-speed broadband becomes more widespread, more individuals will have the means to access online entertainment. This will lead to an even greater demand for streaming content, driving the creation of more original content and the evolution of business models.

Secondly, advancements in technology will continue to influence the way we consume online entertainment. The development of virtual reality (VR) and augmented reality (AR) technologies holds significant potential for immersive and interactive entertainment experiences. These technologies may reshape the way we interact with content, blurring the lines between the physical and digital worlds.

Lastly, the increasing global reach of streaming platforms is likely to result in a more diverse and inclusive entertainment landscape. As creators from different cultures and regions gain access to global audiences, we can anticipate a richer and more varied range of content. This can promote cultural exchange and provide opportunities for underrepresented voices to be heard.

*SECTION 3: CHALLENGES AND OPPORTUNITIES IN THE
INFORMATION AGE*

In conclusion, the rise of streaming platforms has transformed the entertainment industry and the way we consume media. These platforms have provided consumers with unprecedented access to a diverse range of content while offering creators new opportunities for distribution and monetization. However, challenges such as fair compensation, content fragmentation, and piracy persist. Looking ahead, we can expect further advancements in technology, the expansion of streaming platforms, and a more diverse and inclusive entertainment landscape. The future of online entertainment promises exciting possibilities for both creators and consumers alike.

Recommended Resources:

1. *Streaming, Sharing, Stealing: Big Data and the Future of Entertainment* by Michael D. Smith and Rahul Telang.

2. *The Netflix Effect: Technology and Entertainment in the 21st Century* by Kevin McDonald.

3. *Streaming, Sharing, Stealing: How Big Data and Pirates are Transforming the Entertainment Industry* by Michael D. Smith and Rahul Telang.

Try it Yourself: Reflect on your own consumption of entertainment. How has the rise of streaming platforms and digital distribution influenced your viewing and listening habits? Consider the advantages and disadvantages of this shift and discuss how it has impacted the overall entertainment industry.

Subsection: Digital Divide and the Accessibility Gap

In today's interconnected world, the rapid advancement of technology has transformed many aspects of our lives. However, not everyone has equal access to digital tools and resources, leading to a digital divide that exacerbates existing social and economic inequalities. In this subsection, we will explore the concept of the digital divide, its causes and consequences, and potential solutions to bridge the accessibility gap.

Understanding the Digital Divide

The digital divide refers to the gap between individuals and communities that have access to digital technologies, such as the internet, computers, and mobile devices, and those who do not. This divide can be seen both within countries (often along socio-economic lines) and between countries (highlighting global disparities).

CHAPTER 2: THE INFORMATION AGE AND DIGITAL REVOLUTION

Causes of the Digital Divide There are various factors contributing to the digital divide:

1. Economic Factors: Limited financial means can hinder access to digital technologies. High costs of devices, internet subscriptions, and infrastructure development can be prohibitive, particularly for individuals in low-income communities and developing countries.

2. Infrastructure Availability: Unequal distribution of internet infrastructure, such as broadband connectivity and cellular networks, can create disparities in digital access. Rural and remote areas are particularly affected due to limited infrastructure development.

3. Education and Skills Gap: Lack of digital literacy and necessary skills to navigate and effectively utilize technology can further widen the digital divide. Without proper training and education, individuals may struggle to leverage digital tools for personal and professional growth.

Consequences of the Digital Divide The digital divide has significant implications for individuals, communities, and societies at large:

1. Educational Disadvantage: Students without access to digital resources and the internet face challenges in accessing educational material, online learning platforms, and academic opportunities. This hampers their ability to compete on an equal footing with their digitally equipped peers.

2. Economic Inequality: The digital divide perpetuates economic inequalities by limiting access to online job opportunities, digital markets, and financial services. This further marginalizes disadvantaged communities and inhibits social mobility.

3. Social Exclusion: The lack of digital access hinders communication, information sharing, and social participation. Those without access miss out on the benefits of social networking, online communities, and civic engagement facilitated by digital platforms.

4. Health Disparities: The digital divide can impact access to telemedicine, remote healthcare services, and health information, particularly in underserved areas. This exacerbates health disparities and limits access to vital healthcare resources.

Bridging the Gap: Solutions to the Digital Divide

Addressing the digital divide requires a multi-faceted approach involving governments, organizations, and communities. Here are some potential strategies to bridge the accessibility gap:

SECTION 3: CHALLENGES AND OPPORTUNITIES IN THE INFORMATION AGE 175

1.   **Infrastructure Development**   Investment in internet infrastructure, particularly in rural and underserved areas, is crucial to expanding digital access. Governments and organizations can collaborate to enhance broadband connectivity, establish public Wi-Fi hotspots, and improve cellular network coverage in marginalized regions.

2.   **Affordability Initiatives**   To make digital technologies more accessible, policymakers can implement programs to reduce the cost barrier. This may include subsidizing device costs, providing discounted internet plans, and incentivizing private sector participation in bridging the affordability gap.

3.   **Digital Skills Training**   Promoting digital literacy and offering training programs are essential to empower individuals with the necessary skills to utilize digital tools effectively. Educational institutions and community organizations can offer courses, workshops, and online resources to enhance digital competencies.

4.   **Public-Private Partnerships**   Collaboration between governments, private companies, and non-profit organizations can leverage resources and expertise to bridge the digital divide. Such partnerships can facilitate the deployment of technology infrastructure, provide funding for initiatives, and support community-driven access projects.

5. **Content and Language Localization**   Making digital content available in local languages and tailoring it to diverse cultural contexts can enhance accessibility. Localization efforts should prioritize the inclusion of marginalized communities, ensuring that they have access to relevant and culturally appropriate digital content.

6. **Community Empowerment**   Engaging local communities and involving them in decision-making processes helps ensure that initiatives address their unique needs. Community-centric approaches foster a sense of ownership, promote sustainable solutions, and empower individuals to take an active role in bridging the digital divide.

Case Study: Grameenphone Community Information Centers (CICs)

A notable example of bridging the digital divide is the Grameenphone Community Information Centers (CICs) in Bangladesh. The CIC initiative, launched by

1CHAPTER 2: THE INFORMATION AGE AND DIGITAL REVOLUTION

Grameenphone in collaboration with local partners, aims to provide digital access and services to underserved rural communities.

CICs are equipped with computers, internet connectivity, and trained personnel to assist community members in utilizing digital resources. The centers offer services such as internet browsing, e-learning, online job searching, and access to government services. Furthermore, CICs organize training programs to enhance digital literacy and skills.

This community-driven approach addresses the digital divide by empowering rural communities, enabling access to information, and fostering socio-economic development. By providing digital tools and resources, CICs contribute to narrowing the accessibility gap and promoting inclusive growth.

Conclusion

The digital divide poses significant challenges to achieving a more equitable and inclusive society in the digital age. By understanding its causes and consequences, and taking decisive actions, we can work towards bridging the accessibility gap. Through targeted infrastructure development, affordability initiatives, digital skills training, and community empowerment, we can create a more inclusive and connected world, ensuring that no one is left behind in the transformative power of the digital era.

SECTION 3: CHALLENGES AND OPPORTUNITIES IN THE
INFORMATION AGE

Exercises

1. Conduct research on initiatives aimed at bridging the digital divide in your country or region. Identify key strategies and assess their effectiveness. Discuss any challenges or limitations faced in implementing these initiatives.

2. Imagine you are designing a digital literacy training program for a rural community with limited internet access. Outline a curriculum that covers essential digital skills and consider any unique challenges specific to the community.

3. Investigate the concept of community-owned networks (CONs) as a potential solution for bridging the digital divide. Compare and contrast the advantages and disadvantages of CONs with traditional internet service providers.

4. Explore the role of international organizations, such as the United Nations and UNESCO, in addressing the digital divide on a global scale. Assess the effectiveness of their efforts and propose additional measures that could be taken.

5. Analyze the impact of the COVID-19 pandemic on the digital divide. How has the shift to remote learning and work accentuated existing inequalities? Discuss potential strategies to mitigate these disparities in the post-pandemic world.

Additional Resources

1. World Bank: Digital Dividends - www.worldbank.org/en/publication/wdr2016

2. United Nations Development Programme: Bridging the Digital Divide - www.undp.org/content/undp/en/home/librarypage/democratic-governance/digital-divide

3. UNESCO: Promoting Effective Policies for the Digital Era - www.unesco.org/new/en/communication-and-information/resources/publications-and-com

4. International Telecommunication Union: Measuring Digital Development - www.itu.int/en/ITU-D/Statistics/Pages/publications/mis2020.aspx

5. The Guardian: The Widening Global Digital Divide - www.theguardian.com/world/2021/mar/30/the-widening-global-digital-divide

Tricks and Caveats

- When designing interventions to bridge the digital divide, it is essential to consider the unique challenges faced by different communities, including language barriers, cultural considerations, and socio-economic disparities.

- Sustainable solutions require long-term planning, resources, and collaboration between various stakeholders. It is crucial to ensure the continuity and scalability of initiatives beyond short-term projects.

178CHAPTER 2: THE INFORMATION AGE AND DIGITAL REVOLUTION

- Digital literacy programs should not only focus on technical skills but also emphasize critical thinking, online safety, and responsible digital citizenship to empower individuals to navigate the digital landscape effectively.
- Monitoring and evaluation play a vital role in assessing the impact of digital divide initiatives. Collecting data on access, usage, and outcomes helps identify areas of improvement and inform evidence-based decision-making.

Chapter 3: Globalization and the Interconnected World

Section 1: The Rise of Global Trade

Subsection: The World Trade Organization and the Expansion of Free Trade

In this subsection, we will explore the role of the World Trade Organization (WTO) in promoting and facilitating the expansion of free trade. We will delve into the establishment and structure of the WTO, its key principles, and the benefits and challenges of free trade. We will also examine the impact of globalization on the global economy and the role of the WTO in regulating international trade.

The World Trade Organization (WTO)

The World Trade Organization (WTO) is an intergovernmental organization that serves as the global governing body for international trade. It was established in 1995 as the successor to the General Agreement on Tariffs and Trade (GATT). The WTO aims to promote and facilitate the growth of international trade by providing a platform for negotiations, dispute settlement, and the development of trade rules.

The WTO operates on the basis of the principles of non-discrimination, transparency, and predictability. Its main functions include the negotiation of trade agreements, the resolution of trade disputes, and the monitoring of national trade policies. The WTO has a membership of 164 countries, representing over 98% of global trade.

Key Principles of the WTO

The WTO is guided by several key principles that underpin its operations and objectives:

1. Most-Favored-Nation (MFN) Principle: This principle states that any favorable treatment granted to one country must be extended to all member countries, ensuring non-discrimination and equal access to markets.

2. National Treatment: This principle requires that imported and domestically produced goods be treated equally, preventing discrimination against foreign products in favor of domestic ones.

3. Transparency: The WTO promotes transparency in trade policies and practices, ensuring that countries provide timely, accurate, and comprehensive information about their trade measures.

4. Predictability: The WTO aims to create a stable and predictable trading environment by providing a set of rules and regulations that govern international trade.

5. Trade Liberalization: The WTO encourages its members to reduce trade barriers such as tariffs and quotas to promote the free flow of goods and services across borders.

Benefits of Free Trade

Free trade, facilitated by the WTO, offers numerous benefits for countries and the global economy:

1. Economic Growth: Free trade promotes economic growth by expanding market access and creating opportunities for businesses to expand their operations internationally.

2. Improved Efficiency: Free trade encourages countries to specialize in producing goods and services in which they have a comparative advantage, leading to increased efficiency and productivity.

3. Consumer Welfare: Free trade provides consumers with access to a wider variety of goods and services at competitive prices, enhancing consumer welfare and choice.

4. Foreign Direct Investment (FDI): Free trade attracts foreign investment by offering a favorable environment for businesses, stimulating economic growth, job creation, and technological transfer.

5. Poverty Reduction: Free trade has the potential to reduce poverty by creating employment opportunities, fostering economic development, and reducing income disparities between nations.

SECTION 1: THE RISE OF GLOBAL TRADE

Challenges of Free Trade

While free trade brings numerous benefits, it also presents certain challenges that need to be addressed:

1. Vulnerability to Economic Shocks: Increased integration through free trade can make countries more vulnerable to economic shocks, such as financial crises or global recessions.

2. Job Displacement: Free trade can lead to job displacement as industries face competition from imports or relocation to countries with lower labor costs. However, it also promotes job creation in industries that benefit from increased exports.

3. Income Inequality: Free trade can exacerbate income inequality within countries, particularly if the gains from trade are not distributed equitably.

4. Environmental Impact: The expansion of trade can put pressure on natural resources and contribute to environmental degradation, which necessitates the implementation of sustainable practices.

5. Loss of Sovereignty: Some argue that international trade agreements, such as those negotiated by the WTO, limit a country's sovereignty by requiring compliance with global rules and regulations.

The Role of WTO in Regulating International Trade

The WTO plays a crucial role in regulating international trade through its various functions:

1. Trade Negotiations: The WTO facilitates negotiations among member countries to develop trade agreements that aim to lower trade barriers and promote fair competition.

2. Dispute Settlement: The WTO provides a platform for resolving trade disputes between member countries through a formal dispute settlement mechanism, enforcing the rules and regulations of international trade.

3. Trade Policy Review: The WTO conducts regular reviews of member countries' trade policies to ensure transparency, monitor compliance with WTO rules, and identify potential trade barriers.

4. Technical Assistance and Capacity Building: The WTO provides technical assistance and capacity-building programs to help developing countries participate effectively in global trade and benefit from free trade opportunities.

5. Outreach and Public Education: The WTO engages in outreach activities to enhance public understanding of its work and the benefits of free trade, promoting a more inclusive and informed global trade community.

CHAPTER 3: GLOBALIZATION AND THE INTERCONNECTED WORLD

In conclusion, the World Trade Organization (WTO) plays a crucial role in promoting and facilitating the expansion of free trade. By establishing and enforcing rules that govern international trade, the WTO promotes a transparent and predictable global trading system. Free trade, facilitated by the WTO, brings numerous economic benefits, including economic growth, improved efficiency, and enhanced consumer welfare. However, it also presents challenges such as job displacement and income inequality, which require effective policy measures to address. The WTO's role in regulating international trade through negotiations, dispute settlement, and policy reviews is vital for maintaining a fair and inclusive global trading system.

Subsection: The Role of Transnational Corporations in Globalization

Transnational corporations (TNCs) play a crucial role in shaping and driving the process of globalization. These are large companies that operate in multiple countries and possess significant economic power and influence. In this subsection, we will explore the various ways in which TNCs contribute to globalization, the benefits and challenges associated with their activities, and the impact they have on the global economy.

Understanding Transnational Corporations

To understand the role of TNCs in globalization, we need to first define what they are. A transnational corporation is a company that engages in productive activities spanning multiple countries. These corporations have headquarters in one country, but their operations, investments, and assets are spread across different nations. TNCs can be found in various sectors, including manufacturing, services, technology, and finance.

Driving Forces of Transnational Corporations

The expansion of TNCs and their increasing influence in the global economy can be attributed to several driving forces:

- Market opportunities: TNCs expand their operations globally to tap into new markets and reach a wider customer base. They seek opportunities in emerging economies with growing consumer demand and investment prospects.

SECTION 1: THE RISE OF GLOBAL TRADE

- Access to resources: TNCs often move their production or extractive activities to countries rich in natural resources, such as oil, minerals, or agricultural commodities, in order to secure a reliable supply chain.

- Lower production costs: TNCs benefit from cost differentials between countries, such as lower labor costs or favorable regulations, and establish production facilities in countries with cheaper inputs.

- Technological advancements: TNCs leverage their technological capabilities and expertise to expand their reach and compete globally. They invest in research and development, acquire new technologies, and transfer knowledge and innovation across borders.

- Favorable policies: Many countries actively attract TNCs by implementing policies that promote investment, provide tax incentives, and offer regulatory flexibility. This creates a favorable business environment for TNCs to operate and expand globally.

Contributions of Transnational Corporations to Globalization

Transnational corporations have made significant contributions to the process of globalization. Their activities have transformed the global economic landscape in the following ways:

1. Economic growth and development: TNCs contribute to economic growth by generating employment, promoting technological advancements, and attracting foreign direct investment. They often establish production facilities in developing countries, creating job opportunities and transferring skills and knowledge to the local workforce.

2. Integration of global markets: TNCs facilitate the integration of markets worldwide by establishing production networks, supply chains, and distribution channels across countries. They enable the flow of goods, services, and capital across borders, leading to the interconnectedness of national economies.

3. Transfer of technology and innovation: TNCs bring advanced technologies, production techniques, and management practices to host countries. Through research and development activities, they contribute to technological progress and innovation, improving productivity and competitiveness in both home and host countries.

CHAPTER 3: GLOBALIZATION AND THE INTERCONNECTED WORLD

4. Infrastructure development: TNCs often invest in infrastructure projects, such as roads, ports, and telecommunications, to support their operations. This infrastructure development benefits not only the companies but also the local communities and economies by improving connectivity and facilitating trade.

5. Trade and export promotion: TNCs are major players in international trade, accounting for a significant share of global exports and imports. By participating in global value chains, they enable countries to access international markets and participate in global trade, thereby promoting economic growth and development.

Challenges and Criticisms

While transnational corporations have contributed to globalization, their activities have also faced criticisms and posed challenges to various stakeholders:

- Labor and human rights concerns: TNCs have been criticized for exploiting cheap labor, violating workers' rights, and contributing to poor working conditions, particularly in developing countries. There have been instances of labor rights abuses, including low wages, long working hours, and unsafe working conditions.

- Environmental impact: The activities of TNCs, such as resource extraction, energy consumption, and waste generation, can have significant environmental consequences. They have been accused of environmental degradation, pollution, and unsustainable practices, leading to concerns about climate change and biodiversity loss.

- Inequality and distributional effects: TNCs' activities can exacerbate income inequality and wealth disparities within and between countries. They often concentrate profits, resources, and economic opportunities in the hands of a few, leading to social unrest, economic imbalances, and exclusion of marginalized communities.

- Tax avoidance and financial secrecy: Some TNCs engage in aggressive tax planning strategies to minimize their tax liabilities, leading to revenue losses for both host and home countries. Additionally, the complex organizational structures and lack of transparency in TNC operations contribute to global financial secrecy.

SECTION 1: THE RISE OF GLOBAL TRADE

- Political influence: TNCs' economic power and size can provide them with significant political influence, enabling them to shape policies and regulations in their favor. This can undermine democratic processes and decision-making, leading to concerns about corporate capture and undue influence.

Addressing the Challenges

Addressing the challenges associated with the role of transnational corporations in globalization requires a multi-faceted approach involving governments, civil society, and the private sector:

- Enhanced corporate social responsibility: TNCs need to adopt ethical business practices, respect human rights, and ensure decent working conditions. They should implement responsible supply chain management, engage with local communities, and promote sustainable development.

- Strengthened regulation and governance: Governments should develop and enforce robust regulations to hold TNCs accountable for their actions. This includes labor and environmental standards, tax regulations, and measures to combat corruption and financial secrecy.

- International cooperation: Global cooperation is crucial to address the challenges posed by TNCs. This includes international agreements on tax, labor standards, environmental protection, and corporate governance. Multilateral organizations, such as the United Nations and the World Trade Organization, play a significant role in facilitating international cooperation.

- Civil society engagement: Civil society organizations, including labor unions, NGOs, and consumer groups, play a vital role in advocating for responsible business practices, monitoring corporate activities, and holding TNCs accountable. Increased transparency and access to information are essential in enabling civil society engagement.

Conclusion

Transnational corporations have become key drivers of globalization, shaping the global economy and influencing various aspects of society. While they have contributed to economic growth, technological advancements, and market integration, their activities have also raised concerns about labor rights, environmental impact, inequality, and political influence. Addressing these challenges requires a collaborative effort involving governments, civil society, and the private sector to ensure that TNCs operate responsibly and promote sustainable development in a globalized world.

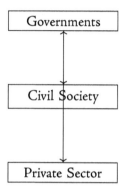

In this interconnected network, governments, civil society, and the private sector must work together to regulate TNCs, promote responsible business practices, and ensure that the benefits of globalization are shared equitably. Only through this collaborative approach can we maximize the positive contributions of TNCs while mitigating the challenges and negative impacts associated with their operations.

SECTION 1: THE RISE OF GLOBAL TRADE 187

Exercises

1. Discuss the driving forces that have contributed to the expansion of transnational corporations in the era of globalization.

2. Analyze the contributions of transnational corporations to the global economy, highlighting their role in economic growth, technology transfer, and market integration.

3. Evaluate the challenges and criticisms associated with the activities of transnational corporations, focusing on labor rights, environmental impact, and income inequality.

4. Propose strategies to address the challenges posed by transnational corporations, considering the importance of corporate social responsibility, strengthened regulation, and international cooperation.

5. Research and analyze a case study of a transnational corporation that faced criticism for its business practices. Identify the key issues, impacts, and the company's response to address these concerns.

Further Reading

1. Dicken, P. (2015). *Global Shift: Mapping the Changing Contours of the World Economy* (7th ed.). Sage.

2. Hirst, P., & Thompson, G. (2009). *Globalization in Question* (3rd ed.). Polity.

3. Kolk, A. (2016). *The Social Responsibility of International Business: From Ethics and the Environment to CSR and Sustainable Development* (2nd ed.). Oxford University Press.

4. Palan, R., Murphy, R., & Chavagneux, C. (2017). *Tax Havens: How Globalization Really Works.* University of Chicago Press.

5. UNCTAD. (2019). *World Investment Report 2019: Special Economic Zones.* United Nations Conference on Trade and Development.

Note: The exercises and further reading are meant to encourage critical thinking and provide additional resources for those interested in studying the role of transnational corporations in globalization further.

Subsection: International Supply Chains and the Global Economy

In today's interconnected world, international supply chains play a vital role in shaping the global economy. A supply chain refers to the network of organizations, resources, activities, and information involved in the production and distribution of goods or services. These supply chains are increasingly global in nature, with goods and components being sourced from different countries, manufactured in various locations, and then distributed worldwide.

The Importance of International Supply Chains

International supply chains have become essential for businesses seeking to optimize their operations and gain a competitive edge in the global market. By sourcing materials and components from different countries, companies can take advantage of cost efficiencies, access specialized resources, and tap into global talent pools. This allows them to produce goods at a lower cost compared to domestic production, leading to increased profitability.

Moreover, international supply chains enable companies to meet customer demands for a wide variety of products and customization options. By manufacturing goods in different locations, companies can reduce lead times and respond rapidly to changes in market demand, thereby staying competitive in an ever-evolving global marketplace.

From a macroeconomic perspective, international supply chains contribute to economic growth by fostering interdependence among countries and promoting global trade. They facilitate the exchange of goods, capital, and knowledge across borders, creating opportunities for countries to specialize in the production of certain goods or services based on their comparative advantages. This specialization leads to increased efficiency and productivity, driving overall economic development.

Challenges in International Supply Chains

While international supply chains offer numerous benefits, they also present challenges that businesses must navigate to ensure smooth operations and minimize disruptions. One of the main challenges is the complexity inherent in managing global networks of suppliers, manufacturers, logistics providers, and customers.

Coordination and communication between various stakeholders become crucial for effective supply chain management. Cultural differences, language barriers, and legal and regulatory variations across countries can further complicate the coordination process. It requires strong leadership, effective collaboration, and the use of appropriate technologies to overcome these challenges and maintain a seamless flow of goods and information.

SECTION 1: THE RISE OF GLOBAL TRADE 189

Supply chain disruptions caused by natural disasters, geopolitical events, or economic crises also pose significant challenges. These disruptions can lead to delays, increased costs, and shortages, impacting the overall efficiency and profitability of supply chains. Businesses need to develop robust risk management strategies, such as diversifying suppliers, establishing contingency plans, and implementing real-time monitoring systems, to mitigate the impact of such disruptions.

The Role of Technology in International Supply Chains

Technology plays a crucial role in optimizing international supply chains and addressing the challenges associated with them. Advanced supply chain management systems, powered by technologies such as cloud computing, big data analytics, and artificial intelligence (AI), enable businesses to streamline their operations, gain real-time visibility into their supply chains, and make data-driven decisions.

For instance, cloud-based platforms facilitate collaboration and information sharing among supply chain partners, improving transparency and coordination. Big data analytics can help identify patterns, predict demand fluctuations, and optimize inventory levels, reducing costs and enhancing customer service. AI and machine learning algorithms can automate routine tasks, optimize routes, and improve forecasting accuracy, enabling businesses to respond more effectively to market changes and disruptions.

Blockchain technology also holds significant promise in enhancing supply chain transparency and traceability. By creating an immutable and decentralized ledger of transactions, blockchain can verify and track the movement of goods across the supply chain, ensuring authenticity, reducing the risk of counterfeit products, and promoting ethical sourcing practices.

Case Study: Apple Inc. and its Global Supply Chain

A prominent example of a company with a complex international supply chain is Apple Inc. As a global technology leader, Apple relies on an extensive network of suppliers, mainly located in Asia, to manufacture its products. The company's supply chain encompasses multiple tiers, with components sourced from various countries and assembled in factories in China.

Apple's supply chain management strategy focuses on close collaboration with suppliers, rigorous quality control measures, and continuous innovation. The company works closely with its suppliers to ensure compliance with ethical standards, environmental regulations, and labor practices. It also invests in supplier development programs to enhance capabilities and sustainability throughout the supply chain.

However, Apple's supply chain has faced challenges, such as labor rights issues, environmental concerns, and disruptions caused by natural disasters. These challenges have led Apple to reassess its supply chain practices and implement measures to improve working conditions, reduce its environmental footprint, and increase supply chain resilience.

Conclusion

International supply chains are essential drivers of the global economy, enabling businesses to optimize their operations, meet customer demands, and foster economic growth. However, managing and navigating these supply chains require effective coordination, risk management strategies, and the adoption of technology-enabled solutions. As businesses continue to expand their global reach, the ability to adapt to evolving supply chain dynamics and address challenges will be crucial for their success in the interconnected world of the global economy.

Subsection: The Impact of Globalization on Developing Countries

Globalization has had a significant impact on developing countries, both positive and negative. In this subsection, we will explore the various ways in which globalization has influenced the economic, social, and cultural landscapes of these nations.

Economic Effects

One of the main advantages of globalization for developing countries is the potential for economic growth and development. Through globalization, these countries have gained access to international markets, increased foreign direct investments, and expanded their export opportunities. This has led to increased employment, rising income levels, and improvements in living standards.

Moreover, globalization has facilitated the transfer of technology, knowledge, and managerial expertise to developing countries. This has enabled them to enhance their productive capacity and compete more effectively in the global economy. For instance, multinational corporations often establish operations in these countries to take advantage of lower production costs and resource availability.

However, it is important to acknowledge that globalization has also created challenges for developing countries. Economic liberalization and the removal of

SECTION 1: THE RISE OF GLOBAL TRADE 191

trade barriers have exposed domestic industries to intense competition from foreign firms. This has led to job dislocation, income inequality, and social unrest, particularly in sectors that are unable to compete globally.

Case Study: Textile Industry in Bangladesh The textile industry in Bangladesh serves as a salient example of the complex effects of globalization on developing countries. The country has emerged as a major player in the global apparel market, thanks to its low-cost labor and preferential trade agreements. However, the reliance on a single industry has made Bangladesh vulnerable to fluctuations in global demand and changes in trade policies. Additionally, the working conditions in the garment factories have raised concerns about labor rights and social standards.

Social Effects

Globalization has also had profound social effects on developing countries. It has led to increased cultural exchange, the spread of ideas, and the transformation of social norms. This has both positive and negative implications for these societies.

On the positive side, globalization has provided developing countries with opportunities to integrate into the global community, learn from other cultures, and diversify their cultural offerings. This has contributed to greater cultural awareness, tolerance, and appreciation. Additionally, increased access to information and communication technologies has enabled people in rural areas to connect with the rest of the world and access educational resources.

Nevertheless, the process of globalization has also raised concerns about cultural homogenization and the erosion of indigenous traditions and values. The dominance of Western cultural products and media has been criticized for crowding out local cultural expression and promoting a consumerist lifestyle.

Case Study: Impact of Hollywood Movies in India The Indian film industry, popularly known as Bollywood, has faced challenges due to the global reach of Hollywood. While globalization has increased the international recognition and market for Indian films, it has also resulted in the adoption of Western storytelling techniques and the dilution of traditional Indian narratives. This has sparked debates about the preservation of cultural authenticity and the impact of globalization on local creativity.

Environmental Effects

Globalization has both positive and negative implications for the environment in developing countries. On the positive side, increased trade and collaboration have provided opportunities for countries to address global environmental challenges collectively. International agreements and initiatives have been established to promote sustainable development, reduce greenhouse gas emissions, and protect biodiversity.

However, the negative effects of globalization on the environment cannot be ignored. The pursuit of economic growth and the desire to attract foreign investments have, in some cases, resulted in unsustainable exploitation of natural resources and environmental degradation. Moreover, the transportation of goods across long distances has contributed to greenhouse gas emissions and climate change.

Case Study: Deforestation in the Amazon The Amazon rainforest, often referred to as the "lungs of the Earth," has been severely affected by globalization. The demand for agricultural products, such as soybeans and beef, has led to extensive deforestation to make way for large-scale farming operations. This has not only resulted in the loss of biodiversity but also contributed to carbon emissions and climate change.

Challenges and Opportunities

The impact of globalization on developing countries is complex and multifaceted. While globalization has presented opportunities for economic growth, technological advancement, and cultural exchange, it has also posed challenges in terms of job displacement, income inequality, and environmental degradation.

To fully exploit the benefits and address the challenges, developing countries need to adopt policies and strategies that promote inclusive growth, protect the environment, and preserve cultural diversity. This requires investment in education and skills development, the establishment of social safety nets, and the adoption of sustainable business practices.

Furthermore, international cooperation and collaboration are crucial to ensuring that the benefits of globalization are shared equitably among all nations. Developing countries, in partnership with developed nations, must work together to address common issues such as poverty, climate change, and access to technology.

SECTION 1: THE RISE OF GLOBAL TRADE 193

Key Takeaways

In summary, globalization has had a significant impact on developing countries. It has brought both opportunities and challenges, particularly in the economic, social, and environmental spheres. Developing countries have experienced economic growth, improved living standards, and increased access to global markets. However, globalization has also contributed to job displacement, income inequality, cultural homogenization, and environmental degradation. To navigate the complexities of globalization, developing countries must pursue inclusive and sustainable development strategies while fostering international cooperation.

Subsection: Economic Inequality and the Pursuit of Social Justice

Economic inequality is a pressing issue in our contemporary world, and addressing this problem is crucial for the pursuit of social justice. In this subsection, we will explore the causes and consequences of economic inequality, discuss different approaches to reducing inequality, and examine the role of social justice in promoting a fairer society.

Causes of Economic Inequality

Economic inequality can arise from various factors, including disparities in income, wealth, and opportunities. One of the key drivers of inequality is the unequal distribution of resources, such as education, healthcare, and job opportunities. Lack of access to quality education and healthcare can limit individuals' upward mobility and perpetuate intergenerational poverty.

Another contributing factor is the concentration of wealth and power in the hands of a few individuals or corporations. This concentration can result from factors such as monopolistic practices, tax policies that favor the wealthy, and the influence of money in politics. These factors create a vicious cycle where the rich get richer while the poor struggle to escape poverty.

Furthermore, globalization and technological advancements have also played a role in exacerbating economic inequality. While globalization has created economic opportunities and lifted many out of poverty, it has also widened the gap between the rich and the poor in both developed and developing countries. Technological advancements have led to automation and the displacement of workers, disproportionately affecting low-skilled workers.

Consequences of Economic Inequality

Economic inequality has far-reaching consequences that extend beyond the financial realm. It impacts various aspects of individuals' lives, including their health, education, social mobility, and overall well-being.

Health outcomes are strongly correlated with socioeconomic status. Studies have shown that individuals from lower income brackets have higher rates of chronic diseases, shorter life expectancies, and limited access to healthcare services. Additionally, children from economically disadvantaged backgrounds often face limited educational opportunities, perpetuating the cycle of inequality.

Social mobility, or the ability of individuals to move up the socioeconomic ladder, is also affected by economic inequality. High levels of inequality can hinder social mobility, making it harder for individuals to improve their economic circumstances and escape poverty.

Moreover, economic inequality can have negative social and political implications. It can lead to social unrest, increased crime rates, and political polarization. When a significant portion of the population feels marginalized and excluded from economic opportunities, it can undermine social cohesion and stability.

Approaches to Reducing Economic Inequality

Addressing economic inequality requires a multipronged approach that combines policies aimed at both wealth redistribution and increasing individual opportunities. Here are some key approaches to reducing economic inequality:

1. Progressive Taxation: Implementing a progressive tax system, where higher income earners are taxed at higher rates, can help redistribute wealth and reduce income disparities. The additional revenue generated can be used to fund social programs and initiatives aimed at reducing inequality.

2. Social Safety Nets: Establishing robust social safety nets, such as unemployment benefits, healthcare subsidies, and affordable housing programs, can provide a safety net for individuals facing economic hardships. These programs help alleviate poverty and reduce inequality by ensuring basic needs are met.

3. Education and Skills Development: Investing in education and skills development is crucial for reducing inequality. Ensuring access to quality education, vocational training, and lifelong learning opportunities can equip individuals with the necessary skills to succeed in the modern economy and break the cycle of poverty.

SECTION 1: THE RISE OF GLOBAL TRADE

4. Labor Market Reforms: Implementing labor market reforms can help improve workers' rights and bargaining power. This includes promoting fair wages, protecting workers' rights to organize and negotiate collective agreements, and combatting precarious employment.

5. Wealth and Corporate Regulation: Implementing measures to address wealth concentration and corporate power can contribute to reducing inequality. This can include stricter antitrust laws, closing tax loopholes, and promoting corporate social responsibility.

Social Justice and Economic Inequality

The pursuit of social justice is closely intertwined with addressing economic inequality. Social justice refers to the fair and equitable distribution of resources, opportunities, and privileges within society. It seeks to ensure that all individuals, regardless of their background or socioeconomic status, have access to the same basic rights and opportunities.

Reducing economic inequality is a fundamental aspect of social justice. By creating a more equitable distribution of wealth and resources, we can foster a society where every individual has equal opportunities to succeed and thrive. Social justice also involves addressing systemic barriers and discrimination that perpetuate inequality, such as racism, sexism, and other forms of discrimination.

Promoting social justice requires collective action from policymakers, civil society organizations, and individuals. It involves advocating for policy changes that tackle inequality, challenging discriminatory practices, and fostering a culture of inclusivity and respect.

Example: Universal Basic Income

One innovative approach to reducing economic inequality and promoting social justice is the concept of a Universal Basic Income (UBI). UBI is a system in which every citizen receives a regular, unconditional cash transfer from the government, regardless of their employment status or income level.

UBI aims to provide a basic level of financial security to all individuals, ensuring that everyone has access to necessities such as food, shelter, and healthcare. It acknowledges that inequality is not solely a result of individual effort but is influenced by societal factors beyond an individual's control.

Proponents of UBI argue that it can help alleviate poverty, reduce inequality, and provide individuals with the freedom to pursue their aspirations and interests.

It can also serve as a safety net in times of economic instability and job displacement due to automation.

However, implementing UBI raises complex questions related to funding, sustainability, and potential unintended consequences. It requires careful consideration of the economic implications, as well as adjustments to existing social welfare programs. Rigorous testing and evaluation of UBI pilot programs are crucial to understanding its effectiveness and potential long-term impacts.

Conclusion

Economic inequality is a significant societal challenge that demands attention and action. By understanding its causes and consequences, exploring approaches to reducing inequality, and embracing the principles of social justice, we can work towards creating a fairer and more equitable society. The pursuit of social justice requires collective efforts to dismantle systemic barriers and ensure that every individual has equal opportunities and access to resources, ultimately creating a more just and inclusive world.

Subsection: The Rise of Financial Globalization and the Global Economy

The rise of financial globalization has had a profound impact on the global economy, transforming the way countries interact and conduct business. In this subsection, we will explore the key drivers and consequences of financial globalization, as well as the challenges it poses to national economies and global governance.

Background and Key Concepts

Financial globalization refers to the integration of financial markets and institutions across national borders. It encompasses the free flow of capital, financial assets, and services, allowing investors and borrowers to access funding and opportunities on a global scale. This process has been facilitated by advancements in technology, deregulation of financial systems, and the liberalization of capital accounts.

One of the key concepts in understanding financial globalization is the internationalization of finance. This involves the growing interconnectedness of financial markets and the increasing cross-border movement of financial assets, such as stocks, bonds, and derivatives.

Another important concept is the emergence of multinational financial institutions, such as banks, insurance companies, and investment firms. These

SECTION 1: THE RISE OF GLOBAL TRADE

institutions operate across multiple jurisdictions and play a pivotal role in facilitating global financial transactions.

Drivers of Financial Globalization

There are several factors that have driven the rise of financial globalization:

1. Technological advancements: The development of information and communication technologies, such as the internet and electronic payment systems, has greatly facilitated the flow of capital across borders. It has also made it easier for investors to access information, monitor investments, and execute transactions in real-time.

2. Deregulation and liberalization: Many countries have implemented policies to liberalize their financial systems, removing restrictions on cross-border capital flows, and easing regulations on financial institutions. This has created a favorable environment for financial globalization, attracting investors and fostering competition.

3. Financial innovation: The development of new financial instruments and techniques, such as securitization and derivatives, has opened up new avenues for investment and risk management. These innovations have fueled financial globalization by increasing the liquidity and efficiency of global financial markets.

4. Economic integration: The growth of global trade and investment flows has created a need for efficient and accessible financial services. As countries become more interconnected through trade and investment, the demand for cross-border financial transactions and services has increased.

Consequences of Financial Globalization

The rise of financial globalization has had both positive and negative consequences for the global economy:

1. Increased capital flows: Financial globalization has facilitated the movement of capital from countries with surplus savings to those in need of investment. This has helped fund economic development, infrastructure projects, and technological advancements in emerging economies.

2. Access to financing: Financial globalization has provided companies, governments, and individuals with greater access to international capital markets. This has enabled them to borrow at lower costs and access a wider range of financial products and services.

CHAPTER 3: GLOBALIZATION AND THE INTERCONNECTED WORLD

3. Portfolio diversification: Investors can now diversify their portfolios by investing in a wide range of assets across different countries and regions. This diversification helps reduce risk and increase potential returns.

4. Financial instability: The rapid flow of capital across borders can amplify financial shocks and increase the vulnerability of economies to financial crises. The 2008 global financial crisis is a stark example of how interconnectedness in the global financial system can transmit and amplify shocks worldwide.

5. Unequal distribution of benefits: Financial globalization has not benefitted all economies equally. Developing countries may face challenges in attracting capital and may be vulnerable to sudden stops or reversals of capital flows. This can result in financial instability and economic instability.

6. Regulatory challenges: Financial globalization has posed challenges for regulators and policymakers. The global nature of finance makes it difficult to regulate and supervise financial institutions effectively. Coordination among different regulatory bodies and countries is crucial to ensure financial stability and protect consumers.

Addressing the Challenges

To mitigate the risks and maximize the benefits of financial globalization, policymakers and international organizations have taken steps to address the challenges it poses:

1. Strengthening financial regulation: Regulatory frameworks need to be robust and adaptable to changes in the global financial landscape. Greater coordination among regulators and international organizations is crucial to address regulatory arbitrage and ensure financial stability.

2. Enhancing global governance: Global governance mechanisms, such as the International Monetary Fund (IMF) and the Financial Stability Board (FSB), play a vital role in promoting financial stability and coordinating policy responses. Reforms to these institutions may be necessary to improve their effectiveness and promote inclusivity.

3. Promoting financial inclusion: Efforts should be made to ensure that the benefits of financial globalization are shared more equitably. This includes promoting financial inclusion, particularly in underserved areas and among marginalized populations. Access to affordable and responsible financial services can help reduce poverty and promote inclusive economic growth.

4. Managing capital flows: Policymakers need to be vigilant of the risks associated with capital flows, particularly for emerging economies. The use of macroprudential tools, such as capital flow management measures and foreign

SECTION 1: THE RISE OF GLOBAL TRADE
199

exchange interventions, can help prevent excessive volatility and mitigate the risks of financial instability.

5. Fostering international cooperation: Collaboration among countries is essential to address challenges associated with financial globalization. This includes sharing best practices, exchanging information, and coordinating policy responses to crises.

Conclusion

The rise of financial globalization has fundamentally transformed the global economy, offering new opportunities for growth and development. However, it also poses significant challenges that require careful management and coordination among policymakers, regulators, and international organizations. By addressing these challenges and promoting inclusive and sustainable finance, we can harness the benefits of financial globalization while safeguarding global financial stability.

Subsection: The Role of Multilateral Organizations in Global Governance

In today's interconnected world, the challenges we face are increasingly complex and often transcend national boundaries. Issues such as climate change, terrorism, and economic inequality require global cooperation and collective action. Multilateral organizations play a crucial role in addressing these global challenges and fostering international collaboration. In this subsection, we will explore the role of multilateral organizations in global governance, their functions, and their impact on shaping global policies and regulations.

Functions of Multilateral Organizations

Multilateral organizations, also known as international organizations, are entities comprised of multiple sovereign states that come together to cooperate on common goals and address shared concerns. These organizations serve several key functions in global governance:

1. **Facilitating Cooperation and Coordination:** Multilateral organizations provide a platform for countries to come together and discuss common issues, share information, and coordinate their efforts. They act as forums for negotiation and consensus-building among member states.

2. **Setting Standards and Regulations:** Multilateral organizations develop and promote international standards, norms, and rules in various sectors. They establish guidelines and regulations to govern areas such as trade, human rights,

CHAPTER 3: GLOBALIZATION AND THE INTERCONNECTED WORLD

the environment, and finance, providing a universal framework for countries to follow.

3. **Monitoring and Compliance:** Multilateral organizations oversee the implementation and adherence to agreed-upon standards and regulations. They monitor the actions of member states, provide assessments and recommendations, and facilitate dispute settlement processes.

4. **Providing Technical Expertise and Support:** Multilateral organizations offer technical expertise, research, and knowledge sharing to support member states in addressing specific challenges. They provide capacity-building programs and assist in policy formulation and implementation.

5. **Coordination of Humanitarian Efforts:** In times of crises such as natural disasters or conflicts, multilateral organizations coordinate emergency response efforts, provide humanitarian aid, and assist in rebuilding affected areas. They ensure a more efficient and effective response by pooling resources and expertise.

Prominent Multilateral Organizations

Several multilateral organizations play a significant role in global governance across various domains. Let's explore some of the most prominent ones:

1. **United Nations (UN):** The United Nations is the most well-known and comprehensive multilateral organization. Established in 1945, it comprises 193 member states and aims to maintain international peace and security, promote sustainable development, protect human rights, and foster social progress. The UN consists of several specialized agencies, programs, and bodies, including the Security Council, General Assembly, and Economic and Social Council.

2. **World Health Organization (WHO):** The WHO is a specialized agency of the UN responsible for global public health. It coordinates international efforts to combat diseases, sets health standards, provides technical assistance to countries, and promotes research and development for improved healthcare.

3. **International Monetary Fund (IMF):** The IMF is an international financial institution that aims to ensure global financial stability and promote economic growth. It provides financial assistance, policy advice, and technical expertise to member countries, monitors the global economy, and facilitates cooperation on international monetary issues.

4. **World Trade Organization (WTO):** The WTO is a global organization that deals with international trade rules between nations. It aims to foster free and fair trade by reducing barriers, resolving trade disputes, and promoting transparency in global trade relations. The WTO also provides a platform for negotiations on various trade-related issues.

SECTION 1: THE RISE OF GLOBAL TRADE

5. **World Bank**: The World Bank is an international financial institution that provides loans, grants, and technical assistance to developing countries for development projects. It focuses on reducing poverty, promoting inclusive growth, and supporting sustainable development.

Impact and Challenges

Multilateral organizations have had a significant impact on global governance, fostering cooperation, and addressing global challenges. However, they also face several challenges:

1. **Political Realities**: Multilateral organizations operate in a complex geopolitical landscape where national interests and power dynamics can impede decision-making and consensus. The diverse priorities and perspectives of member states can slow down progress on critical issues.

2. **Relevance and Effectiveness**: Critics argue that some multilateral organizations need to adapt to the rapidly changing global landscape and evolving challenges to remain relevant and effective. Reforms and restructuring may be necessary to enhance the decision-making process and increase responsiveness.

3. **Funding and Resource Constraints**: Multilateral organizations rely on member contributions and voluntary funding, which can be limited and unpredictable. Adequate resources are essential for carrying out their functions effectively and addressing global needs.

4. **Coordination and Fragmentation**: The proliferation of multilateral organizations and the overlapping mandates of some can lead to fragmentation and duplication of efforts. Enhancing coordination and coherence among different organizations is crucial for maximizing their impact.

5. **Representation and Inclusivity**: Ensuring fair representation and participation of all member states, particularly smaller and developing countries, is essential for the legitimacy and effectiveness of multilateral organizations. Efforts to enhance inclusivity and diversity are ongoing.

Despite these challenges, multilateral organizations remain vital in addressing global governance issues and fostering international cooperation. Their role in setting standards, coordinating efforts, and providing technical expertise is crucial for tackling the complex challenges of our interconnected world.

Key Takeaways

- Multilateral organizations play a crucial role in global governance by facilitating cooperation, setting standards and regulations, monitoring compliance, providing

CHAPTER 3: GLOBALIZATION AND THE INTERCONNECTED WORLD

technical expertise, and coordinating humanitarian efforts.

- Prominent multilateral organizations include the United Nations, World Health Organization, International Monetary Fund, World Trade Organization, and World Bank.

- Multilateral organizations face challenges such as political realities, relevance, funding constraints, coordination issues, and representation.

- Despite these challenges, multilateral organizations remain essential in addressing global challenges and fostering international cooperation. Their role in setting standards and coordinating efforts is vital for tackling complex global issues.

Subsection: The Debate on Protectionism vs. Free Market Capitalism

In this subsection, we will explore the ongoing debate between protectionism and free market capitalism. These two economic ideologies represent contrasting approaches to international trade and have significant implications for globalization and economic growth. Understanding the arguments and consequences of each perspective is crucial in comprehending the complexities of the global economy.

Introduction

Protectionism and free market capitalism embody different approaches to trade and economic policy. Protectionism refers to the use of trade barriers, such as tariffs and quotas, to shield domestic industries from foreign competition and promote domestic production. Free market capitalism, on the other hand, advocates for minimal government intervention in trade and supports unrestricted movement of goods and services.

The issue of protectionism vs. free market capitalism has been a subject of intense debate among economists, policymakers, and business leaders. It raises questions about the effects of trade on employment, economic growth, income distribution, and national security. Additionally, the rise of populist movements and nationalist sentiment in recent years has further fueled discussions on the merits and drawbacks of global trade.

Arguments for Protectionism

Proponents of protectionism argue that it is necessary to safeguard domestic industries and promote economic sovereignty. Here are some key arguments in favor of protectionism:

SECTION 1: THE RISE OF GLOBAL TRADE

1. **Protecting Domestic Industries:** Protectionists argue that imposing trade barriers can shield domestic industries from unfair competition by foreign companies that benefit from lower wages, lax environmental regulations, or government subsidies. By restricting imports, protectionism aims to create a level playing field for domestic producers.

2. **Preserving Jobs:** Critics of free trade argue that the removal of trade barriers can lead to job losses as companies move production to countries with lower labor costs. Protectionism, they claim, can help preserve domestic employment by limiting the flow of goods and services from abroad.

3. **National Security:** Some argue that protectionism is necessary to protect national security interests. By reducing reliance on foreign suppliers for critical goods and services, countries can ensure their economic resilience in times of geopolitical tensions or conflicts.

4. **Industrial Policy:** Protectionism can be seen as a tool for fostering targeted industries and promoting economic diversification. By sheltering nascent industries from foreign competition, governments can nurture their growth and development.

Arguments for Free Market Capitalism

Advocates of free market capitalism contend that unrestricted international trade brings numerous benefits and outweighs the drawbacks. Here are some key arguments in support of free market capitalism:

1. **Efficiency and Lower Prices:** Supporters of free trade argue that allowing goods and services to move freely across borders promotes efficiency, specialization, and economies of scale. By benefiting from comparative advantages, countries can produce goods at lower costs, resulting in lower prices for consumers.

2. **Increased Consumer Choice:** Free trade expands consumer choices by enabling access to a wider range of goods and services. When trade restrictions are reduced, consumers can enjoy a broader selection of products, including those not available or more expensive domestically.

3. **Economic Growth and Innovation:** Opening up to international trade can spur economic growth and drive innovation. By allowing companies to tap into larger markets, trade facilitates economies of scale, encourages

investment, and fosters competition, all of which contribute to economic development.

4. **Wealth Creation and Poverty Reduction:** Free trade has the potential to create wealth and alleviate poverty by expanding market opportunities, attracting foreign investment, and promoting economic integration. Developing countries, in particular, can benefit from increased export opportunities and technology transfer.

Trade-offs and Challenges

The debate between protectionism and free market capitalism is complex and nuanced, with trade-offs and challenges for both approaches. It is essential to consider the following factors:

- **Global Supply Chains:** Protectionist policies can disrupt global supply chains, which may have far-reaching effects on various industries and slow down economic growth. Additionally, dependencies on specific markets for inputs or finished goods can increase vulnerability to trade disruptions.

- **Retaliation and Trade Wars:** Imposing trade barriers can result in retaliatory actions by other countries, leading to trade wars and escalating tensions. These conflicts can have significant economic repercussions and harm global trade and cooperation.

- **Inequality and Distributional Effects:** Free trade can exacerbate income inequality, as certain industries or regions may suffer job losses or wage stagnation. Addressing these distributional effects is crucial to ensure that the benefits of trade are equitably shared.

- **Risks of Protectionism:** While protectionism may offer short-term benefits for some industries, it can hinder long-term competitiveness and innovation. Insulating domestic industries from competition may discourage efficiency improvements and technological advancements.

Real-World Examples

To illustrate the impact of the protectionism vs. free market capitalism debate, let's consider a couple of real-world examples:

SECTION 1: THE RISE OF GLOBAL TRADE 205

1. **The Smoot-Hawley Tariff Act (1930):** The enactment of this protectionist legislation by the United States significantly raised tariffs on imported goods. While it aimed to promote domestic industries during the Great Depression, it led to retaliatory actions by trading partners and contributed to a decline in global trade.

2. **European Union (EU) and the Single Market:** The EU represents an example of a regional bloc that promotes free movement of goods, services, capital, and labor. The creation of a single market has facilitated trade among member states and contributed to economic growth and integration.

Conclusion

The debate between protectionism and free market capitalism reflects the ongoing tensions in the global economy. Finding a balance between protecting domestic industries and reaping the benefits of global trade is a complex challenge faced by policymakers worldwide.

Ultimately, the choice between protectionism and free market capitalism depends on several factors, including a country's economic situation, geopolitical context, and societal values. Striking a balance that fosters economic growth, innovation, and social welfare requires careful consideration and ongoing dialogue.

Subsection: The Effects of Globalization on Local Cultures

Globalization has had a profound impact on local cultures around the world. As societies become increasingly interconnected through trade, communication, and migration, the boundaries between different cultures begin to blur. While globalization has brought numerous benefits and opportunities, it has also raised concerns about the preservation and identity of local cultures. In this subsection, we will explore the effects of globalization on local cultures, examining both the positive and negative aspects.

Cultural diversity and hybridization

One of the key effects of globalization on local cultures is the emergence of cultural diversity and hybridization. As different cultures come into contact with one another, they often influence and borrow from each other, leading to the creation of new cultural forms. For example, the fusion of musical styles from different regions has given rise to genres such as jazz, reggae, and hip-hop. Similarly, the blending of culinary traditions has resulted in the popularity of fusion cuisine.

This cultural hybridization can lead to a rich and vibrant exchange of ideas, practices, and values. It promotes creativity, innovation, and understanding between cultures. However, it also raises concerns about cultural appropriation and the potential loss of authenticity. It is important to strike a balance between celebrating cultural diversity and respecting the origins and significance of different cultural practices.

Homogenization and cultural imperialism

While globalization encourages cultural diversity, it also poses a risk of homogenization and cultural imperialism. As Western cultural values and practices permeate into various societies through media, technology, and consumerism, local cultures may face the threat of being overshadowed or marginalized. For instance, the dominance of Hollywood movies and Western fashion trends can erode indigenous cultural expressions and traditions.

Moreover, multinational corporations often introduce global brands and products that homogenize cultural experiences and preferences. This can be seen in the proliferation of global fast-food chains and the spread of Western consumer culture. Such homogenization can erode local traditions and lead to a loss of cultural identity and uniqueness.

Revitalization and cultural resilience

Despite the risks posed by globalization, many local cultures have shown remarkable resilience and adaptability. In response to the challenges brought about by external influences, communities have sought to revitalize and reclaim their cultural heritage. This can take various forms, including the revitalization of traditional crafts, languages, rituals, and festivals.

Additionally, cultural preservation efforts are being supported through policies, education, and tourism. Many governments recognize the importance of safeguarding their cultural heritage and promoting cultural diversity. The UNESCO World Heritage Sites program, for example, aims to protect and promote sites of outstanding universal value, highlighting the significance of cultural diversity.

Digital technologies and cultural expression

The rise of digital technologies, particularly the internet and social media, has provided new avenues for cultural expression and preservation. Local communities

SECTION 1: THE RISE OF GLOBAL TRADE 207

can now share their traditions, stories, and art forms with a global audience, fostering cross-cultural dialogue and appreciation.

Furthermore, digital platforms have empowered individuals and communities to document and archive their cultural practices. This not only preserves cultural heritage but also allows for the transmission of knowledge and traditions to future generations. Online forums, blogs, and virtual museums have become invaluable resources for learning about and engaging with diverse cultures.

Challenges and future considerations

While globalization has undoubtedly expanded access to diverse cultures, it is essential to address the challenges it presents. Governments, organizations, and individuals must work together to ensure the sustainable development and preservation of local cultures. This involves:

1. Promoting cultural diversity: Encouraging the celebration of cultural diversity and fostering intercultural dialogue and understanding. 2. Supporting local artists and artisans: Providing opportunities and resources for local artists and artisans to showcase and sustain their cultural practices. 3. Educating about cultural heritage: Incorporating cultural heritage education into school curricula to raise awareness and appreciation of local traditions. 4. Balancing economic development and cultural preservation: Finding a balance between economic growth and cultural preservation to ensure local communities benefit from globalization without compromising their cultural integrity.

In conclusion, globalization has both positive and negative effects on local cultures. While it leads to cultural hybridization and the risk of cultural homogenization, it also provides opportunities for cultural revitalization, digital preservation, and cross-cultural exchange. By promoting cultural diversity and finding ways to support and protect local cultures, we can ensure that globalization remains a force for cultural enrichment rather than cultural erasure.

Subsection: Globalization and the Environment: Challenges and Opportunities

In the era of globalization, the interconnectedness of nations has brought about numerous opportunities and challenges for the environment. The increasing flow of goods, services, and information across borders has had profound implications for the natural world. In this subsection, we will explore the various challenges posed by globalization to the environment, as well as the potential opportunities for sustainable development.

The Challenge of Environmental Degradation

One of the key challenges of globalization is the accelerated rate of environmental degradation. As economic activities expand, so does the extraction of natural resources, deforestation, and pollution. The pursuit of economic growth often comes at the expense of environmental conservation, leading to habitat destruction, loss of biodiversity, and climate change.

Rapid industrialization in developing countries, driven by globalization, has resulted in increased emissions of greenhouse gases and air pollutants. This not only contributes to climate change but also leads to air and water pollution, posing significant health risks to both humans and ecosystems.

Furthermore, the globalization of agriculture has led to increased use of chemical fertilizers, pesticides, and genetically modified organisms (GMOs), which have adverse effects on soil quality and biodiversity. Large-scale industrial farming practices also contribute to deforestation as forests are cleared for agricultural land.

Opportunities for Sustainable Development

Despite these challenges, globalization also presents opportunities for promoting sustainable development and mitigating environmental harm. Through international cooperation and the sharing of knowledge and best practices, we can work towards addressing the negative impacts of globalization on the environment.

One opportunity lies in the promotion of green technologies and renewable energy sources. As nations become more interconnected, they can collaborate on research and development initiatives to advance clean energy solutions such as solar power, wind energy, and geothermal energy. The transfer of environmentally friendly technologies from developed to developing countries can aid in reducing their dependence on fossil fuels and promote sustainable economic growth.

Globalization also offers opportunities for the exchange of environmental policies and regulations. By sharing successful strategies for conservation, waste management, and pollution control, nations can learn from each other's experiences and implement effective measures to protect the environment. International agreements, such as the Paris Agreement on climate change, provide a framework for collective action and cooperation in addressing global environmental challenges.

Moreover, globalization enables the formation of global environmental movements and grassroots organizations. Through social media and other online platforms, individuals from diverse backgrounds can come together to raise awareness about environmental issues and advocate for change. These movements

SECTION 1: THE RISE OF GLOBAL TRADE 209

have the potential to pressure governments and corporations to adopt more environmentally sustainable practices.

Case Study: E-Waste Management

The globalization of technology has brought about a new challenge in the form of electronic waste or e-waste. Electronic devices, such as computers, smartphones, and televisions, have a short lifespan and often end up in landfills or are exported to developing countries for improper disposal.

E-waste contains hazardous materials, including heavy metals and toxic chemicals, which can contaminate soil and water sources. To address this issue, the Basel Convention on the Control of Transboundary Movements of Hazardous Wastes and Their Disposal aims to regulate the international trade of e-waste and promote environmentally sound management practices.

One opportunity emerging from this challenge is the development of recycling and resource recovery industries. By implementing proper e-waste management systems, valuable metals and materials can be extracted from discarded electronic devices, reducing the demand for virgin resources. This not only mitigates environmental harm but also creates economic opportunities for job creation and the growth of a circular economy.

Conclusion

Globalization has both positive and negative impacts on the environment. While it poses significant challenges in terms of environmental degradation and resource depletion, it also offers opportunities for sustainable development through international cooperation, technology transfer, and the formation of global environmental movements.

To harness these opportunities, it is crucial for nations to adopt a comprehensive approach towards environmental protection. This includes implementing effective policies and regulations, investing in green technologies, promoting sustainable consumption and production patterns, and fostering international collaboration. By doing so, we can ensure that globalization becomes a force for positive environmental change and contribute to a more sustainable future.

Section 2: Migration and the Movement of People

Subsection: The Causes and Consequences of Forced Migration

Forced migration is a complex issue that has significant social, economic, and political consequences. This subsection explores the causes of forced migration as well as the impact it has on individuals, communities, and society as a whole.

Causes of Forced Migration

There are several factors that contribute to forced migration. It is essential to understand these causes in order to address the root causes and develop strategies to prevent or mitigate forced migration.

1. **Conflict and War** One of the primary causes of forced migration is armed conflict and war. When conflicts erupt, people are forced to flee their homes to seek safety and refuge in other regions or countries. They leave behind their homes, communities, and livelihoods in search of a secure environment. The displacement caused by conflict often leads to internal displacement or cross-border movement of refugees.

2. **Persecution and Human Rights Violations** Persecution based on race, ethnicity, religion, political opinion, or social group identity is another significant cause of forced migration. People facing persecution often have no choice but to flee their homes and seek asylum in other countries. Political repression, discriminatory policies, and violence can force individuals and communities to leave their countries in search of safety and protection.

3. **Environmental Factors** Environmental factors, such as natural disasters and climate change, can also contribute to forced migration. The increasing frequency and intensity of natural disasters, such as hurricanes, floods, droughts, and wildfires, can render land uninhabitable and destroy homes and infrastructure. Climate change, including rising sea levels and temperature changes, can exacerbate existing environmental challenges and lead to forced migration.

4. **Socioeconomic Factors** Socioeconomic factors, including poverty, inequality, and lack of economic opportunities, play a significant role in forced migration. People often leave their homes in search of better economic prospects, access to education, healthcare, and a higher quality of life. Economic disparities within and

SECTION 2: MIGRATION AND THE MOVEMENT OF PEOPLE   211

between countries can create push factors that force individuals and families to migrate.

Consequences of Forced Migration

Forced migration has far-reaching consequences for individuals, communities, and societies. It disrupts lives, separates families, and poses significant challenges for both the displaced individuals and the host communities.

1. Humanitarian Crisis   Forced migration often leads to humanitarian crises. Displaced individuals face numerous challenges, including limited access to basic necessities such as food, clean water, healthcare, and shelter. Refugee camps and temporary settlements may lack adequate infrastructure and resources to support the needs of the displaced population. This can result in a further deterioration of living conditions and the spread of diseases.

2. Social and Cultural Impact   Forced migration can have a profound social and cultural impact on individuals and communities. Displaced individuals often face discrimination, stigmatization, and marginalization, which can lead to social exclusion and hinder their integration into the host society. The loss of cultural identity and the disruption of social networks can also have long-term effects on the well-being and mental health of the displaced individuals.

3. Economic Implications   Forced migration can have significant economic implications for both the displaced population and the host communities. Displaced individuals may struggle to find employment and access economic opportunities, leading to increased poverty and dependency on humanitarian aid. Host communities may experience strained resources and competition for jobs and services, which can create social tensions.

4. Political and Security Challenges   Forced migration can also present political and security challenges. The mass movement of people across borders can strain the capacity of governments to manage and respond effectively. It can disrupt social cohesion, fuel xenophobia and nativist sentiments, and potentially contribute to social unrest and conflicts between different ethnic or religious groups.

Addressing Forced Migration

Addressing forced migration requires a comprehensive and collaborative approach involving governments, international organizations, civil society, and the international community. It is crucial to tackle the root causes of forced migration and provide support and protection to displaced individuals and communities.

1. **Conflict Prevention and Resolution** Efforts should be made to prevent and resolve conflicts through diplomatic means, mediation, and peacebuilding initiatives. Investing in conflict prevention and resolution can help reduce the number of people forced to flee their homes due to armed conflict and war.

2. **Protection and Assistance** Displaced individuals should be provided with legal protection, access to basic services, and humanitarian assistance. This includes ensuring their safety, upholding their human rights, and addressing their immediate needs, such as food, shelter, healthcare, and education.

3. **Sustainable Development** Promoting sustainable development and addressing socioeconomic inequalities can help address the root causes of forced migration. Investments in education, infrastructure, healthcare, and job creation can provide individuals with opportunities in their home countries, reducing the need to migrate.

4. **International Cooperation** International cooperation plays a critical role in addressing forced migration. Collaboration between governments, international organizations, and civil society is essential to develop effective migration policies, share responsibilities, and support the integration of displaced individuals into host communities.

Case Study: Syrian Refugee Crisis

The Syrian refugee crisis serves as a significant example of forced migration and its consequences. The ongoing conflict in Syria has forced millions of Syrians to flee their homes, seeking refuge in neighboring countries and beyond. The influx of refugees has strained the resources and infrastructure of host countries and has had political, social, and economic ramifications for the entire region.

The Syrian refugee crisis highlights the urgency of international cooperation, humanitarian aid, and long-term solutions to address forced migration. It underscores the need for a comprehensive approach that considers the causes, consequences, and potential solutions to forced migration in the contemporary world.

Conclusion

Forced migration is a complex issue with profound consequences. Understanding the causes of forced migration and its impact is crucial in developing effective strategies to address this global challenge. By addressing the root causes, providing protection and assistance to displaced individuals, and promoting international cooperation, we can work towards creating a world where forced migration is minimized, and individuals can live in peace and security in their own communities.

Subsection: Refugee Crises and the Role of Humanitarian Organizations

Refugee crises are an unfortunate reality of our contemporary world, with millions of people being displaced from their homes due to conflict, persecution, or natural disasters. In this subsection, we will explore the causes and consequences of these crises and the crucial role played by humanitarian organizations in providing aid and support to refugees.

Causes of Refugee Crises

Refugee crises can have various causes, each with its own complexities and challenges. Some of the main causes include:

1. Conflict: Armed conflicts, such as civil wars or international disputes, often result in mass displacement of people. For example, the ongoing Syrian civil war has led to millions of Syrians seeking refuge in neighboring countries and beyond.

2. Persecution: Individuals or groups who face persecution based on their race, religion, nationality, political opinion, or membership in a particular social group might be forced to flee their home countries. The Rohingya crisis in Myanmar is a stark example of persecution leading to mass displacement.

3. Environmental disasters: Natural disasters, such as earthquakes, floods, or droughts, can render areas uninhabitable, forcing people to leave their homes. The 2010 earthquake in Haiti, for instance, caused widespread displacement and compelled many Haitians to seek refuge elsewhere.

Consequences of Refugee Crises

Refugee crises have far-reaching consequences, affecting both the refugees and the countries that host them. Some of the key consequences include:

1. Humanitarian crisis: Refugees often face acute challenges, including lack of shelter, food, healthcare, and educational opportunities. They are also vulnerable to exploitation, violence, and human rights abuses.

2. Strain on host countries: Countries hosting large numbers of refugees may struggle to provide basic services and infrastructure to both their existing population and the influx of refugees. This strain can lead to social, economic, and political tensions.

3. Global security concerns: In some cases, terrorist organizations or extremist groups may exploit refugee flows to infiltrate host countries, posing a security threat. This connection requires careful management and screening procedures.

Role of Humanitarian Organizations

Humanitarian organizations play a vital role in responding to refugee crises. These organizations provide various forms of assistance to refugees, including:

1. Emergency aid: Humanitarian organizations deliver life-saving assistance, such as food, clean water, medical care, and shelter, to meet the immediate needs of refugees.

2. Protection and advocacy: Humanitarian organizations work to protect the rights of refugees and advocate for their access to legal protection and services. They also raise awareness about the plight of refugees and promote solutions to address their needs.

3. Long-term support and development: Humanitarian organizations assist in the long-term resettlement and integration of refugees by providing education, vocational training, and livelihood support. They aim to empower refugees to rebuild their lives and contribute to their host communities.

4. Coordination and collaboration: Humanitarian organizations collaborate with governments, international agencies, and local communities to ensure a coordinated and effective response to refugee crises. This collaboration helps maximize resources, avoid duplication, and enhance the overall humanitarian response.

Challenges and Solutions

The response to refugee crises faces several challenges, but innovative solutions are continually evolving. Some of the key challenges include:

SECTION 2: MIGRATION AND THE MOVEMENT OF PEOPLE 215

1. Funding: Humanitarian organizations rely on donor funding to carry out their work. However, securing and sustaining adequate funding for long-term refugee assistance remains a challenge.

2. Access and security: Humanitarian organizations often face access constraints and security risks due to the volatile environments where refugee crises occur. Ensuring the safety of aid workers and maintaining consistent access to refugees require strategic planning and coordination.

3. Lack of legal frameworks: In many cases, there is a lack of comprehensive legal frameworks to protect the rights of refugees. Advocacy efforts are essential to encourage governments to enact and implement laws that safeguard the rights of refugees.

4. Public perception and xenophobia: Negative public perception and xenophobic attitudes towards refugees can hinder their integration and make it difficult for them to access support services. Education, awareness campaigns, and community engagement are crucial to address these challenges.

Innovative solutions and good practices are emerging to overcome these challenges:

1. Multi-stakeholder partnerships: Governments, NGOs, corporations, and local communities can collaborate to mobilize resources, share expertise, and address the complex needs of refugees.

2. Technology-driven solutions: Humanitarian organizations are leveraging technology to improve the efficiency of their operations, enhance data management, and provide innovative solutions for refugee challenges, such as digital identification systems or mobile applications for access to information and services.

3. Empowering refugees: Recognizing the skills and potential that refugees bring, empowering them through education, vocational training, and entrepreneurship programs can not only help them rebuild their lives but also contribute to the development of host communities.

Conclusion

Refugee crises present immense humanitarian challenges, but through the concerted efforts of humanitarian organizations and collaborations among various stakeholders, solutions can be found. Addressing the root causes, providing essential assistance, and promoting the rights and integration of refugees are the key steps towards mitigating the impact of refugee crises and shaping a more inclusive and compassionate world.

Subsection: Immigration Policies and the Challenges of Integration

In this subsection, we will explore the complexities surrounding immigration policies and the challenges associated with the integration of immigrants into host societies. Immigration is a significant aspect of globalization, shaping demographic changes and cultural diversity across the world. As countries strive to manage and regulate migration, they face various political, economic, and social dilemmas. This subsection examines the underlying principles, key issues, and potential solutions related to immigration policies and the integration of immigrants.

Overview of Immigration Policies

Immigration policies refer to the laws, regulations, and procedures established by national governments to control the entry and stay of foreign nationals within their territories. These policies are influenced by factors such as national security concerns, economic needs, humanitarian considerations, and cultural preservation. Immigration policies can range from strict restrictions to open-door policies that facilitate the movement of people across borders.

The principles and goals underlying immigration policies vary across countries. Some countries prioritize attracting high-skilled immigrants to fill labor market gaps and contribute to economic growth. Others focus on family reunification, human rights, or providing humanitarian assistance to refugees and asylum seekers. It is important to note that immigration policies can change over time in response to shifting demographics, political dynamics, and public sentiment.

Key Challenges of Integration

Integration refers to the process by which immigrants become full members of the receiving society, both economically and socially. Successful integration involves economic participation, social inclusion, and the preservation of cultural diversity. However, integration can be a complex and multifaceted task that poses several challenges:

1. **Economic Integration:** Immigrants often face barriers in accessing employment opportunities that match their skills and qualifications. Language proficiency, recognition of foreign credentials, and discrimination in the job market are some of the key obstacles. Additionally, the impact of immigrant labor on wages and job competition can be a concern for native-born workers.

2. **Social and Cultural Integration:** Social integration encompasses the inclusion of immigrants in social networks, institutions, and community life.

SECTION 2: MIGRATION AND THE MOVEMENT OF PEOPLE 217

Cultural integration refers to the adaptation and acceptance of cultural norms and values of the host society while preserving elements of the immigrants' own cultural identity. Language barriers, cultural differences, social prejudice, and discrimination can make social and cultural integration challenging for immigrants.

3. Education and Integration of Children: Education plays a crucial role in the integration of immigrant children. Access to quality education, language support programs, cultural sensitivity in schools, and the involvement of parents are key factors in promoting successful integration. However, immigrant children may face obstacles such as language barriers, limited access to educational resources, and socio-economic disadvantages.

4. Public Perception and Political Support: The public's perception of immigration and the political discourse surrounding it can influence the integration process. Negative stereotypes, anti-immigrant sentiments, and xenophobic attitudes can hinder the integration of immigrants. Conversely, positive public opinion, inclusive policies, and initiatives promoting social cohesion can foster integration.

Potential Solutions

Addressing the challenges of immigration integration requires a comprehensive approach involving various stakeholders, including governments, civil society, immigrants themselves, and host communities. Here are some potential solutions:

1. Enhancing Language Acquisition and Skills Training: Providing language courses and skills training programs can facilitate immigrants' entry into the labor market and improve their economic integration. Language proficiency enables better communication and social integration, while skills training equips immigrants with marketable skills aligned with the host country's labor market needs.

2. Promoting Diversity and Inclusion Policies: Implementing diversity and inclusion policies in education, workplaces, and communities can foster social integration and combat discrimination. These policies create environments where immigrants feel valued and have equal opportunities to participate in various spheres of society.

3. Strengthening Support Networks and Social Services: Establishing support networks, community centers, and social services specifically aimed at assisting immigrants can facilitate their integration. These resources provide guidance on navigating the host society, accessing social benefits, and addressing specific challenges faced by the immigrant population.

4. Encouraging Intercultural Exchange and Dialogue: Promoting intercultural exchange programs, cultural events, and platforms for dialogue between immigrant and host communities can foster mutual understanding and appreciation. These initiatives help dispel stereotypes, build social cohesion, and create opportunities for cultural exchange.

5. **Implementing Comprehensive Immigration Policies:** Governments can design immigration policies that balance national security, economic needs, and humanitarian considerations. Comprehensive policies should include clear pathways to legal status, streamlined procedures, and support for family reunification. Flexible immigration policies can contribute to successful integration by recognizing the diversity and potential contributions of immigrants.

6. **Public Awareness and Education:** Raising public awareness about the benefits of immigration, dispelling myths, and combating prejudice through education campaigns can create a more positive environment for integration. Educating the public about the economic, cultural, and social contributions of immigrants helps to challenge negative narratives and promote social cohesion.

It is important to note that the challenges and potential solutions outlined above are not exhaustive, and the needs and circumstances may differ based on specific contexts. Flexibility, adaptation, and ongoing evaluation of policies and programs are essential for effectively addressing the challenges of immigration policies and the integration of immigrants.

Case Study: Canada's Immigration and Integration Model

One example of a country that has made significant progress in immigration policies and integration is Canada. With a long history of immigration, Canada has developed a comprehensive model that focuses on economic integration, social inclusion, and cultural diversity.

Canada's immigration system is based on a points system that evaluates applicants based on factors such as education, work experience, language proficiency, and adaptability. This system aims to attract skilled immigrants who can contribute to the country's economy and help address labor market needs. Additionally, Canada emphasizes family reunification as a key element of its immigration policy.

To address the challenges of integration, Canada provides various support programs, language training, and settlement services to assist newcomers in their transition. The government also encourages intercultural exchange and promotes diversity through policies aimed at combatting discrimination and ensuring equal opportunities for all.

Canada's success in immigrant integration can be attributed to its commitment to social cohesion, inclusivity, and multiculturalism. The Canadian model serves as a valuable example for other countries seeking to develop effective immigration policies and promote integration.

Conclusion

Immigration policies play a significant role in shaping the movement of people across borders, and the successful integration of immigrants is crucial for the social, cultural, and economic fabric of host societies. By understanding the challenges and potential solutions associated with immigration policies and integration, countries can develop more effective strategies to meet the needs of both immigrants and their receiving communities. Embracing diversity, promoting inclusion, and fostering dialogue are vital components of creating cohesive and prosperous societies in an interconnected world.

Subsection: Brain Drain and the Impact on Developing Countries

Brain drain refers to the emigration or migration of highly skilled individuals, particularly professionals, from developing countries to developed countries. This phenomenon has significant implications for the socio-economic development of the countries experiencing the brain drain. In this subsection, we will explore the concept of brain drain, its causes, and its impact on developing countries. We will also discuss potential strategies to mitigate the negative effects of brain drain.

Understanding Brain Drain

Brain drain occurs when individuals with advanced skills, knowledge, and expertise leave their home countries to seek better opportunities abroad. This trend is particularly prevalent in sectors such as healthcare, engineering, science, and technology. The departure of these skilled individuals poses challenges for the countries they leave behind, as it hampers the development and progress of key sectors that depend on their expertise.

The phenomenon of brain drain is driven by various factors, including economic, political, and social reasons. Economic factors, such as higher wages and better job prospects in developed countries, serve as a strong pull for skilled individuals. Political instability, lack of career advancement opportunities, limited access to resources and infrastructure, and inadequate working conditions also contribute to brain drain.

Causes of Brain Drain

1. Economic Factors: Skilled professionals are often attracted to developed countries that offer higher salaries, better living standards, and greater career prospects. The lure of better economic opportunities is a significant driver of brain drain.

2. Education and Research Facilities: Developing countries may lack adequate educational institutions and research facilities that can provide opportunities for professionals to pursue advanced studies and engage in cutting-edge research.

3. Political and Social Factors: Political instability, social unrest, and lack of social security in developing countries can lead professionals to seek stability and security in more developed nations.

4. Quality of Life: Factors such as healthcare facilities, infrastructure, safety, and overall quality of life play a crucial role in influencing individuals' decisions to emigrate.

5. Migration Policies: Immigration policies in developed countries that prioritize skilled professionals further exacerbate brain drain by attracting talent from developing countries.

Impacts of Brain Drain

The brain drain phenomenon has significant ramifications for developing countries:

1. Loss of Human Capital: Developing countries invest considerable resources in educating and training professionals, only to experience the loss of these skilled individuals. This deprives the countries of the human capital needed for their socio-economic development.

2. Shortage of Skilled Workers: Brain drain creates a shortage of skilled professionals in crucial sectors, such as healthcare and technology. The scarcity of skilled workers impedes the delivery of critical services and hampers the growth of industries that require specialized expertise.

3. Reduced Innovation and Research: The departure of skilled researchers and scientists limits the capacity of developing countries to innovate and contribute to scientific advancements. This contributes to a reliance on developed countries for technological progress.

4. Economic Consequences: Brain drain affects the economy of developing countries by reducing productivity, hindering economic growth, and impeding the development of key industries. It can also lead to a loss of tax revenue and increased dependence on foreign expertise.

SECTION 2: MIGRATION AND THE MOVEMENT OF PEOPLE

5. Social Impact: Brain drain can have adverse social consequences, including a loss of role models for aspiring professionals, increasing inequality, and exacerbating social issues in developing countries.

Mitigating Brain Drain

Addressing brain drain requires a multi-faceted approach involving the collaboration of governments, educational institutions, and international organizations. Some potential strategies include:

1. Strengthening Domestic Opportunities: Developing countries should focus on improving education and research facilities, offering competitive salaries, and creating an enabling environment for professional growth and advancement.

2. Incentives for Return: Governments can implement policies and programs aimed at attracting expatriate professionals back to their home countries. This may include offering financial incentives, career opportunities, and improved working conditions.

3. Collaboration and Partnerships: Developing countries can foster partnerships with developed nations to create opportunities for knowledge-sharing, capacity-building, and joint research initiatives.

4. Retaining Talent: Developing countries should prioritize initiatives to retain skilled professionals by providing career development opportunities, creating a conducive work environment, and offering competitive compensation packages.

5. Emphasizing Technological Advancements: Investing in technology and innovation can help mitigate the brain drain impact by creating opportunities for professionals to contribute to their home countries' technological advancements.

6. Diaspora Engagement: Governments can actively engage with their diaspora communities, leveraging their skills, expertise, and networks to contribute to the development of their home countries.

It is important for developing countries to adopt a comprehensive and proactive approach to mitigate brain drain and harness the potential of skilled professionals for their own development.

Case Study: Brain Drain in the Healthcare Sector

To illustrate the impact of brain drain, let us consider the healthcare sector in a developing country. Skilled doctors, nurses, and healthcare professionals often migrate to developed countries in search of better career prospects and remuneration. The consequences of brain drain in this sector are profound:

1. Shortage of Healthcare Professionals: The departure of skilled medical practitioners creates a shortage of healthcare professionals, leading to inadequate healthcare services and long waiting times for patients.

2. Disruption of Training and Education: Brain drain hampers the training and education of future healthcare professionals, as experienced practitioners leave teaching and mentoring positions vacant.

3. Decreased Quality of Care: The loss of experienced doctors and nurses negatively affects the quality of healthcare services, as less-experienced professionals may struggle to provide the same level of care.

4. Economic Loss: Developing countries invest significant resources in training healthcare professionals. When these professionals emigrate, it represents a loss of investment for the country.

To address brain drain in the healthcare sector, governments can implement measures such as improving working conditions, offering competitive salaries, providing opportunities for professional development, and leveraging technology to enhance healthcare delivery.

Conclusion

Brain drain has far-reaching implications for developing countries, affecting their economic growth, innovation capacity, and social well-being. To mitigate the negative impact, it is essential for governments, educational institutions, and international organizations to collaborate and implement strategies that address the underlying causes of brain drain. By creating conducive environments, offering attractive opportunities, and retaining skilled professionals, developing countries can navigate the challenges posed by brain drain and pave the way for sustainable development.

Subsection: Cultural Diversity and the Globalization of Diaspora Communities

In this subsection, we will explore the concept of cultural diversity and its relationship with the globalization of diaspora communities. Cultural diversity refers to the existence of multiple cultures within a society, while the globalization of diaspora communities highlights how these diverse cultures interact and evolve in a global context. This subsection will delve into the factors contributing to cultural diversity, the impact of globalization on diaspora communities, and the challenges and opportunities presented by this phenomenon.

SECTION 2: MIGRATION AND THE MOVEMENT OF PEOPLE   223

Factors Contributing to Cultural Diversity

Cultural diversity arises from various factors, including historical events, migration, and globalization. Historical events, such as colonization and decolonization, have played a significant role in shaping cultural diversity. The establishment of colonies by European powers led to the movement of people from different regions, resulting in the mixing of cultures and the emergence of new cultural identities.

Migration is another key factor contributing to cultural diversity. Individuals and communities may migrate voluntarily or forcibly, seeking better economic opportunities, escaping persecution, or due to environmental factors. As people settle in new locations, they bring with them their traditions, languages, and customs, enriching the cultural fabric of their host communities.

Globalization has further accelerated cultural diversity by promoting interactions between different cultures. Advances in transportation and communication technology have facilitated the movement of people, ideas, and cultural artifacts across borders, leading to cultural exchange and hybridization. This interconnectedness has created opportunities for diaspora communities to maintain their cultural heritage and connect with their home countries.

Impact of Globalization on Diaspora Communities

Globalization has had a profound impact on diaspora communities, both positive and negative. On one hand, it has provided diaspora communities with greater opportunities to preserve and celebrate their cultural identities. Through globalization, diaspora communities can maintain connections with their home countries, participate in cultural festivals, and engage in transnational networks.

Additionally, globalization has created economic opportunities for diaspora communities. Many diaspora communities have leveraged their unique cultural knowledge and skills to establish businesses and contribute to the local economy. For example, the Chinese diaspora has played a significant role in promoting trade between China and their host countries.

On the other hand, globalization has also posed challenges for diaspora communities. Cultural assimilation can be a concern as diaspora communities navigate the dominant culture of their host countries. The pressure to conform to mainstream norms and values can lead to the erosion of cultural practices and languages.

Furthermore, globalization can exacerbate issues of identity and belonging within diaspora communities. The process of acculturation can be complex, as individuals and communities navigate between multiple cultural identities. This

CHAPTER 3: GLOBALIZATION AND THE INTERCONNECTED WORLD

can result in a sense of cultural dislocation and the need to negotiate between different cultural expectations.

Challenges and Opportunities

The globalization of diaspora communities presents both challenges and opportunities. One of the main challenges is the preservation of cultural heritage. Diaspora communities often face the risk of cultural assimilation, making it crucial to find innovative ways to transmit cultural knowledge and practices to future generations. This could involve organizing cultural festivals, language classes, and community events that celebrate diverse cultural traditions.

Another challenge is the promotion of inclusivity and equality within diaspora communities. Infighting or the exclusion of certain groups based on socio-cultural differences can hinder the unity and progress of the community as a whole. Creating platforms for open dialogue and fostering an environment that values diversity can help overcome these challenges.

Despite the challenges, the globalization of diaspora communities also presents numerous opportunities. Diaspora communities can act as bridges between their home countries and host countries, facilitating cultural exchanges and promoting mutual understanding. This can be achieved through initiatives such as cultural exchange programs, collaborations in the arts, and intercultural dialogues.

Additionally, diaspora communities can contribute to the economic development of both their home countries and host countries. By leveraging their cultural knowledge and networks, they can facilitate trade, business partnerships, and investments. Such economic collaborations can create opportunities for both sides to benefit and foster greater intercultural understanding.

Example: The Impact of the Indian Diaspora

An example of the impact of diaspora communities on cultural diversity and globalization is the Indian diaspora. The Indian diaspora is one of the largest and most diverse diaspora communities globally, with significant populations in countries such as the United States, the United Kingdom, Canada, and the Gulf countries.

The Indian diaspora has played a crucial role in shaping cultural diversity, particularly in terms of food, music, and literature. Indian cuisine, such as curry, has become popular worldwide, blending with local cuisines and creating unique fusion dishes. Bollywood, the Indian film industry, has gained international popularity, influencing global entertainment and fashion trends.

SECTION 2: MIGRATION AND THE MOVEMENT OF PEOPLE 225

Additionally, the Indian diaspora has created economic and trade opportunities. Indian professionals and entrepreneurs have excelled in various fields, contributing to the technology industry, academia, and the arts. They have also fostered trade partnerships between India and their host countries, facilitating economic growth and cultural exchange.

However, the Indian diaspora also faces challenges, such as maintaining cultural traditions and languages across generations. Efforts are being made to establish community centers, language schools, and cultural organizations to preserve Indian cultural heritage within the diaspora.

In conclusion, the globalization of diaspora communities has greatly impacted cultural diversity and cultural exchange in today's interconnected world. By understanding the factors contributing to cultural diversity, the impact of globalization on diaspora communities, and the challenges and opportunities presented, we can appreciate the rich tapestry of human cultures and work towards promoting inclusivity and mutual understanding.

Subsection: Human Trafficking and Modern-Day Slavery

Human trafficking and modern-day slavery are grave issues that continue to persist in the contemporary world, affecting millions of individuals worldwide. This subsection will delve into the complexities of human trafficking, its causes, consequences, and potential solutions. We will explore various aspects of this global problem, including its definition, forms, impacts, and efforts to combat it.

Definition and Forms of Human Trafficking

Human trafficking refers to the recruitment, transportation, transfer, harboring, or receipt of individuals through means such as force, coercion, deception, or abuse of power for the purpose of exploitation. It is a modern form of slavery that exploits victims for forced labor, sexual exploitation, organ trafficking, and other forms of abuse.

There are different forms of human trafficking, each with its distinct characteristics and challenges. These include:

- **Sex Trafficking:** Involves the recruitment, transportation, or harboring of individuals, usually women and children, through force or deception for the purpose of sexual exploitation. This form of trafficking is prevalent in the commercial sex industry, including brothels, escort services, and online platforms.

- **Labor Trafficking:** Involves the exploitation of individuals, often migrant workers, through forced labor in sectors such as agriculture, construction, manufacturing, domestic work, and mining. Victims of labor trafficking endure harsh working conditions, non-existent or minimal wages, and physical and psychological abuse.

- **Child Trafficking:** Refers to the trafficking of children for various forms of exploitation, including sexual exploitation, child soldiers, forced labor, and child marriages. Children are particularly vulnerable due to their age, lack of awareness, and dependence on adults.

- **Organ Trafficking:** Involves the illegal trade of organs, where individuals are coerced or deceived into donating their organs for transplantation or harvested through illicit means. Organ trafficking poses significant ethical dilemmas and is driven by the demand for organs and the lack of legal and regulated organ donation systems.

Causes and Consequences of Human Trafficking

Human trafficking is a complex issue influenced by a range of factors. Understanding the causes helps in developing effective strategies to combat this crime. Some key causes of human trafficking include:

- **Poverty and Economic Inequality:** Poverty and lack of economic opportunities are strong push factors that make individuals vulnerable to trafficking. In many cases, traffickers prey on individuals seeking better economic prospects, offering false promises of employment or education.

- **Gender Inequality and Discrimination:** Gender discrimination plays a significant role in perpetuating human trafficking. Women and girls are disproportionately affected by trafficking due to social and economic inequalities, limited access to education, and discriminatory societal norms.

- **Armed Conflict and Political Instability:** Regions plagued by armed conflict and political instability create fertile ground for human trafficking. Displaced individuals, refugees, and those living in conflict zones are particularly vulnerable to exploitation by traffickers.

- **Corruption and Weak Governance:** Corrupt officials and weak governance structures facilitate trafficking networks by allowing traffickers to operate with impunity. Lack of effective law enforcement, judicial systems, and

SECTION 2: MIGRATION AND THE MOVEMENT OF PEOPLE   227

proper implementation of anti-trafficking measures contribute to the growth of this illicit activity.

The consequences of human trafficking are severe and far-reaching, affecting individuals, communities, and societies as a whole. Victims of trafficking suffer physical and psychological abuse, their fundamental human rights are violated, and they often live in fear and isolation. The impact ripples beyond the victims themselves, extending to their families and communities. Human trafficking undermines social stability, fosters inequality, and perpetuates cycles of violence and exploitation.

Efforts to Combat Human Trafficking

Addressing human trafficking requires a comprehensive approach encompassing prevention, protection, prosecution, and partnerships. Various actors, including governments, international organizations, civil society, and the private sector, play a crucial role in combating this crime.

- **Legislation and Law Enforcement:** Enacting and enforcing robust legislation is essential to combat human trafficking. Countries should criminalize all forms of trafficking, provide adequate resources for law enforcement agencies, and strengthen international cooperation to dismantle trafficking networks.

- **Victim Protection and Support:** Protecting and supporting victims of trafficking is of utmost importance. This includes providing safe shelters, medical and psychological care, legal support, and access to education and vocational training to facilitate their reintegration into society.

- **Prevention and Awareness:** Prevention efforts should focus on addressing the root causes of trafficking, such as poverty, discrimination, and lack of opportunities. Raising awareness among vulnerable populations, educating the public, and implementing targeted campaigns are crucial in preventing individuals from falling prey to traffickers.

- **International Cooperation:** Cooperation between countries is necessary to combat transnational trafficking networks. Sharing information, intelligence, best practices, and harmonizing anti-trafficking efforts at the regional and international levels are vital.

- **Public-Private Partnerships:** Collaboration between governments, civil society organizations, and the private sector can yield significant results in tackling human trafficking. Private sector engagement can involve implementing ethical supply chain practices, supporting victims' economic empowerment, and leveraging technology to identify and disrupt trafficking networks.

Unconventional Approach: Empowering Survivors through Entrepreneurship

One unconventional approach to combating human trafficking is empowering survivors through entrepreneurship. Providing survivors with the necessary skills, training, and resources to start their own businesses or gain meaningful employment can significantly contribute to their rehabilitation and reintegration into society. Entrepreneurship can offer survivors economic independence, boost their self-esteem, and provide a sustainable livelihood. This approach not only provides survivors with a sense of purpose but also addresses the root causes of vulnerability that lead to trafficking, such as lack of economic opportunities and social exclusion.

Organizations and initiatives focusing on survivor-led entrepreneurship can offer mentorship, access to capital, business development training, and networking opportunities. By supporting survivor-led businesses, individuals and communities can contribute to breaking the cycle of exploitation and empower survivors to become agents of change in the fight against human trafficking.

Conclusion

Human trafficking and modern-day slavery remain significant challenges in the contemporary world. This subsection has explored the definition and forms of human trafficking, its causes and consequences, as well as efforts to combat this heinous crime. By addressing the root causes, strengthening legislation and enforcement, providing comprehensive victim support, and fostering international cooperation and partnerships, we can collectively work towards ending human trafficking and ensuring that every individual enjoys their basic human rights and freedoms.

Subsection: Environmental Migration and Climate Change

Environmental migration refers to the movement of people from their homes or communities due to the degradation or destruction of their natural environment, which is primarily caused by climate change. Climate change is one of the greatest challenges of our time, and its impacts are being felt around the world. Rising

SECTION 2: MIGRATION AND THE MOVEMENT OF PEOPLE   229

temperatures, extreme weather events, sea-level rise, and other environmental changes are displacing communities and forcing people to migrate in search of better living conditions and opportunities.

Causes and Consequences of Environmental Migration

The causes of environmental migration can be categorized into gradual, sudden and catastrophic events. Gradual environmental changes, such as desertification, land degradation, and slow-onset sea-level rise, can directly affect the resources that communities depend on for their livelihoods. Sudden events, such as storms, floods, and wildfires, can destroy homes and infrastructure, making it uninhabitable. Catastrophic events, such as earthquakes, tsunamis, and hurricanes, can result in large-scale displacement and the destruction of entire communities.

The consequences of environmental migration are vast and impact not only the individuals and communities who are forced to migrate but also the areas they migrate to. For those who are displaced, loss of homes, livelihoods, and community ties can lead to increased poverty, food insecurity, and vulnerability to exploitation and violence. Migration can also put pressure on the areas where people migrate to, straining resources, infrastructure, and social services. This can exacerbate social tensions and contribute to conflicts and instability.

The Role of Climate Change in Environmental Migration

Climate change is a major driver of environmental migration. Rising global temperatures are causing changes in weather patterns and more frequent and intense extreme weather events. For example, prolonged droughts can lead to failed crops and the loss of livelihoods, forcing farmers to abandon their land and seek opportunities elsewhere. Similarly, sea-level rise and coastal erosion can render coastal communities uninhabitable, causing people to relocate to safer areas.

The effects of climate change are also interlinked with other social, economic, and political factors. Poverty, lack of access to resources, and weak governance can exacerbate the impacts of climate change and increase the vulnerability of communities to environmental migration. Additionally, conflicts and political instability can be both a cause and consequence of environmental migration, as competition for scarce resources can escalate tensions and lead to displacement.

Addressing Environmental Migration and Climate Change

Addressing environmental migration requires a comprehensive approach that integrates climate change adaptation, disaster risk reduction, and sustainable development strategies. Here are some key considerations and approaches:

1. Climate Change Adaptation: Building resilience in vulnerable communities through measures such as improving early warning systems, enhancing infrastructure, diversifying livelihoods, and promoting sustainable land and water management.

2. Sustainable Development: Promoting sustainable development practices that reduce poverty, inequality, and dependence on environmentally vulnerable sectors. This includes investments in renewable energy, sustainable agriculture, and eco-tourism.

3. Disaster Risk Reduction: Strengthening disaster preparedness and response capacity to minimize the impacts of environmental hazards. This includes investing in early warning systems, evacuation plans, and infrastructure that can withstand extreme weather events.

4. International Cooperation: Collaborating at the global level to address climate change and its impacts. This includes providing financial and technical assistance to developing countries, supporting capacity-building initiatives, and fostering knowledge-sharing and technology transfer.

5. Social Safety Nets: Establishing social protection programs that provide support and assistance to affected communities, including access to healthcare, education, and income support.

It is important to recognize that environmental migration is a complex and multi-faceted issue, with no easy solutions. It requires a holistic and inclusive approach that takes into account the needs and rights of affected communities and ensures that their voices are heard in decision-making processes.

Case Study: Climate-Induced Migration in Bangladesh

Bangladesh is one of the most vulnerable countries to climate change due to its geographical location and high population density. The country faces threats from sea-level rise, increased flooding, and more frequent cyclones— all of which are putting strain on its agricultural and coastal areas.

As a result, a significant number of people in Bangladesh have been internally displaced or have migrated to urban areas in search of better opportunities. The effects of environmental migration can be seen in cities like Dhaka, where rapid urbanization has led to overcrowding, inadequate infrastructure, and the emergence of informal settlements.

To address the issue, the government of Bangladesh has implemented various initiatives. These include the construction of climate-resilient infrastructure, the promotion of sustainable agriculture practices, and the development of early

SECTION 2: MIGRATION AND THE MOVEMENT OF PEOPLE   231

warning systems for natural disasters. The government has also worked closely with international organizations and received support for projects aimed at building resilience in vulnerable communities.

Despite these efforts, challenges remain in addressing the complex and interconnected issues of climate change and environmental migration. Long-term solutions require not only immediate actions but also a focus on sustainable development, social inclusion, and global cooperation.

Conclusion

Environmental migration is a growing phenomenon that is largely driven by climate change. It poses significant challenges for individuals, communities, and societies, as well as opportunities for adaptation and transformation. By recognizing the causes and consequences of environmental migration and taking comprehensive actions, we can work towards building a more resilient and sustainable future. The global community must come together to address the impacts of climate change, protect vulnerable populations, and promote a just and equitable response to environmental migration.

Subsection: The Rise of Xenophobia and Anti-Immigrant Sentiment

In recent years, there has been a concerning rise in xenophobia and anti-immigrant sentiment across the globe. This section will explore the factors contributing to this phenomenon, its impact on individuals and societies, and potential solutions to address this issue.

Understanding Xenophobia and Anti-Immigrant Sentiment

Xenophobia refers to the fear or hatred of strangers or foreigners, while anti-immigrant sentiment encompasses negative attitudes and discrimination towards immigrants. These sentiments are often rooted in a combination of cultural, economic, and political factors.

Cultural Factors: Differences in language, religion, customs, and traditions can foster a sense of cultural threat or anxiety among host populations. Fear of change or perceived threats to national identity can fuel xenophobia and anti-immigrant sentiment.

Economic Factors: Economic downturns or periods of instability may create an environment where immigrants are scapegoated as taking jobs, draining resources, or burdening social welfare systems. This perception can contribute to anti-immigrant sentiment.

Political Factors: Politicians and political parties sometimes exploit public anxieties by promoting xenophobia and anti-immigrant rhetoric. This can be driven by a variety of factors, including nationalism, populism, and the pursuit of political gain.

Impact of Xenophobia and Anti-Immigrant Sentiment

Xenophobia and anti-immigrant sentiment have significant human and societal consequences. They perpetuate discrimination, marginalization, and social exclusion. Additionally, they can hinder economic growth and social cohesion, while also breeding hostility and conflict within communities.

Individuals who experience xenophobia and anti-immigrant sentiment may face discrimination in employment, education, housing, and access to social services. They may also encounter hate crimes, harassment, and prejudice in their daily lives. Psychological well-being can be negatively affected, leading to stress, anxiety, and a decreased sense of belonging.

At the societal level, xenophobia and anti-immigrant sentiment can erode social cohesion and trust. They divide communities along ethnic and cultural lines, hindering cooperation and solidarity. These sentiments may also lead to the creation of discriminatory policies and practices.

Addressing Xenophobia and Anti-Immigrant Sentiment

Countering xenophobia and anti-immigrant sentiment requires a multi-faceted approach involving various stakeholders, including governments, civil society organizations, and individuals. Here are some strategies to address this issue:

1. Education and Awareness: Promote education programs that raise awareness of the positive contributions immigrants make to society. Foster dialogue, cultural exchange, and understanding among diverse communities.

2. Policy Interventions: Implement policies that promote inclusivity, diversity, and equal rights for all residents, regardless of their immigration status. Reform immigration policies to facilitate integration and provide support for migrants.

3. Economic Integration: Create economic opportunities for immigrants to integrate into the labor market. Encourage skills training and job placement programs that address the concerns of both native-born and immigrant populations.

SECTION 2: MIGRATION AND THE MOVEMENT OF PEOPLE 233

4. Social Integration: Foster inclusive communities by promoting social interaction, dialogue, and cooperation among diverse groups. Support initiatives that promote intercultural understanding and cooperation.

5. Media and Public Discourse: Encourage responsible media reporting that avoids sensationalism and stereotypes. Promote positive narratives about immigration and challenge negative stereotypes through public discourse.

6. Combating Discrimination: Enforce legislation against discrimination and hate crimes. Provide legal support and access to justice for victims of xenophobic acts.

7. Grassroots Initiatives: Support grassroots organizations that work to counter xenophobia and promote social cohesion. Encourage community engagement and activism against discrimination.

It is important to recognize that addressing xenophobia and anti-immigrant sentiment requires sustained efforts, as it is deeply rooted in societal attitudes and prejudices. By implementing these strategies, societies can create more inclusive and accepting environments for all individuals, regardless of their cultural or national background.

Note: This section aims to provide a comprehensive overview of the rise of xenophobia and anti-immigrant sentiment and potential solutions. It is essential to consult additional resources and research for a more in-depth understanding of this complex issue.

Subsection: Remittances and the Economic Impact on Sending Countries

Remittances, the transfer of money by individuals working abroad to their home countries, have become an increasingly important topic in the context of globalization. In this subsection, we will explore the economic impact of remittances on sending countries. We will examine how remittances affect the overall economy, the household level, and the potential challenges and opportunities they present.

The Importance of Remittances

Remittances have become a significant source of income for many developing countries. According to the World Bank, global remittances reached a record high of $689 billion in 2018, providing crucial financial support to millions of households. For many sending countries, remittances often exceed official development assistance and foreign direct investment.

Economic Impact on Sending Countries

The economic impact of remittances on sending countries can be analyzed from different perspectives.

1. **Macroeconomic Impact:** Remittances play a crucial role in shaping the macroeconomic landscape of sending countries. They contribute to foreign exchange earnings, which can boost the country's foreign currency reserves and stabilize exchange rates. Moreover, remittances can stimulate aggregate demand, leading to increased consumption and investment, thereby driving economic growth.

2. **Poverty Alleviation:** Remittances are often instrumental in reducing poverty in sending countries. They provide families with a stable source of income, enabling them to meet basic needs such as food, education, and healthcare. In some cases, remittances have led to a decline in poverty rates and improved living standards.

3. **Investment and Entrepreneurship:** Remittances can also spur entrepreneurship and investment in sending countries. Some remittance recipients use the funds to start businesses, thus contributing to the development of the local economy. Additionally, remittances can serve as a source of capital for investment in sectors such as housing, infrastructure, and agriculture.

4. **Social and Cultural Impact:** Beyond the economic aspects, remittances can have social and cultural implications. They provide families with the means to maintain connections and support social ties across borders. Remittances can also

SECTION 2: MIGRATION AND THE MOVEMENT OF PEOPLE 235

influence cultural patterns, as they may result in changes in consumption patterns and attitudes toward education and healthcare.

Challenges and Opportunities

While remittances offer numerous benefits, they also present challenges and potential risks for sending countries. It is important to understand and address these issues to maximize the positive impact of remittances.

1. **Dependency:** Overreliance on remittances can create a dependency syndrome in sending countries. This reliance may discourage investment in other sectors, potentially leading to an imbalanced economy. Governments should promote economic diversification to mitigate this risk.

2. **Brain Drain:** One of the indirect consequences of remittances is the brain drain phenomenon. Skilled individuals often migrate to find higher-paying jobs, leaving behind a shortage of skilled labor in sending countries. Policies should be implemented to balance the outflow of human capital with efforts to enhance education and skills development.

3. **Financial Inclusion:** Many remittance recipients in sending countries lack access to formal financial services. This limits their ability to save or invest the funds effectively. Governments and financial institutions should prioritize financial inclusion initiatives to provide individuals with access to safe, affordable, and convenient financial services.

4. **Remittance Costs:** The cost of remittance transfers can be high, particularly for low-income families. High transaction costs reduce the economic benefits for both senders and recipients. Encouraging competition among remittance service providers and promoting technological innovations can help reduce costs and make remittance flows more efficient.

Case Study: The Philippines

The Philippines provides an interesting case study to examine the economic impact of remittances. The country is one of the world's largest recipients of remittances, with millions of Filipinos working abroad. Remittances have contributed significantly to the Philippine economy, accounting for approximately 10% of the country's GDP.

The influx of remittances has helped alleviate poverty in many parts of the Philippines. Families receiving remittances have been able to afford education, healthcare, and housing improvements. Moreover, remittances have supported local businesses and stimulated economic activities in rural areas.

Despite the positive impact, challenges remain in maximizing the potential benefits of remittances. The Philippine government has implemented various programs to promote financial literacy, entrepreneurship, and investment. Efforts are also being made to address the brain drain issue by investing in education and skills training.

Conclusion

Remittances play a crucial role in the economic development of sending countries. They contribute to poverty reduction, economic growth, investment, and social stability. However, challenges such as dependency, brain drain, financial exclusion, and high transaction costs must be addressed to fully harness the potential of remittances.

Understanding the economic impact of remittances is essential for policymakers, economists, and individuals considering working abroad. By recognizing both the opportunities and challenges associated with remittances, sending countries can develop strategies to maximize the benefits for their economies and societies.

Subsection: The Future of Migration in a Globalized World

Migration has always been a significant aspect of human history. People have moved from one place to another in search of new opportunities, better living conditions, or to escape from conflict and persecution. In the context of a globalized world, migration has become more complex and interconnected. In this subsection, we will explore the future of migration, considering the challenges, opportunities, and potential solutions in a world where boundaries are increasingly blurred.

The Role of Technology in Migration

Technology has played a crucial role in shaping the migration patterns of today and will continue to influence future migration trends. Advancements in transportation and communication have made it easier for individuals to move across borders and stay connected with their home countries. The internet, social media, and mobile applications have transformed the way people gather information about migration opportunities, connect with potential employers or sponsors, and maintain ties with their communities.

As technology continues to advance, we can expect further changes in the ways migration occurs. For example, virtual reality could enable individuals to explore their destination countries and assess potential job opportunities without

SECTION 2: MIGRATION AND THE MOVEMENT OF PEOPLE

physically traveling. Artificial intelligence could assist in streamlining visa processes and improving the efficiency of immigration systems. These technological advancements have the potential to both facilitate and complicate migration processes, presenting both opportunities and challenges for policymakers and migrants alike.

Climate Change and Migration

One of the most pressing challenges in the future of migration is the impact of climate change. As global temperatures rise and extreme weather events become more frequent, people living in vulnerable areas may be forced to migrate in search of safer and more stable environments. This phenomenon, known as climate migration or environmental migration, poses significant challenges for both sending and receiving countries.

To address the potential increase in climate-induced migration, policymakers will need to develop comprehensive strategies that promote climate adaptation and resilience in vulnerable regions. International cooperation will be crucial in providing assistance and support to communities affected by climate change, both in terms of mitigation efforts and the management of migration flows. Additionally, efforts to reduce greenhouse gas emissions and mitigate the effects of climate change can help alleviate the need for mass migration in the first place.

Integration and Social Cohesion

In a globalized world, migration has become more diverse, with people moving across borders for various reasons, including economic, educational, and humanitarian purposes. One of the key challenges for receiving countries is ensuring the successful integration of migrants into their societies while maintaining social cohesion.

Intercultural exchange programs, language training, and comprehensive support systems can facilitate the integration process and foster social cohesion. Education and awareness campaigns aimed at countering xenophobia and promoting understanding can also contribute to creating inclusive societies. It is important that policymakers and communities work together to address the concerns and needs of both migrants and the host population, promoting a sense of belonging and cooperation.

The Economic Implications of Migration

Migration has significant economic implications for both sending and receiving countries. Migrants often contribute to the economic development of their host countries through their labor, skills, and entrepreneurship. They fill labor market gaps, drive innovation, and contribute to economic growth. However, migration can also put pressure on local labor markets and public resources, leading to concerns about job competition and the provision of social services.

To maximize the potential benefits of migration, it is essential to develop policies that facilitate the integration of migrants into the labor market and ensure their access to decent work and fair wages. Creating pathways for migrants to acquire necessary skills and qualifications, along with adopting inclusive labor market policies, can help foster economic integration and reduce inequalities. Responsible and ethical recruitment practices and the protection of migrants' rights are also crucial aspects to consider.

Digital Solutions for Migration Challenges

In the digital age, various innovative solutions can help address the challenges associated with migration. Digital platforms and tools can facilitate information sharing and provide access to services, such as language learning, job matching, and legal assistance. For example, online platforms connecting refugees and host communities can enable better coordination of support and resources, promoting social integration and mutual understanding.

To realize the potential of digital solutions, it is important to address the digital divide and ensure equal access to technology and internet connectivity. Efforts should be made to bridge the gap between technology developers and policymakers, fostering collaboration and the development of tools that cater to the specific needs of migrants and their host communities.

Unconventional Solution: Microfinance for Migrants

Microfinance, the provision of small loans and financial services to low-income individuals, has been used as a tool for poverty reduction and economic empowerment in various contexts. In the context of migration, microfinance can play a significant role in supporting migrants in their entrepreneurial endeavors and facilitating their economic integration.

By providing access to affordable credit and financial services, microfinance institutions can help migrants establish businesses, generate income, and

SECTION 2: MIGRATION AND THE MOVEMENT OF PEOPLE 239

contribute to local economies. Additionally, microfinance can empower migrants by promoting financial literacy and fostering long-term financial stability.

To implement this unconventional solution, partnerships between microfinance institutions, governments, and migration support organizations are crucial. Financial education programs tailored to the needs of migrants, along with regulatory frameworks that facilitate access to microfinance services for migrants, are essential components of this approach.

Conclusion

The future of migration in a globalized world presents both challenges and opportunities. As technology advances, policymakers need to adapt migration policies to harness the benefits of technological innovations while addressing the associated challenges. Climate change will continue to shape migration patterns, necessitating global cooperation and proactive strategies to mitigate its adverse effects. Integration and social cohesion are critical for creating inclusive societies that benefit both migrants and host communities. Additionally, the economic implications of migration highlight the importance of labor market integration and the protection of migrants' rights.

Digital solutions and unconventional approaches, such as microfinance, offer promising avenues for addressing the challenges associated with migration. By embracing innovation, fostering collaboration, and adopting comprehensive and inclusive policies, the future of migration can be shaped in a way that benefits individuals, societies, and economies across the globe.

Further Reading:

1. Castles, S., de Haas, H., & Miller, M. J. (2014). *The Age of Migration: International Population Movements in the Modern World.* Palgrave Macmillan.

2. Collyer, M. (Ed.). (2014). *The Routledge Handbook of Diaspora Studies.* Routledge.

3. International Organization for Migration. (2020). *Addressing the Challenges of Climate Change and Migration.* Retrieved from `https://publications.iom.int/system/files/pdf/icmc_ issue_briefing_climate_change_june_2020.pdf`

Key Terms: technology, climate change, integration, social cohesion, labor market, microfinance

Section 3: Global Challenges and Collaborative Solutions

Subsection: Climate Change and the Need for Sustainable Development

Climate change is one of the most pressing challenges facing our world today. It refers to the long-term changes in temperature, precipitation patterns, sea level rise, and extreme weather events, among others, resulting from the increase in greenhouse gas emissions from human activities. The consequences of climate change can be detrimental, affecting ecosystems, agriculture, water resources, and human health. To address this issue, sustainable development is vital.

Sustainable development is an approach that aims to meet the needs of the present generation without compromising the ability of future generations to meet their own needs. It recognizes the interdependence of social, economic, and environmental factors and seeks to find a balance between them. In the context of climate change, sustainable development offers solutions to mitigate its effects and adapt to its impacts.

To understand the need for sustainable development in the face of climate change, it is crucial to examine the causes and consequences of this global phenomenon. The main driver of climate change is the burning of fossil fuels such as coal, oil, and natural gas, which release carbon dioxide (CO_2) and other greenhouse gases into the atmosphere. Deforestation, industrial activities, and agricultural practices also contribute to greenhouse gas emissions.

The consequences of climate change range from rising temperatures and sea levels to more frequent and intense extreme weather events. These changes pose significant threats to ecosystems, biodiversity, and human societies. For instance, increased temperatures can lead to the melting of polar ice caps, resulting in rising sea levels that endanger coastal communities. Extreme weather events, such as hurricanes and droughts, can cause extensive damage to infrastructure, agriculture, and livelihoods.

To address climate change and work towards sustainable development, several key strategies can be implemented.

1. **Reducing Greenhouse Gas Emissions:** The primary focus should be on decreasing the emission of greenhouse gases. This can be achieved by transitioning to renewable and clean energy sources such as solar, wind, and hydropower. Additionally, improving energy efficiency in industries, transportation, and buildings can significantly reduce emissions.

SECTION 3: GLOBAL CHALLENGES AND COLLABORATIVE SOLUTIONS

2. **Conservation and Sustainable Land Use:** Protecting forests, promoting afforestation and reforestation, and implementing sustainable agricultural practices can help sequester carbon dioxide and preserve biodiversity. Sustainable land use practices also involve minimizing deforestation, preventing soil erosion, and promoting sustainable farming techniques.

3. **Adaptation Measures:** As climate change is already occurring, it is crucial to adapt to its impacts. This includes developing climate-resilient infrastructure, implementing water management strategies, and creating early warning systems for extreme weather events. It is essential to build adaptive capacity in vulnerable communities and enhance their ability to cope with changing climatic conditions.

4. **International Cooperation and Policy Frameworks:** Addressing climate change requires global cooperation. International agreements such as the Paris Agreement aim to limit global warming to well below 2 degrees Celsius above pre-industrial levels. Countries must work together to set targets, share knowledge, and provide financial and technological support to developing nations.

5. **Education and Awareness:** Raising awareness about climate change and sustainable practices is crucial for driving behavioral change. Education plays a vital role in fostering a sense of responsibility towards the environment and promoting sustainable lifestyles.

While the need for sustainable development in combating climate change is evident, the transition may present challenges. Some key challenges include the high initial costs of renewable energy infrastructure, the need for technology transfer to developing countries, and the resistance to change from vested interests in fossil fuel industries. However, the economic, social, and environmental benefits of sustainable development far outweigh these challenges.

For example, investing in renewable energy sources not only reduces greenhouse gas emissions but also creates new job opportunities and stimulates economic growth. Sustainable land use practices not only sequester carbon dioxide but also protect ecosystems, preserve biodiversity, and enhance food security.

In conclusion, climate change poses a significant threat to our planet, and sustainable development is essential to mitigate its effects and ensure a better future for all. By reducing greenhouse gas emissions, implementing conservation measures, promoting adaptation strategies, fostering international cooperation, and raising awareness, we can work towards a sustainable and resilient world. It is crucial to act now and embrace sustainable development principles to combat climate change effectively.

Subsection: International Cooperation on Pandemics and Global Health

In today's interconnected world, pandemics and global health issues pose significant challenges that require international cooperation and collaboration. The recent COVID-19 pandemic, for example, has demonstrated the urgent need for countries to work together to effectively respond to and mitigate the impact of such health crises. In this subsection, we will explore the importance of international cooperation in addressing pandemics and global health issues, the role of international organizations, challenges faced, and potential solutions.

The Importance of International Cooperation

Pandemics do not recognize borders, and their spread can be rapid and devastating. Therefore, international cooperation is crucial for the following reasons:

1. Early Detection and Rapid Response: By sharing information and collaborating on surveillance systems, countries can detect and respond to outbreaks more quickly. Early detection enables timely interventions, such as implementing travel restrictions and quarantine measures, which can help contain and control the spread of infectious diseases.

2. Resource Sharing and Capacity Building: International cooperation promotes the sharing of resources, expertise, and technology, which are often limited in some regions. Collaborative efforts can help strengthen healthcare infrastructure, enhance diagnostic capabilities, and improve treatment and vaccine development.

3. Coordination of Efforts: By coordinating efforts, countries can avoid duplication of resources and minimize gaps in the response. This ensures a more effective and efficient allocation of resources, such as medical supplies, personnel, and logistics, to areas most in need during a pandemic.

4. Health Diplomacy: International cooperation fosters goodwill and strengthens diplomatic ties among nations. By working together to address global health challenges, countries can build mutual trust and enhance cooperation in other areas.

Role of International Organizations

Various international organizations play a crucial role in facilitating global cooperation and collaboration on pandemics and global health issues. The following organizations are key players in this regard:

SECTION 3: GLOBAL CHALLENGES AND COLLABORATIVE SOLUTIONS 243

1. World Health Organization (WHO): As the leading global health authority, the WHO provides technical expertise, guidance, and coordination during pandemics. It facilitates information sharing, data analysis, and best practice recommendations among member countries. The WHO also supports the development and distribution of vaccines and treatments.

2. Centers for Disease Control and Prevention (CDC): The CDC, based in the United States, is a vital institution for global health security. It provides technical assistance, training, and capacity building to partner countries, helping them strengthen their disease surveillance, laboratory capacities, and emergency response systems.

3. World Bank: The World Bank provides funding and financial support to countries to strengthen their healthcare systems and respond effectively to pandemics. It also assists in the development and implementation of health policies, strategies, and projects.

4. Gavi, the Vaccine Alliance: Gavi is a public-private partnership that focuses on expanding access to vaccines in low-income countries. It plays a critical role in ensuring equitable distribution of vaccines during pandemics and supports immunization programs globally.

Challenges Faced

Despite the importance of international cooperation, several challenges hinder effective collaboration in addressing pandemics and global health issues:

1. Political Barriers: Political tensions and conflicts between countries can impede cooperation and hinder the sharing of critical health information and resources. Geopolitical rivalries may also undermine the establishment of transparent and effective global health governance structures.

2. Unequal Access to Resources: Disparities in resources, including healthcare infrastructure, medical supplies, and funding, can hinder the ability of some countries to respond adequately to pandemics. Limited access to technology and expertise further exacerbate these inequalities.

3. Differing Priorities and Agendas: Countries may prioritize their domestic concerns over global health cooperation, leading to fragmented responses and inadequate international coordination. Conflicting agendas and competing political interests can hinder the establishment of unified strategies for pandemic response.

4. Legal and Regulatory Frameworks: Differences in legal and regulatory frameworks across countries can pose challenges to harmonization of policies and the development of common guidelines for pandemic response. Disparities in

intellectual property rights and regulatory processes may hinder access to vaccines and treatments.

Potential Solutions

Addressing the challenges of international cooperation on pandemics and global health requires concerted efforts and innovative solutions. Here are some potential strategies:

1. Strengthening Global Health Governance: There is a need for enhanced global health governance mechanisms that promote transparency, accountability, and equitable decision-making. This could involve strengthening the role and authority of existing organizations like the WHO and establishing agreements on data sharing, resource allocation, and coordinated response strategies.

2. Investing in Healthcare Infrastructure: International financial institutions and donor countries should prioritize investments in healthcare infrastructure, especially in low-income countries. This includes improving healthcare facilities, training healthcare workers, and establishing robust disease surveillance systems.

3. Technology Transfer and Capacity Building: Developed countries should support technology transfer initiatives to enhance the capabilities of developing countries in diagnostics, vaccine production, and research. Capacity building programs should be implemented to ensure that healthcare professionals in resource-limited settings have the necessary skills and knowledge to respond effectively to pandemics.

4. Addressing Legal and Regulatory Challenges: International agreements and frameworks should be developed to address legal and regulatory challenges in areas such as intellectual property rights, drug approval processes, and vaccine distribution. This would promote equitable access to lifesaving medicines and technologies during pandemics.

In conclusion, international cooperation is essential to effectively address pandemics and global health issues. By recognizing the importance of collaboration, strengthening global health governance, and addressing challenges, countries can better prepare for and respond to future health crises. This will ensure a more resilient and interconnected world where global health security is prioritized, and the impact of pandemics is minimized.

Bibliography

[1] World Health Organization. (2021). COVID-19 pandemic. *https://www.who.int/emergencies/diseases/novel-coronavirus-2019*. Accessed August 15, 2021.

[2] Centers for Disease Control and Prevention. (2021). International Activities. *https://www.cdc.gov/globalhealth/index.html*. Accessed August 15, 2021.

[3] World Bank. (2021). Health. *https://www.worldbank.org/en/topic/health*. Accessed August 15, 2021.

[4] Gavi, the Vaccine Alliance. (2021). Gavi's vision and mission. *https://www.gavi.org/about/mission*. Accessed August 15, 2021.

[5] Frieden, T. R., Dasgupta, S., McClelland, A., & Scales, D. (2010). A new era for global health: international cooperation for health in the 21st century. *Journal of public health policy*, 31(1), 1-26.

Subsection: Terrorism and the Battle against Extremism

Terrorism has become one of the most pressing global challenges in the contemporary world. It poses a threat to peace, stability, and security, not only in specific regions but also on a global scale. This subsection will explore the nature of terrorism, the factors contributing to its rise, and the strategies employed to combat it.

Understanding Terrorism

Terrorism can be defined as the use of violence, intimidation, or coercion to achieve political, ideological, or religious objectives. It is typically carried out by non-state actors, often referred to as terrorist organizations or extremist groups, who use violence against civilians or non-combatants to instill fear and advance their agenda.

Terrorist acts can take various forms, including bombings, assassinations, hijackings, and cyber-attacks. The motivations behind terrorism can vary greatly, ranging from separatism and nationalism to religious fundamentalism and ideological extremism.

Root Causes of Terrorism

To effectively combat terrorism, it is crucial to understand its root causes. While there is no single explanation for why individuals or groups turn to terrorism, several factors contribute to its emergence and sustenance:

1. Socioeconomic factors: Poverty, unemployment, social inequality, and lack of education can create fertile ground for the recruitment and radicalization of individuals who feel marginalized or disenfranchised.

2. Political grievances: Political oppression, state repression, and discrimination can foster a sense of injustice and fuel radical ideologies among certain groups, leading to acts of terrorism.

3. Ideological and religious extremism: The manipulation of religious beliefs and ideologies, often by radicalized religious leaders or charismatic individuals, can motivate individuals to resort to terrorism as a means of advancing their religious or ideological agenda.

4. State sponsorship and foreign intervention: In some cases, state actors have been known to support and sponsor terrorist organizations either directly or indirectly, while foreign intervention in regional conflicts can exacerbate existing tensions and grievances, providing fertile ground for extremist ideologies to thrive.

Strategies to Counter Terrorism

The battle against terrorism requires a multi-faceted and comprehensive approach that addresses its root causes while simultaneously targeting terrorist organizations and their infrastructure. Here are some strategies employed to counter terrorism:

1. Intelligence and information sharing: Effective intelligence gathering and sharing among national and international security agencies are crucial in identifying and tracking terrorist networks. This includes monitoring online platforms and social media, which have become key recruitment and propaganda tools for extremist groups.

2. Law enforcement and military operations: Proactive law enforcement efforts, such as arrests, disruption of terror plots, and targeted military operations against

BIBLIOGRAPHY

terrorist strongholds, are essential to dismantle terrorist networks and disrupt their activities.

3. International cooperation: Terrorism is a transnational threat that requires international cooperation and collaboration. Sharing intelligence, coordinating efforts, and implementing joint operations can enhance the effectiveness of counterterrorism measures.

4. Addressing root causes: Addressing the underlying social, economic, and political factors that contribute to terrorism is essential. This includes efforts to reduce poverty, inequality, and social exclusion, as well as promoting inclusive governance and respect for human rights.

5. Countering extremist ideologies: Governments, civil society organizations, and religious leaders must work together to challenge and counter extremist ideologies. This involves promoting alternate narratives, religious tolerance, and inclusive values to undermine the appeal of radical ideologies.

6. Rehabilitation and reintegration: Providing support and rehabilitation programs for individuals who have been radicalized or involved in terrorist activities can help facilitate their reintegration into society and prevent future acts of violence.

Case Study: Countering ISIS

The rise of the Islamic State of Iraq and Syria (ISIS) in the early 2010s presented a significant challenge to global security. ISIS utilized sophisticated propaganda methods and social media platforms to recruit individuals from around the world and establish a self-proclaimed caliphate.

To counter ISIS, a comprehensive approach combining military action, intelligence cooperation, and efforts to address root causes was implemented. Military operations led by regional and international coalitions targeted ISIS-held territories, successfully retaking key cities and diminishing its territorial control.

Simultaneously, intelligence sharing and international cooperation played a crucial role in tracking foreign fighters, disrupting financial networks, and countering the spread of propaganda. Efforts were also made to address the underlying grievances by promoting good governance, promoting stability, and supporting the rehabilitation of individuals affected by ISIS ideology.

Ethical Considerations and Future Challenges

While combating terrorism is essential for global security, it is important to recognize the ethical dilemmas and potential dangers associated with counterterrorism measures. In some cases, efforts to combat terrorism may infringe upon civil liberties, human rights, and privacy rights. Striking the balance between security and individual rights remains a challenge.

Moreover, the evolving nature of terrorism, including the emergence of lone wolf attacks and the exploitation of technology, presents ongoing challenges. The increasing use of encryption, the dark web, and emerging technologies such as artificial intelligence and drones by terrorist actors require continuous adaptation and innovation in counterterrorism strategies.

In conclusion, the battle against terrorism and extremism requires a multi-faceted approach that addresses the root causes, dismantles terrorist networks, and promotes international cooperation. By understanding the nature of terrorism, its underlying causes, and effective strategies to counter it, we can work towards a safer and more secure world.

Subsection: Nuclear Proliferation and Arms Control Agreements

Nuclear proliferation refers to the spread of nuclear weapons and technology to non-nuclear-weapon states. This is a significant concern for international security because it increases the risk of nuclear war, nuclear terrorism, and regional instability. In response to this threat, the international community has developed and implemented a framework of arms control agreements aimed at reducing the proliferation and promoting disarmament.

Background

The atomic bombings of Hiroshima and Nagasaki in 1945 marked the beginning of the nuclear age. Soon after, the Soviet Union developed its own nuclear weapons, and the world witnessed the start of the arms race between the United States and the Soviet Union. This rivalry led to the proliferation of nuclear weapons to other countries, including the United Kingdom, France, China, and eventually, India, Pakistan, and North Korea.

The Treaty on the Non-Proliferation of Nuclear Weapons (NPT), which entered into force in 1970, remains the cornerstone of global efforts to prevent the spread of nuclear weapons. The NPT has three main pillars: non-proliferation, disarmament, and the peaceful use of nuclear energy.

Principles of the NPT

The NPT recognizes the five original nuclear-weapon states (the United States, Russia, the United Kingdom, France, and China) as nuclear-weapon states, while

BIBLIOGRAPHY 249

preventing the proliferation of nuclear weapons to other countries. Under the treaty, non-nuclear-weapon states commit not to acquire nuclear weapons, in exchange for assistance with the peaceful use of nuclear energy and a commitment from nuclear-weapon states to disarm.

The NPT also established the International Atomic Energy Agency (IAEA) to verify compliance with the treaty and promote the peaceful use of nuclear energy. The IAEA conducts inspections of nuclear facilities and ensures that countries are using nuclear materials solely for peaceful purposes.

Challenges of Nuclear Proliferation

Despite the efforts made under the NPT, nuclear proliferation remains a challenge. Some countries, such as North Korea and Iran, have pursued nuclear weapons programs, leading to tensions and concerns within the international community. Additionally, the fear of terrorist groups acquiring nuclear weapons or materials poses a significant security risk.

Arms Control Agreements

To address the challenges posed by nuclear proliferation, a series of arms control agreements have been established. These agreements aim to limit the number of nuclear weapons, prevent their use, enhance security, and promote disarmament.

One of the most significant arms control agreements is the Strategic Arms Reduction Treaty (START). The START treaty was signed between the United States and Russia in 1991, and subsequent agreements were made to further reduce the number of deployed strategic nuclear weapons. The New START treaty, signed in 2010, limits the number of deployed strategic nuclear warheads and delivery systems.

Another important arms control agreement is the Comprehensive Nuclear-Test-Ban Treaty (CTBT). Although the treaty has not yet entered into force, it bans all nuclear explosions, whether for military or peaceful purposes. The CTBT aims to prevent the development of advanced nuclear weapons and improve international security.

Verification and Compliance

Ensuring compliance with arms control agreements is crucial for their effectiveness. The IAEA plays a fundamental role in verifying compliance with the NPT and other nuclear-related treaties. The agency conducts regular inspections and monitors nuclear activities to ensure that countries are adhering to their commitments.

Verification measures include on-site inspections, the use of surveillance equipment, and the analysis of nuclear samples. The IAEA also relies on the cooperation of member states to report on their nuclear activities accurately. While there are challenges in detecting covert nuclear programs, concerted international efforts have improved the effectiveness of verification and compliance measures.

Contemporary Challenges

In today's complex geopolitical landscape, nuclear proliferation and arms control remain significant challenges. Some countries, such as North Korea, continue to defy international norms and pursue nuclear weapons. Advances in technology, such as cyber warfare and delivery systems, pose additional challenges to arms control and verification efforts.

Furthermore, arms control agreements face the challenge of maintaining political will and cooperation among states. As geopolitical tensions rise, there is a risk of a new nuclear arms race, as seen in recent developments between the United States, Russia, and China.

Conclusion

Nuclear proliferation and arms control agreements are critical issues in contemporary international relations. The threat of nuclear weapons demands continued efforts to prevent their spread, promote disarmament, and enhance global security. As the world grapples with new challenges and emerging technologies, it is crucial to maintain and strengthen existing arms control frameworks while seeking innovative solutions to address contemporary issues. Only through international cooperation and a commitment to non-proliferation can we ensure a safer and more secure world for future generations.

Additional Resources

1. International Atomic Energy Agency (IAEA) - Official website providing information on nuclear energy, non-proliferation, and peaceful uses of nuclear technology: https://www.iaea.org/

2. Arms Control Association - A nonprofit organization dedicated to promoting effective arms control policies and agreements: https://www.armscontrol.org/

BIBLIOGRAPHY   251

3. United Nations Office for Disarmament Affairs - Provides resources and information on disarmament and non-proliferation efforts: `https://www.un.org/disarmament/`

4. The Nonproliferation Review - A scholarly journal focusing on the political, scientific, and technical aspects of nonproliferation: `https://nonproliferation.org/nonproliferation-review/`

Subsection: Cyber Warfare and Defending against Cyber Attacks

In today's interconnected world, where information is exchanged and stored electronically, the importance of cybersecurity cannot be overstated. Cyber warfare has emerged as a significant threat, with state-sponsored actors, organized crime groups, and hacktivists targeting critical infrastructure, governments, and businesses. This subsection explores the concept of cyber warfare, the various types of cyber attacks, and the strategies employed to defend against them.

Understanding Cyber Warfare

Cyber warfare refers to the use of digital attacks to disrupt, destroy, or manipulate computer systems or networks for political, ideological, or military purposes. It encompasses a wide range of activities, including espionage, sabotage, propaganda dissemination, and disruption of critical infrastructure. The motivation behind cyber warfare can vary, ranging from political coercion to economic gain to advancing military objectives.

Types of Cyber Attacks

There are several types of cyber attacks commonly employed by attackers. Understanding these attack vectors is crucial for developing effective defensive strategies. Some key types of cyber attacks include:

- **Malware**: Malicious software, such as viruses, worms, and Trojans, is designed to infiltrate systems or networks, causing damage, stealing sensitive information, or providing unauthorized access to attackers.

- **Phishing**: Phishing attacks involve deceptive emails, messages, or websites that trick users into divulging their sensitive information, such as passwords or credit card details. These attacks are often aimed at stealing financial information or gaining unauthorized access to systems.

- **Denial of Service (DoS) and Distributed Denial of Service (DDoS) Attacks:** These attacks overwhelm a target system or network with a flood of traffic, making it inaccessible to legitimate users. DDoS attacks involve multiple compromised systems working together to launch the attack, making them even more potent.

- **Man-in-the-Middle (MitM) Attacks:** In MitM attacks, an attacker intercepts communication between two parties without their knowledge and can eavesdrop on or manipulate the communication. This attack vector is commonly used to steal sensitive information, such as usernames and passwords.

- **SQL Injection:** SQL injection attacks exploit vulnerabilities in web applications that allow attackers to insert malicious SQL queries into the underlying database. This can lead to unauthorized access, data theft, or even manipulation of the database.

- **Ransomware:** Ransomware is a type of malware that encrypts a victim's files, holding them hostage until a ransom is paid. This type of attack has become increasingly prevalent, causing significant financial losses and disruptions.

Defending against Cyber Attacks

Defending against cyber attacks requires a multi-layered approach that combines technical measures, awareness training, and incident response capabilities. Some key strategies for defending against cyber attacks include:

- **Firewalls and Intrusion Prevention Systems:** Firewalls and intrusion prevention systems form the first line of defense against cyber attacks. They monitor network traffic, filter out malicious packets, and detect and block unauthorized access attempts.

- **Secure Network Architecture:** Implementing a secure network architecture involves segmenting networks, implementing access controls, and ensuring proper network configuration. This can limit the impact of a successful attack and minimize lateral movement by attackers.

- **Regular Patching and System Updates:** Keeping software and systems up to date with the latest patches and updates is crucial to address known vulnerabilities. Attackers often exploit unpatched systems to gain unauthorized access.

BIBLIOGRAPHY 253

- **Strong Authentication and Access Controls:** Implementing strong authentication mechanisms, such as two-factor authentication, and enforcing access controls help prevent unauthorized access to systems and sensitive information.

- **Employee Training and Awareness:** Educating employees about cybersecurity best practices, such as recognizing phishing attempts, avoiding suspicious downloads, and practicing good password hygiene, can significantly reduce the risk of successful attacks.

- **Incident Response Planning:** Developing an incident response plan is essential to minimize the impact of a successful attack. This includes pre-defined procedures for identifying and containing cyber attacks, investigating incidents, and restoring affected systems.

Real-World Example: Stuxnet

One notable example of cyber warfare is the Stuxnet worm, discovered in 2010. Stuxnet was designed to target and disrupt Iran's nuclear program by sabotaging industrial control systems. The worm exploited multiple vulnerabilities, including zero-day exploits, and specifically targeted programmable logic controllers (PLCs) used in centrifuge control.

Stuxnet's sophistication and complexity indicated the involvement of a well-resourced and highly skilled attacker, widely believed to be a joint effort by the United States and Israel. The attack demonstrated the potential of cyber weapons to cause physical destruction and highlighted the need for robust cybersecurity measures to defend against such advanced threats.

Resources for Further Learning

Keeping up with the rapidly evolving landscape of cyber warfare and defense requires continuous learning. Here are some recommended resources for further exploration:

- **Books:**

  - "Countdown to Zero Day: Stuxnet and the Launch of the World's First Digital Weapon" by Kim Zetter
  - "The Art of Intrusion: The Real Stories Behind the Exploits of Hackers, Intruders, and Deceivers" by Kevin D. Mitnick

- "Cybersecurity and Cyberwar: What Everyone Needs to Know" by P.W. Singer and Allan Friedman

- **Online Courses and Certifications:**

  - Cybrary (www.cybrary.it): Offers a wide range of free and paid online cybersecurity courses, covering topics such as ethical hacking, incident response, and network defense.
  - Certified Information Systems Security Professional (CISSP): A globally recognized certification that validates expertise in designing, implementing, and managing cybersecurity programs.

- **Industry Conferences:**

  - Black Hat (www.blackhat.com): An annual conference focusing on the latest in information security research, development, and trends.
  - DEF CON (www.defcon.org): One of the world's largest and most notable hacker conventions, featuring a wide array of presentations, workshops, and challenges.

Conclusion

In an increasingly digitized world, the threat of cyber warfare and cyber attacks continues to grow. Understanding the various types of cyber attacks and implementing robust defensive strategies are critical in safeguarding critical systems and sensitive information. By staying informed, adopting best practices, and continually enhancing cybersecurity measures, individuals and organizations can help defend against the ever-evolving landscape of cyber threats.

Subsection: Global Poverty and the Pursuit of Economic Equality

Global poverty is a pressing issue that continues to affect millions of people around the world. In this subsection, we will explore the causes of global poverty and examine the different strategies and initiatives aimed at promoting economic equality.

Understanding Global Poverty

Global poverty refers to the condition of individuals or communities who lack the resources necessary to meet their basic needs, such as food, shelter, and healthcare.

It is characterized by low income, limited access to education and healthcare, inadequate housing, and chronic malnutrition.

There are various causes of global poverty, including:

+ **Economic factors:** Limited economic opportunities, income inequality, lack of access to credit and financial resources, and underdeveloped infrastructure contribute to the perpetuation of poverty.

+ **Political factors:** Corruption, weak governance, and political instability create barriers to poverty alleviation efforts and hinder the implementation of effective policies.

+ **Social factors:** Discrimination, social exclusion, and unequal power dynamics contribute to the persistence of poverty, particularly affecting marginalized groups such as women, ethnic minorities, and indigenous communities.

+ **Environmental factors:** Natural disasters, climate change, and environmental degradation have devastating effects on vulnerable populations, exacerbating poverty and hindering development.

To address global poverty, it is essential to prioritize economic equality and implement strategies that promote inclusive growth and provide equal opportunities for all individuals to improve their living conditions.

International Efforts to Alleviate Global Poverty

The pursuit of economic equality and poverty eradication has been a priority for international organizations, governments, and civil society. Here are some key initiatives and strategies:

+ **Millennium Development Goals (MDGs):** Adopted by the United Nations (UN) in 2000 and succeeded by the Sustainable Development Goals (SDGs) in 2015, the MDGs aimed to reduce poverty, hunger, disease, and inequality. These goals provided a roadmap for global poverty reduction and served as a catalyst for international cooperation.

+ **Foreign Aid and Development Assistance:** Developed countries provide financial assistance, technical expertise, and resources to developing nations to support their economic development and poverty reduction efforts. Official Development Assistance (ODA) has played a crucial role in promoting economic equality and social progress.

- **Microfinance and Microcredit:** Microfinance programs offer financial services, including small loans, savings accounts, and insurance, to individuals who lack access to traditional banking services. By empowering individuals to start or expand small businesses, microfinance helps alleviate poverty and promote economic self-sufficiency.

- **Education for All:** Access to quality education is a fundamental right and a powerful tool for breaking the cycle of poverty. Initiatives such as the Global Partnership for Education (GPE) aim to ensure that all children have equal access to education, particularly in low-income countries.

- **Social Safety Nets:** Governments and international organizations implement social safety net programs that provide financial assistance, healthcare, and education to the most vulnerable individuals and households. These programs help protect people from falling into extreme poverty during crisis situations.

Challenges and Solutions

While progress has been made in reducing global poverty, significant challenges remain. Here are some key challenges and potential solutions:

- **Income Inequality:** Addressing income inequality is crucial for promoting economic equality. Governments can implement progressive taxation policies, invest in social welfare programs, and promote fair labor practices to reduce income disparities.

- **Access to Basic Services:** Ensuring universal access to healthcare, education, clean water, and sanitation is essential for poverty reduction. Governments, in collaboration with international organizations, need to invest in infrastructure and social services to improve access for marginalized communities.

- **Climate Change and Environmental Sustainability:** Climate change disproportionately affects the poor and exacerbates existing vulnerabilities. Adaptation and mitigation measures, such as promoting renewable energy, sustainable agriculture, and disaster preparedness, are crucial for building resilience and reducing poverty.

- **Promoting Gender Equality:** Empowering women and promoting gender equality are pivotal for poverty reduction. Enhancing women's access to education, healthcare, economic opportunities, and decision-making processes can lead to more inclusive and equitable societies.

+ **Enhancing Productive Employment:** Creating decent and sustainable jobs is essential for poverty reduction. Governments need to prioritize investment in sectors that generate employment opportunities, promote entrepreneurship, and provide skills training for individuals to secure stable and well-paying jobs.

+ **Addressing Conflict and Political Instability:** Conflict and political instability perpetuate poverty and hinder development efforts. Promoting peace, ensuring good governance, and addressing the root causes of conflicts are necessary steps for poverty alleviation.

+ **Promoting Fair Trade Practices:** Addressing the imbalances in global trade is crucial for poverty reduction. Promoting fair trade practices, reducing trade barriers, and supporting market access for developing countries can contribute to more equitable economic growth.

Example: The Grameen Bank

An example of an initiative that has successfully tackled global poverty is the Grameen Bank in Bangladesh. Founded by Nobel laureate Muhammad Yunus, the bank provides microcredit to impoverished individuals, particularly women, to start their own businesses. The Grameen Bank has empowered millions of people to lift themselves out of poverty, demonstrating the power of microfinance in promoting economic equality.

Resources for Further Exploration

+ World Bank - https://www.worldbank.org/

+ United Nations Development Programme (UNDP) - https://www.undp.org/

+ The Borgen Project - https://borgenproject.org/

+ Oxfam International - https://www.oxfam.org/

Conclusion

Achieving economic equality and alleviating global poverty require a comprehensive and multidimensional approach. By addressing the root causes of poverty, promoting inclusive growth, and implementing targeted initiatives, we can work towards creating a more equitable and sustainable world. Collaboration between governments, international organizations, civil society, and individuals is crucial for achieving these goals and ensuring a brighter future for all.

Subsection: Human Rights and the Quest for Universal Standards

Human rights are fundamental principles that aim to protect the inherent dignity and worth of every individual, regardless of their nationality, race, gender, or any other characteristic. The quest for universal standards of human rights has been a central focus of international organizations and activists seeking to promote equality, justice, and freedom for all.

Background

The concept of human rights has evolved over centuries, influenced by philosophical and legal traditions which recognize the inherent value of every human being. The Universal Declaration of Human Rights (UDHR), adopted by the United Nations General Assembly in 1948, marked a milestone in the articulation of human rights principles at the global level. The UDHR enshrines a set of fundamental rights and freedoms that should be universally protected, including civil, political, economic, social, and cultural rights.

Principles and Key Concepts

1. Universality: Human rights are universal and apply to all individuals, regardless of their nationality, ethnic origin, or any other factor. They are based on the inherent dignity of every human being and are not subject to national or cultural relativism.

2. Equality and Non-Discrimination: Human rights should be enjoyed by all individuals without distinction or discrimination of any kind. They ensure that all people are treated with equal dignity and respect, irrespective of their characteristics or social status.

3. Inalienability: Human rights are inherent to all individuals and cannot be taken away or forfeited. They cannot be renounced or revoked, even in times of crisis or conflict.

BIBLIOGRAPHY

4. Indivisibility: Human rights are interrelated, interdependent, and indivisible. The realization of one right often depends on the enjoyment of other rights. For example, access to education is essential for the full exercise of the right to freedom of thought, conscience, and belief.

5. Accountability: States, as duty-bearers, have the primary responsibility to respect, protect, and fulfill human rights. Individuals and non-state actors also have a role to play in promoting and safeguarding human rights.

International Framework for Human Rights

1. United Nations Human Rights Council: The UN Human Rights Council is the main intergovernmental body responsible for promoting and protecting human rights globally. It reviews the human rights situation in member states, issues resolutions and recommendations, and conducts inquiries into human rights violations.

2. International Covenant on Civil and Political Rights (ICCPR): The ICCPR is a key international treaty that protects civil and political rights, such as the right to life, freedom of expression, and the right to a fair trial. States that have ratified the ICCPR are legally bound to uphold these rights.

3. International Covenant on Economic, Social, and Cultural Rights (ICESCR): The ICESCR protects economic, social, and cultural rights, including the right to work, the right to education, and the right to an adequate standard of living. It provides a comprehensive framework for states to address issues such as poverty, inequality, and social exclusion.

Challenges and Achievements

Despite significant progress, the realization of universal human rights faces numerous challenges. Some of these challenges include:

1. Cultural Relativism: The idea that human rights are culturally determined and vary across societies has been used to justify certain practices that violate human rights. Balancing universal standards with cultural diversity remains a complex issue.

2. Weak Implementation and Enforcement: Many states struggle to implement and enforce human rights standards effectively. Lack of resources, political will, and corruption often hinder progress in protecting and promoting human rights.

3. Gender Inequality: Women and girls continue to face discrimination and violence, highlighting the need to address gender inequality and promote gender-responsive policies and laws.

4. Violations in Conflict Situations: Armed conflicts and political instability create an environment conducive to human rights abuses. The protection of civilians and the prevention of atrocities require concerted international efforts.

Despite these challenges, significant achievements have been made in the quest for universal human rights standards. Examples include:

1. The Abolition of Apartheid: The dismantling of apartheid in South Africa in the 1990s marked a major victory in the fight against racial discrimination and segregation.

2. Advancements in LGBTQ+ Rights: Many countries have adopted legislation to protect the rights of LGBTQ+ individuals, including granting marriage equality and combating discrimination based on sexual orientation and gender identity.

3. International Criminal Court: The establishment of the International Criminal Court (ICC) in 2002 represents a significant step towards ensuring accountability for individuals responsible for war crimes, crimes against humanity, and genocide.

4. Nuremberg Trials: The Nuremberg Trials after World War II set a precedent for holding individuals accountable for crimes against humanity, establishing the principle that human rights violations should not go unpunished.

Contemporary Issues

1. Freedom of Expression: The digital age has raised new challenges for the protection of freedom of expression, including issues related to online censorship, surveillance, and the spread of disinformation.

2. Refugees and Asylum Seekers: The global refugee crisis highlights the importance of protecting the human rights of displaced persons, ensuring access to asylum, and promoting the integration of refugees into host communities.

3. Indigenous Peoples' Rights: Efforts to recognize and protect the collective rights of indigenous peoples, including their land rights and cultural heritage, continue to be significant issues globally.

4. Economic Inequality: Addressing economic inequalities and ensuring equitable access to resources and opportunities are ongoing challenges to the realization of economic and social rights.

Exercises

1. Research and analyze a recent human rights violation and discuss the international response to the situation.

BIBLIOGRAPHY   261

2. Identify a country that has made significant progress in promoting gender equality and discuss the strategies and policies that have contributed to these advancements.

3. Investigate a case of discrimination or persecution against a minority group and propose strategies to address the issue and promote inclusion.

4. Conduct a comparative analysis of the human rights frameworks in different regions and evaluate their effectiveness in protecting and promoting human rights.

Additional Resources

1. United Nations Human Rights Council: `https://www.ohchr.org/EN/HRBodies/HRC/Pages/HRCIndex.aspx`

2. Amnesty International: `https://www.amnesty.org`

3. Human Rights Watch: `https://www.hrw.org`

4. Stanford Encyclopedia of Philosophy - Human Rights: `https://plato.stanford.edu/entries/rights-human/`

By promoting universal standards of human rights, we can work towards creating a more equal, just, and inclusive world. The journey towards universal human rights continues, and it is crucial for individuals, governments, and international organizations to collaborate in upholding and advancing these fundamental principles.

Subsection: Gender Equality and Empowerment of Women

Gender equality and the empowerment of women have been long-fought battles in societies around the world. Throughout history, women have faced discrimination and unequal treatment in various aspects of life, including education, employment, and social norms. However, in recent decades, there has been significant progress in promoting gender equality and empowering women to achieve their full potential. This subsection explores the challenges, efforts, and achievements in the fight for gender equality and women's empowerment.

The Gender Gap

One of the key issues in achieving gender equality is the existence of a gender gap. This gap manifests in different forms, such as unequal access to education and healthcare, lower participation in the workforce, and limited representation in leadership roles. Understanding the causes and consequences of the gender gap is essential in formulating effective strategies for promoting gender equality.

Causes of the Gender Gap The gender gap can be attributed to various socio-economic and cultural factors. Traditional gender roles and stereotypes play a significant role in perpetuating inequality. In many societies, women are expected to prioritize family responsibilities over career aspirations, limiting their opportunities for professional growth. Additionally, discriminatory laws and policies, such as gender-based violence and unequal pay, further contribute to the gender gap.

Consequences of the Gender Gap The gender gap has profound consequences for individuals, communities, and societies as a whole. When women are underrepresented in decision-making positions, their perspectives and experiences may be overlooked, leading to policies and initiatives that are not inclusive or reflective of diverse needs. Furthermore, the gender gap limits economic growth potential as a significant portion of the talent pool remains untapped. Addressing and closing the gender gap is crucial for achieving social justice, sustainable development, and overall well-being.

Promoting Gender Equality and Women's Empowerment

Efforts to promote gender equality and empower women have gained momentum globally. Governments, international organizations, non-governmental organizations (NGOs), and grassroots movements have played a vital role in driving change. Various strategies and initiatives have been implemented to address the root causes of gender inequality and create a more inclusive and equitable world.

Legal Reforms and Policies Legal reforms and policies have been instrumental in advancing gender equality. Governments have enacted legislation to protect women's rights, eliminate discrimination, and promote equal opportunities. For example, laws addressing gender-based violence, equal pay, and parental leave have been passed in many countries. Additionally, gender quotas and affirmative action policies have been implemented to increase women's representation in political and corporate positions.

Education and Awareness Education plays a crucial role in challenging gender stereotypes and empowering women. By promoting gender-sensitive curricula and providing equal access to quality education, societies can nurture the intellectual, social, and economic potential of women. Education also helps raise awareness about gender issues, fostering a more inclusive and gender-equal society.

BIBLIOGRAPHY

Economic Empowerment   Economic empowerment is essential for enhancing women's status and autonomy.   Efforts to promote financial inclusion, entrepreneurship, and skills development have been instrumental in empowering women economically.   Microfinance initiatives, vocational training programs, and mentorship schemes are examples of interventions aimed at providing women with opportunities for economic self-sufficiency and advancement.

Health and Well-being   Ensuring women's access to quality healthcare and reproductive rights is a significant aspect of gender equality.   Efforts to address reproductive health issues, gender-based violence, and maternal mortality have been prioritized globally.   Additionally, initiatives promoting mental health and well-being and addressing the unique healthcare needs of women have gained recognition.

Challenges and Future Outlook

Despite significant progress, several challenges persist in the journey towards gender equality and women's empowerment.   Deep-rooted patriarchal norms, cultural resistance, and institutional biases continue to hinder progress. Additionally, intersecting forms of discrimination, such as those based on race, class, and sexuality, further complicate efforts to achieve gender equality.

Intersectionality   Recognizing and addressing the intersectional nature of gender inequality is crucial.   Intersectionality acknowledges that individuals may experience multiple forms of discrimination simultaneously and that various dimensions of identity (such as race, class, and gender) intersect to shape different experiences and barriers.   Adopting an intersectional approach allows for a more comprehensive understanding of gender inequality and the development of targeted solutions.

Male Engagement   Engaging men and boys as allies in the fight for gender equality is essential.   Challenging traditional notions of masculinity, promoting healthy relationships, and addressing male privilege are key areas for intervention. Collaborative efforts that involve men and boys alongside women and girls can foster a more inclusive and sustainable approach to achieving gender equality.

Education and Awareness   Continued efforts to promote gender-sensitive education and raise awareness about gender equality are imperative.   Educational institutions and media platforms have a crucial role in challenging gender norms and stereotypes. Promoting critical thinking, empathy, and respect for diversity can contribute to the dismantling of gender-based barriers and the promotion of a more inclusive society.

Supportive Policies and Legislation Strengthening existing policies and legislation to eliminate gender-based discrimination and promote equal opportunities is an ongoing process. Governments and international organizations must ensure the effective implementation of these policies and address any gaps or loopholes. Regular evaluation and monitoring of progress are essential to drive sustainable change.

Sustainable Development Goals The United Nations' Sustainable Development Goals (SDGs) provide a framework for achieving gender equality and women's empowerment. SDG 5 specifically targets gender equality and calls for the elimination of all forms of discrimination against women and girls. Aligning efforts with the SDGs can facilitate global collaboration and prioritize gender equality as a key development agenda.

In conclusion, achieving gender equality and empowering women requires a collective and sustained effort. By addressing the root causes of gender inequality, promoting inclusive policies, and fostering awareness and education, societies can create an environment where all individuals have equal opportunities, rights, and representation. Embracing gender equality and women's empowerment not only benefits women but also contributes to a more just, prosperous, and harmonious world for all.

Subsection: Access to Education and the Globalization of Knowledge

Access to education is a fundamental human right and plays a crucial role in individual development, social progress, and economic growth. In the context of globalization, advancements in technology and the spread of knowledge have revolutionized the way education is accessed and delivered. This subsection explores the challenges and opportunities associated with ensuring equitable access to education in a globalized world.

BIBLIOGRAPHY

The Digital Divide and Educational Inequality

The digital divide refers to the gap between those who have access to digital technologies and those who do not. In the context of education, the digital divide contributes to educational inequality, as disadvantaged communities and individuals are left behind in the digital age. Lack of access to computers, internet connectivity, and digital literacy skills hinder their ability to participate fully in educational opportunities.

To bridge the digital divide, various initiatives have been implemented. One such initiative is the provision of technology resources, such as computers and internet connectivity, to underserved communities. Governments, international organizations, and non-profit organizations have collaborated to set up computer labs and community centers equipped with educational resources. These efforts aim to provide equal access to digital tools and educational opportunities for all.

Open Educational Resources and Massive Open Online Courses

Open Educational Resources (OER) and Massive Open Online Courses (MOOCs) have emerged as powerful tools for expanding access to education. OER are freely accessible learning materials, including textbooks, lectures, and multimedia resources, which can be modified and shared. MOOCs, on the other hand, are online courses open to a large number of participants, regardless of geographical location or prior qualifications.

The availability of OER and MOOCs has enabled learners from all corners of the world to access high-quality educational content and receive certifications from renowned institutions. This has democratized education, empowering individuals who may not have access to traditional educational institutions or resources. Learners can study at their own pace, interact with peers globally, and acquire valuable skills for personal and professional growth.

Educational Exchanges and Study Abroad Programs

Globalization has fostered international collaboration and cultural exchange in the field of education. Educational exchanges and study abroad programs provide students with opportunities to experience different learning environments, immerse themselves in diverse cultures, and develop a global perspective.

Through these programs, students can broaden their knowledge, gain intercultural competencies, and build networks that extend beyond national boundaries. They enhance their understanding of global issues, collaborate with students from different backgrounds, and develop a sense of global citizenship.

Study abroad experiences also contribute to personal growth and foster tolerance and appreciation for diversity.

The Role of Technologies in Access to Education

Advancements in information and communication technologies (ICTs) have revolutionized access to education. Online learning platforms, virtual classrooms, and educational apps provide flexible and interactive learning experiences, transcending geographical barriers. Through these technologies, individuals can access educational content, engage with instructors, and collaborate with peers, regardless of their physical location.

However, it is important to consider the digital divide mentioned earlier. While technologies have the potential to enhance access to education, their widespread adoption is limited by factors such as affordability, infrastructure availability, and digital literacy. Efforts must be made to ensure equitable access to ICTs and provide necessary support and training to promote digital inclusion.

Addressing Educational Inequalities

To address educational inequalities, a multi-faceted approach is required. Governments, educational institutions, and international organizations should collaborate to:

1. Invest in infrastructure: Improve connectivity, provide computers, and establish digital learning centers in underserved areas to bridge the digital divide.

2. Develop digital literacy programs: Offer training and resources to develop digital skills necessary for utilizing technology in education.

3. Support community-based initiatives: Encourage the establishment of community learning centers and partnerships between schools and local organizations to provide accessible education resources.

4. Expand open educational resources: Invest in creating and distributing high-quality OER to ensure that educational materials are freely accessible to all learners.

5. Promote cross-cultural exchanges: Encourage study abroad programs and initiatives that foster global collaboration and cultural understanding.

6. Provide financial assistance: Offer scholarships and grants to individuals from disadvantaged backgrounds, enabling them to access education and training opportunities.

BIBLIOGRAPHY 267

7. Foster public-private partnerships: Collaborate with private sector organizations to leverage their resources and expertise in expanding educational access, particularly in areas where government support is limited.

By implementing these strategies, educational inequalities can be minimized, and access to education can be democratized in the globalized world.

Conclusion

In summary, access to education and the globalization of knowledge are interconnected in the modern world. The digital divide, open educational resources, study abroad programs, and the role of technologies play crucial roles in determining educational opportunities for individuals. Addressing educational inequalities requires a comprehensive approach that combines infrastructure development, digital literacy programs, community-based initiatives, and financial support. By ensuring equitable access to education, societies can empower individuals, foster innovation, and contribute to sustainable global development. The globalization of knowledge has the potential to transform lives and create a more inclusive and interconnected world.

Subsection: International Humanitarian Aid and Disaster Response

In times of crisis and disaster, international humanitarian aid plays a critical role in providing assistance and relief to affected regions. From natural disasters like earthquakes and hurricanes to man-made conflicts and epidemics, the world relies on dedicated organizations and a collaborative response to mitigate suffering and rebuild affected communities. In this subsection, we will explore the principles, challenges, and innovative solutions in the field of international humanitarian aid and disaster response.

Principles of International Humanitarian Aid

International humanitarian aid is guided by a set of principles that ensure effective and ethical assistance to those in need. The following principles form the foundation of humanitarian action:

1. **Humanity:** The principle of humanity emphasizes the importance of saving lives, preventing and alleviating suffering, and upholding human dignity. Humanitarian aid is centered on the needs of affected individuals and communities, regardless of their race, religion, nationality, or political affiliations.

2. **Neutrality:** Neutrality requires humanitarian organizations to provide assistance without taking sides in conflicts or engaging in any political, religious, or military actions. This principle ensures the safety and acceptance of aid workers by all parties involved.

3. **Impartiality:** Impartiality means that humanitarian aid should be provided solely based on the needs of the affected population, without discrimination or favoritism. It ensures that assistance reaches those who are most vulnerable and in urgent need, regardless of any external factors.

4. **Independence:** Humanitarian organizations maintain their independence from political, economic, or military actors to ensure their ability to act according to humanitarian principles. Independence allows aid agencies to prioritize the needs of affected populations objectively and without interference.

5. **Accountability:** Humanitarian actors are accountable to the affected populations and donors for their actions and use of resources. Transparency in funding, operations, and decision-making processes is crucial to maintaining trust and ensuring the effectiveness of aid efforts.

Challenges in International Humanitarian Aid

While the principles of international humanitarian aid provide a framework for effective intervention, several challenges must be addressed to ensure successful disaster response:

1. **Access to Affected Areas:** In conflict zones or regions hit by natural disasters, gaining access to affected areas can be challenging due to security concerns, logistical constraints, or political restrictions. Humanitarian organizations must negotiate access with relevant authorities and ensure the safety of their personnel.

2. **Coordination and Collaboration:** Collaboration among different humanitarian actors, including governments, non-governmental organizations (NGOs), and international agencies, is essential for efficient and effective aid delivery. However, coordination can be complex due to differing mandates, priorities, and approaches. Strengthening coordination mechanisms is crucial to avoid duplication of efforts and maximize resources.

3. **Resource Constraints:** The demand for humanitarian aid often exceeds available resources. Funding shortfalls, limited staffing, and inadequate logistical support can hinder the scale and timeliness of assistance. Building sustainable funding mechanisms and strengthening partnerships is vital to address resource constraints.

4. **Local Context and Cultural Sensitivity:** Understanding the local context, culture, and dynamics is essential for effective humanitarian aid. Cultural sensitivity

BIBLIOGRAPHY

and community engagement ensure that interventions are appropriate and tailored to the specific needs and preferences of the affected population.

5. **Long-term Development:** While immediate relief is crucial, sustainable long-term development efforts are equally important. Humanitarian aid must be integrated with development programs to help affected communities rebuild, recover, and become more resilient to future disasters.

Innovative Solutions in International Humanitarian Aid

Addressing the challenges in international humanitarian aid requires innovative solutions and approaches. Here are some examples of innovative practices and technologies:

1. **Data-driven Decision Making:** Humanitarian organizations are increasingly using data analysis and technology to make informed decisions in aid delivery. The use of satellite imagery, remote sensing, and geographic information systems (GIS) helps identify vulnerable areas, assess needs, and allocate resources efficiently.

2. **Cash Transfers:** Cash-based interventions, such as mobile money transfers, allow affected communities to have choices and participate in their own recovery. Providing cash grants instead of in-kind relief items enables individuals to prioritize their needs according to their specific circumstances.

3. **Mobile Technology:** The widespread use of mobile phones has revolutionized humanitarian aid. SMS-based systems can disseminate critical information, receive feedback from affected populations, and provide targeted assistance through mobile cash transfers and voucher programs.

4. **Local Capacity Building:** Strengthening the capacity of local communities and organizations is crucial for sustainable recovery and resilience. By involving local actors in decision-making processes and providing training and support, international humanitarian aid can empower communities to lead their own recovery efforts.

5. **Humanitarian Innovation Labs:** Humanitarian innovation labs and centers bring together experts, aid workers, and local communities to co-create solutions to complex challenges. These labs foster collaboration, experimentation, and iterative problem-solving, leading to innovative approaches in disaster response.

Case Study: The Rohingya Crisis in Myanmar

The Rohingya crisis, characterized by widespread violence, displacement, and human rights violations, exemplifies the complexities and challenges in international humanitarian aid. Since 2017, thousands of Rohingya Muslims have fled persecution in Myanmar, seeking safety in neighboring Bangladesh. The response to this crisis has involved various humanitarian actors and innovative approaches.

One innovative solution in the Rohingya crisis has been the use of drone technology for rapid needs assessments and mapping of displacement camps. Drones equipped with high-resolution cameras can provide real-time imagery, helping aid agencies identify gaps in services, plan infrastructure development, and monitor the situation.

Another example is the use of blockchain technology to provide transparent and accountable assistance. Blockchain-based systems enable direct transfers of funds and resources to affected individuals, ensuring that aid reaches the intended recipients without intermediaries or corruption.

Additionally, the involvement of local organizations and communities plays a crucial role in responding to the Rohingya crisis. Local NGOs and community-based organizations have been instrumental in providing services and support to the affected population, leveraging their knowledge of the local context and building trust with the Rohingya community.

Resources for Further Exploration

1. Sphere Handbook: The Sphere Handbook provides essential standards and guidelines for humanitarian response, guiding practitioners in delivering quality and accountable assistance. It covers key areas such as water supply, sanitation, nutrition, and shelter.

2. United Nations Office for the Coordination of Humanitarian Affairs (OCHA): OCHA coordinates international humanitarian response and supports countries in disaster response and coordination efforts. Their website provides updates on ongoing crises, resources, and guidelines for effective humanitarian action.

3. ALNAP (Active Learning Network for Accountability and Performance in Humanitarian Action): ALNAP is a global network that promotes learning and accountability in humanitarian action. Their publications and resources offer valuable insights into best practices and lessons learned in humanitarian aid and disaster response.

4. International Federation of Red Cross and Red Crescent Societies (IFRC): The IFRC is a global humanitarian network that provides assistance during emergencies and advocates for the rights of vulnerable populations. Their website offers resources, guidelines, and case studies on disaster response and humanitarian aid.

Key Concepts and Terms

1. Humanitarian Principles 2. Neutrality 3. Impartiality 4. Independence 5. Accountability 6. Access 7. Coordination 8. Cash Transfers 9. Mobile Technology 10. Local Capacity Building 11. Humanitarian Innovation Labs 12. Data-driven Decision Making 13. Rohingya Crisis 14. Blockchain Technology

Exercises

1. Research and analyze a recent humanitarian crisis or disaster. Identify the key challenges faced in the response efforts and propose innovative solutions to address those challenges.

2. Imagine yourself working for a humanitarian organization responding to a natural disaster. Create a comprehensive action plan detailing the steps you would take to ensure efficient and effective aid delivery.

3. Debate the role of technology in humanitarian aid. Discuss the advantages and disadvantages of using technology in disaster response, considering ethical, practical, and cultural implications.

4. Conduct a case study on a specific humanitarian organization or agency involved in disaster response. Analyze their approach, principles, and innovative practices, and evaluate their impact on affected communities.

Conclusion

International humanitarian aid and disaster response are essential components of contemporary history. By understanding the principles, challenges, and innovative solutions in this field, we can work towards building more effective and efficient mechanisms to alleviate human suffering in times of crisis. Through collaboration, innovation, and a commitment to human dignity, we can pave the way for a more resilient and compassionate world.

Index

-effectiveness, 127

ability, 7, 48, 72, 85, 87, 90, 106,
113, 115, 117, 144, 156,
161, 165, 167, 174, 190,
194, 240, 243, 265
abolition, 61
abortion, 65
about, 18, 24, 27, 39, 58, 63, 66–69,
71, 72, 75, 81, 83–85, 93,
97, 98, 101, 102, 106, 113,
114, 125, 126, 131, 132,
134, 135, 137, 149, 159,
161, 164, 172, 180, 185,
191, 202, 205–209, 214,
233, 236, 238, 262, 263
absence, 8, 85, 100
abundance, 84
abuse, 225, 227
academia, 225
acceptance, 66, 68–70, 79, 136, 137
access, 40, 43, 50, 53, 60, 64–66,
82–86, 93, 94, 96, 98, 101,
102, 105, 106, 109,
111–115, 125–127, 129,
139, 140, 152, 159, 161,
164, 165, 168, 169,
171–178, 180, 188,
190–197, 207, 210–212,
214, 215, 219, 228–230,
232, 233, 238, 239, 243,
244, 255, 259–267
accessibility, 69, 86, 93, 97,
103–105, 118, 156, 167,
170, 171, 173–176
account, 19, 137, 164, 230
accountability, 71, 93, 167, 169, 244
accountable, 65, 116, 260, 270
accounting, 155
acculturation, 223
accuracy, 160, 167, 189
achievement, 25, 73
act, 224, 241
action, 5, 16, 54, 71–73, 146, 195,
196, 199, 208, 247, 262,
267, 271
activism, 62, 66, 67, 70–72, 100,
125, 155–159, 233
activist, 61
activity, 54
adaptability, 206, 218
adaptation, 73, 88, 218, 229, 231,
237, 241, 248
addiction, 125
address, 4–6, 22, 23, 35, 42, 43, 45,
49, 54, 55, 65, 66, 90, 98,

102, 112, 118, 129, 134, 136, 137, 146, 149, 167, 175, 187, 190, 192, 195, 198, 199, 207, 209, 210, 212–215, 218, 222, 230–232, 235–238, 240, 242, 244, 247, 249, 250, 255, 259, 261, 263, 264, 266, 271

addressing, 3, 5, 32, 37, 39, 61, 74, 96, 118, 120, 160, 177, 193, 195, 199, 201, 202, 208, 212, 213, 218, 228, 231, 233, 239, 242–244, 258, 262–264

adequacy, 172

adoption, 23, 48, 50, 51, 73, 83, 87, 88, 117, 124, 140, 190–192, 266

advance, 20, 60, 102, 106, 137, 140, 149, 167, 208, 236, 246

advancement, 27, 43, 58, 65, 85, 124, 126, 131, 137, 173, 192, 219, 221, 263

advantage, 21, 180, 188, 190

advent, 83, 97, 101, 120, 124, 171

advertising, 51, 52, 79, 81, 83, 102, 104, 105, 126, 139

advice, 35, 165

advocacy, 49, 66, 72, 158, 214

advocate, 67, 69, 72, 156, 208, 214

affordability, 50, 175, 176, 266

Africa, 16

aftermath, 6, 9, 10, 13, 22, 24

age, 28, 53, 69, 74, 84, 103, 105, 106, 109, 115, 120, 125, 140, 149, 152, 159, 162, 168, 172, 176, 238, 248, 260, 265

agency, 68, 142, 249, 271

agenda, 79, 246

agreement, 34

agriculture, 38, 74, 230, 240

agroecology, 74

aid, 4, 38, 39, 47, 165, 208, 211–215, 267–271

aim, 17, 181, 214, 249, 258, 265

air, 208

Alabama, 61

Alex Comfort, 69

Alexander Graham Bell's, 124

algorithm, 104, 167

alignment, 23

alliance, 23

allocation, 49, 242, 244

allure, 51

alternative, 44, 49, 67, 68, 70, 79, 82, 83, 87, 104

amount, 103, 106, 162

analysis, 19, 53, 131, 161–164, 250, 261

answer, 92

anthem, 63

anti, 23, 63, 71, 231–233

anxiety, 82, 231, 232

apartheid, 63, 260

app, 122

apparel, 191

appeal, 247

application, 135, 137, 167

appreciation, 191, 207, 266

approach, 49, 53, 71, 82, 83, 90, 114, 133, 151, 154, 160, 168, 170, 174, 176, 185, 186, 194, 209, 212, 217, 221, 227–230, 232, 239, 240, 246–248, 252, 258, 263, 266, 267, 271

Index 275

appropriation, 87, 206
approval, 244
arbitrage, 198
architecture, 91, 138, 139
area, 159
array, 93
arrest, 61
art, 87, 207
ascendancy, 6
ascent, 9, 55, 58
Asia, 6, 16, 20, 46, 189
aspect, 104, 169, 195, 216, 236, 263
aspiration, 79
assault, 65
assessment, 136
asset, 54
assimilation, 223, 224
assistance, 4, 34–36, 38, 46, 139,
       181, 212–216, 230, 237,
       238, 266, 267, 270
asylum, 210, 216, 260
attack, 20, 28, 142, 155, 251, 253
attacker, 253
attempt, 39
attention, 72, 79, 85, 86, 100, 196
attorney, 62
audience, 51, 79, 84, 88, 101, 102,
       105, 159, 168, 171, 207
audit, 164
austerity, 36, 49
authentication, 129
authenticity, 161, 189, 191, 206
authority, 93, 244
automate, 99, 189
automation, 58–61, 118, 120, 131,
       133, 134, 144, 146, 193,
       196
autonomy, 66, 68, 106, 263

availability, 51, 68, 72, 81, 97, 99,
       125, 129, 141, 156, 190,
       265, 266
awareness, 66, 71–75, 83, 93, 155,
       156, 158, 191, 207, 208,
       214, 215, 232, 237, 241,
       252, 262–264

b. ", 64
background, 17, 19, 33, 195, 233
baht, 36
balance, 6, 13, 18, 24, 28, 34, 35, 44,
       74, 109, 113, 115, 123,
       125, 137, 161, 205–207,
       240, 248
balancing, 146
bandwidth, 96
Bangladesh, 191, 230, 257, 270
bank, 257
bargaining, 195
barrier, 30, 169, 175
base, 6, 87, 161
basis, 72
battle, 24, 140, 143, 246, 248
battleground, 20
beauty, 80
beef, 192
beginning, 6, 28, 248
behavior, 51, 79, 80, 99, 102, 117,
       144, 160
being, 74, 82, 83, 120, 138, 160,
       167, 188, 194, 206, 211,
       213, 222, 225, 228, 232,
       236, 258, 262, 263
belief, 49, 51, 72, 81, 259
belonging, 80, 124, 223, 232, 237
benefit, 60, 181, 207, 224, 239
Berlin, 30, 32
beta, 137

Betty Friedan, 67, 69
bias, 60, 80, 102, 116, 118, 167
Bing, 104
biodiversity, 74, 136, 192, 208, 240, 241
biotechnology, 135–137
bipolarity, 6, 9
birth, 17, 34, 68, 73
blending, 205, 224
blindness, 137
bloc, 23
block, 5, 114
blockchain, 189, 270
Bob Dylan, 63
body, 35, 80, 259
Bollywood, 191
bombing, 21
book, 19, 72, 122
border, 19, 31, 196, 197, 210
borrowing, 54, 87
bottom, 105
brain, 219–222, 236
brand, 80, 102
breach, 126, 142
breadth, 113
breakdown, 35
breast, 167
breeding, 22, 232
Bretton Woods, 33–37
brick, 51, 97, 169
bridge, 109, 111, 112, 170, 173–175, 177, 238, 265, 266
Britain, 18
broadband, 172, 174, 175
browsing, 105, 106, 176
brutality, 62, 63
bubble, 51–53
budget, 105

buffer, 10
building, 5, 17, 33, 52, 181, 221, 230, 231, 244, 270, 271
burden, 165
bursting, 53
bus, 61, 62
business, 40, 43, 49, 51–53, 124–126, 129, 172, 186, 187, 192, 196, 202, 224, 228
buying, 82, 97
buzzword, 162

cable, 171
call, 55
camera, 139
campaign, 22, 61, 64, 102, 159–161
campaigning, 161
Canada, 218, 224
cancer, 167
capability, 28
capacity, 5, 35, 72, 181, 190, 211, 220–222, 230
capital, 30, 35, 36, 46–48, 51, 188, 196–198, 220, 228
capitalism, 24, 202–205
capture, 86, 99
carbon, 192, 241
care, 125, 165, 167, 214, 222
career, 65, 123, 219–221, 262
Carla L. Klausner, 19
carotene, 137
cartel, 44
case, 5, 16, 24, 42, 43, 62, 67, 126, 155, 157, 161, 164, 187, 261, 271
cash, 98
Castro, 22, 23
categorization, 104

Index 277

cater, 129, 238
Catonsville, 71
cause, 63, 210, 229, 240, 253
caution, 101
ceasefire, 6
ceiling, 67
celebration, 207
celebrity, 80
censorship, 113–115, 260
center, 54, 60
Central Europe, 10
century, 17, 23, 46, 48, 61, 64, 72, 103, 124
certainty, 28
chain, 54, 98, 187–190
challenge, 16, 23, 46, 48, 62, 64, 65, 67, 68, 71, 79, 80, 85, 87, 101, 125, 140, 156, 160, 169, 196, 205, 209, 213, 215, 224, 233, 247–250
change, 23, 24, 31, 32, 45, 61–64, 67, 72–74, 82, 93, 94, 102, 155, 158, 192, 199, 208–210, 216, 228–231, 237, 239–241, 264
changer, 124
characteristic, 258
checking, 152, 160
checkout, 60
Chile, 50
China, 3, 21, 55–58, 114, 189, 223, 248, 250
choice, 49, 50, 97, 100, 180, 205, 210
circuit, 89, 90
citizen, 93, 101
citizenship, 178, 265
city, 18
class, 22, 263

classroom, 168, 169
climate, 22, 27, 45, 61, 73, 74, 82, 192, 199, 208, 210, 228–231, 237, 240, 241
Clinton, 161
cloud, 52, 126, 127, 129, 144, 189
coalition, 16
coercion, 225, 245, 251
cohesion, 17, 83, 194, 211, 218, 232, 233, 237, 239
collaboration, 43, 47, 84, 91, 93, 94, 120, 129, 152, 155, 158, 169, 177, 188, 189, 192, 199, 209, 214, 221, 238, 239, 242–244, 247, 265, 266, 271
collapse, 34, 37, 51–54
collection, 19, 106, 126, 161–164
college, 62
colonization, 223
colonoscopy, 167
color, 63
combat, 71, 141, 155, 161, 225, 226, 228, 241, 245, 246, 248
combination, 30, 46, 50, 53, 138, 231
comfort, 165
command, 29
commerce, 51, 60, 96–100
commercialization, 137
commitment, 30, 39, 47, 218, 250, 271
commodification, 87
communication, 27, 40, 51, 81, 83–87, 100–102, 113, 116, 124–126, 137, 144, 146, 160, 161, 174, 188, 191, 197, 205, 223, 236
communism, 20, 22–24, 38

community, 21, 34, 124, 175–177, 181, 191, 212, 215, 224, 225, 229, 231, 233, 248, 249, 265–267, 270

company, 40, 42, 171, 182, 187, 189

comparison, 82

compatibility, 140

compensation, 172, 173, 221

competition, 10, 24, 27–29, 49, 82, 97, 104, 172, 181, 191, 197, 202, 211, 229, 238

competitiveness, 47

complexity, 188, 253

compliance, 5, 181, 189, 201, 249, 250

compromise, 6

computer, 115, 138–141, 152, 251, 265

computing, 52, 126, 127, 129, 144, 147–149

concentration, 50, 172, 193, 195

concept, 28, 29, 90–93, 109, 126, 131, 140, 144, 173, 196, 219, 222, 251

concern, 20, 21, 25, 29, 71, 72, 113, 172, 223, 248

conclusion, 17, 19, 29, 50, 55, 67, 85, 94, 102, 120, 140, 149, 164, 170, 173, 207, 225, 241, 244, 248, 264

condition, 254

conditionality, 35, 36

conduct, 40, 43, 138, 196

conference, 34

conferencing, 169

confidence, 52, 54

confidentiality, 141

conflict, 4, 5, 8, 10, 17–21, 30, 44, 73, 210, 212, 213, 232, 236, 258

conformity, 70

confrontation, 21, 22, 29

confusion, 160

congestion, 90

Congo, 16

connection, 20, 84, 90, 93, 214

connectivity, 85, 95, 96, 109, 124, 126, 129, 144, 172, 174–176, 238, 265, 266

conscience, 71, 259

consciousness, 70

consensus, 5, 6, 73

consent, 69, 126, 164

consequence, 229

conservation, 44, 45, 73, 75, 208, 241

conservatism, 49

consideration, 118, 196, 205

consolidation, 22, 52

construction, 19, 54, 230

consultation, 136

consumer, 7, 50, 51, 55, 79, 80, 82, 86, 87, 100, 142, 180, 206

consumerism, 70, 81–83, 206

consumerist, 83, 191

consumption, 49, 52, 74, 81–83, 146, 173, 209

contact, 205

content, 51, 52, 86, 87, 103, 113, 114, 136, 139, 140, 160, 168, 171–173, 175, 265

contention, 19

context, 20, 28, 38, 61, 64, 67, 131, 132, 136, 139, 161, 167, 205, 222, 234, 236, 238, 240, 264, 265, 270

continent, 10, 13, 16, 39

contingency, 189

Index

279

continuity, 177

contraception, 65, 68

contrast, 27, 63

control, 16, 18, 24, 29, 68, 88, 106,
113, 114, 137, 138, 146,
164, 189, 195, 208, 216,
242, 247–250

controversy, 58

convenience, 97, 100, 125, 168

convergence, 86, 117, 144

conversation, 84

convertibility, 34

cooperation, 3, 5, 16, 29, 30, 32, 34,
36, 38, 48, 73, 155, 187,
192, 193, 199, 201, 202,
208, 209, 212, 213, 228,
231–233, 237, 239,
241–244, 247, 248, 250

coordination, 55, 188–190, 198,
199, 202, 215, 238, 243

copying, 172

copyright, 172

core, 3, 28, 34, 141, 144

cornerstone, 83

corporation, 40, 182, 187

correction, 51–53, 149

corruption, 22, 79, 259, 270

cost, 127, 129, 131, 175, 188, 191

Costa Rica, 74

counter, 233, 246–248

counterculture, 68

counteroffensive, 20, 21

counterterrorism, 247, 248

country, 20, 22, 28, 37, 40, 55, 74,
126, 153, 177, 181, 182,
191, 205, 218, 221, 222,
261

couple, 204

course, 9, 24, 168

coursework, 169

coverage, 161, 175

crawling, 105

creation, 17, 19, 34, 35, 59–61, 84,
171, 172, 181, 205, 209,
212, 232

creativity, 59, 191, 206

credibility, 29

credit, 53, 54, 98, 142, 238

crime, 194, 226–228, 251

criminal, 152

crisis, 36, 37, 44, 45, 50, 53–55, 82,
198, 212–214, 258, 260,
267, 269–271

criticism, 23, 50, 80, 112, 187

crop, 135, 137

crossing, 31

crunch, 54

cryptography, 149

Cuba, 22, 23

cuisine, 205, 224

cultivation, 136

culture, 7, 70, 78–82, 86–88, 102,
195, 206, 223

curiosity, 93

currency, 34

curriculum, 177

curry, 224

customer, 97–99, 125, 188–190

customization, 97, 188

cut, 135

cyber, 101, 140, 142, 153, 155, 246,
250–254

cyberattack, 155

cyberbullying, 102

cybercrime, 152, 154, 155

cybersecurity, 126, 140–143, 155,
251, 253, 254

cyberterrorism, 152

cycle, 193, 194, 228

damage, 28, 72, 140, 155, 240
dance, 87
data, 52, 60, 89, 90, 97–99, 101,
    106, 113, 114, 117, 125,
    126, 128, 129, 140–142,
    144, 146, 152, 159–165,
    167, 171, 178, 189, 215,
    244
day, 19, 21, 69, 162, 225, 228
de, 67, 69, 71
debate, 51, 71, 202, 204, 205
debt, 49, 53, 58
deception, 225
decision, 5, 6, 35, 55, 60, 66, 80,
    137, 144, 146, 162, 175,
    178, 230, 244, 262
declaration, 3, 17
decline, 45, 52, 54
decoherence, 149
decolonization, 13, 15–17, 223
decrease, 125, 131
defense, 253
deficiency, 137
definition, 225, 228
deforestation, 72, 192, 208
degradation, 27, 69, 181, 192, 193,
    208, 209, 228, 229
delivery, 98, 164, 168, 220, 222, 250,
    271
demand, 54, 59, 60, 63, 71, 82, 95,
    123, 127, 131, 146, 168,
    171, 172, 188, 189, 191,
    192, 197, 209
democracy, 10, 30–32, 73, 113
democratization, 84, 85, 93, 94, 171
demographic, 18, 216
Deng Xiaoping, 55

departure, 219, 220, 222
dependence, 45, 74, 101, 208, 220,
    230
dependency, 16, 211, 236
depletion, 82, 209
deployment, 6, 127, 175
depth, 19, 101
deregulation, 50, 53, 196
desertification, 229
design, 59, 60, 138, 139
designing, 177
desire, 31, 32, 81, 192
destination, 90, 236
destruction, 28, 30, 208, 228, 229,
    253
detection, 167, 242
deterioration, 211
determination, 15, 17, 18, 30
deterrence, 28, 30
deterrent, 28
devaluation, 36
devastation, 34
development, 4, 5, 16, 17, 23,
    27–29, 35–37, 39, 43, 44,
    47, 48, 50, 52, 68, 73–75,
    80, 83, 91, 94, 103, 112,
    113, 120, 124, 126, 135,
    136, 138, 140, 169, 174,
    176, 180, 186, 188, 190,
    192–194, 197, 199,
    207–209, 212, 214, 215,
    219–222, 224, 228, 230,
    231, 236, 238, 240–243,
    262–264, 267, 270
device, 139, 175
Dhaka, 230
diagnosis, 167
diagnostic, 165, 242

Index 281

dialogue, 5, 6, 84, 113, 115, 137, 205, 207, 219, 224, 232, 233
diary, 27
diaspora, 221–225
diffusion, 86, 87
dignity, 106, 258, 271
diligence, 52
dilution, 191
dioxide, 241
disarmament, 29, 30, 248–250
disaster, 229, 230, 267, 268, 271
discipline, 169
discontent, 22
discord, 160
discourse, 79, 93, 101, 114, 160, 233
discovery, 171
discrimination, 4, 61–65, 164, 180, 195, 211, 218, 231–233, 246, 258–264
discussion, 169
disease, 135, 164, 244
disinformation, 149–152, 160, 161, 260
dislocation, 191, 224
dismantling, 260, 264
disobedience, 71
displacement, 5, 18, 59–61, 116, 118, 131, 133, 134, 181, 192, 193, 196, 210, 213, 229, 269, 270
display, 105, 138
disposal, 82, 209
dispute, 181
disruption, 131, 211, 246, 251
dissatisfaction, 82
dissemination, 84, 88, 101, 106, 114, 168, 251
dissent, 70

dissolution, 13, 29
distance, 101, 124
distinction, 258
distress, 53, 54
distribution, 39, 146, 171–174, 188, 193, 195, 198, 202, 243, 244
diversification, 16, 45, 198
diversion, 29
diversity, 66, 73, 87, 88, 93, 113, 192, 205–207, 216, 218, 219, 222–225, 232, 259, 264, 266
divide, 28–30, 85, 96, 109–112, 125, 126, 169, 173–178, 232, 238, 265–267
diving, 91
division, 10, 12, 13, 20, 21, 30–32
document, 93, 207
dollar, 34
dominance, 6, 47, 48, 87, 88, 191, 206
domination, 39, 88
dominos, 20
Donald Trump, 161
donor, 215, 244
door, 106, 216
downturn, 36, 37, 54
draft, 71
drain, 219–222, 236
drive, 129, 162, 238, 264
driver, 54, 220, 229
driving, 9, 40, 47, 123, 158, 172, 182, 187, 188
drone, 270
drug, 244
duplication, 214, 242
duty, 259
dynamic, 90, 99

e, 51, 60, 96–100, 168, 176, 209
Earth, 25, 27, 192
earthquake, 213
ease, 86, 172
East, 30, 31, 33
East Asia, 20, 21
East Berlin, 30
East Germany, 30
East-West, 30
Eastern Europe, 6, 30, 38, 39
echo, 102, 160
eco, 100, 230
economic, 6, 7, 9, 12, 13, 16, 17,
　　22–24, 29, 34–40, 42–61,
　　73, 74, 82, 125, 126, 173,
　　174, 176, 177, 180, 181,
　　183, 185, 187–190,
　　192–199, 202, 205,
　　207–212, 214, 216,
　　218–220, 222–225, 228,
　　229, 231, 232, 234–241,
　　247, 251, 254, 255, 257,
　　258, 260, 262–264
economy, 40, 43–45, 47, 49, 51–55,
　　74, 83, 120–123, 180, 182,
　　185, 187, 190, 194, 196,
　　197, 199, 202, 205, 209,
　　218, 220, 223, 234
ecosystem, 72, 146
edge, 40, 47, 188, 220
education, 4, 60, 61, 64, 66, 69, 73,
　　74, 112, 116, 125, 126,
　　134, 138–140, 155,
　　168–170, 174, 192–194,
　　206, 207, 210, 212, 214,
　　215, 218, 221, 222, 230,
　　232, 235, 236, 239, 246,
　　255, 259, 261–267
effect, 29, 31, 54, 72, 82, 114

effectiveness, 5, 36, 127, 164, 177,
　　196, 247, 249, 250, 261
efficiency, 45, 47, 49, 50, 58, 90, 129,
　　131, 134, 144, 146, 180,
　　188, 189, 197, 215, 237
effort, 97, 152, 186, 195, 253, 264
El Salvador, 23
election, 160, 161
electorate, 159
electricity, 74, 146
electronic, 97, 197, 209
element, 218
email, 101, 124
embargo, 44
emergence, 51, 59, 64, 72, 84, 96,
　　102, 103, 120, 124, 196,
　　205, 223, 230, 246, 248
emigration, 219
empathy, 264
emphasis, 48, 50, 52, 53, 59, 68, 73
employment, 38, 42, 59, 60, 64–66,
　　112, 118, 120, 131, 180,
　　190, 195, 202, 211, 228,
　　232, 261
empowerment, 66, 176, 238, 261,
　　263, 264
emptiness, 82
enactment, 66
encourage, 54, 83, 187, 215
encryption, 98, 164, 248
end, 6, 13, 17, 18, 20, 28, 30–33, 38,
　　71, 209
endeavor, 149
energy, 44, 45, 74, 146, 208, 230,
　　241
enforce, 102, 259
enforcement, 5, 114, 152, 228, 246
engagement, 6, 71, 136, 137, 174,
　　215, 233

Index 283

engine, 52, 103–105
engineering, 101, 135–137, 219
enjoyment, 259
enrichment, 207
entertainment, 86, 93, 116, 139,
140, 171–173, 224
enthusiasm, 23
entrepreneurship, 60, 61, 215, 228,
236, 238, 263
entry, 27, 49, 69, 216
environment, 49, 50, 72–74, 82, 83,
90, 106, 125, 135, 138,
139, 169, 180, 192, 197,
207–210, 221, 224, 228,
231, 260, 264
epicenter, 10
equality, 3, 4, 61–68, 112, 224, 254,
255, 257, 258, 261–264
equipment, 250
equity, 54, 65, 74, 167
era, 6, 13, 16, 17, 27, 29, 33, 118,
176, 187, 207
eradication, 255
erasure, 207
Ernesto "Che" Guevara, 22
erode, 39, 206, 232
erosion, 50, 106, 191, 223, 229
error, 149
escalation, 28, 71
espionage, 251
establishment, 3, 5, 17–19, 23, 37,
43, 47, 71, 72, 192, 223,
243, 266
esteem, 80, 228
ethics, 27, 161
ethnicity, 210
Europe, 6, 10, 12, 13, 17, 38, 40
evacuation, 230
evaluation, 52, 178, 196, 218, 264

evening, 31
event, 17, 20, 22, 24, 30, 31, 33, 36,
53, 58, 72
evidence, 165, 178
evolution, 85, 103–105, 152, 172
example, 6, 16, 36, 47, 59, 60, 63,
71, 74, 79, 80, 87, 105,
122, 137, 146, 155, 164,
189, 191, 198, 205, 206,
212, 213, 218, 219, 223,
224, 229, 236, 238, 241,
242, 257, 259, 262, 270
exchange, 34–36, 83, 87, 91, 93, 98,
113, 125, 135, 144, 172,
188, 191, 192, 199,
206–208, 218, 223–225,
232, 237, 265
exclusion, 211, 224, 228, 232, 236,
247
exclusivity, 172
exercise, 101, 259
existence, 16, 222, 261
expansion, 7, 60, 172, 173, 181, 182,
187
expansionism, 10
expense, 50, 208
experience, 51, 53, 99, 124,
138–140, 165, 169, 211,
218, 220, 232, 265
experimentation, 70
expertise, 4, 84, 175, 190, 201, 202,
215, 219–221, 242, 243,
267
explainability, 167
explanation, 246
exploit, 98, 141, 152, 155, 160, 192,
214, 232
exploitation, 16, 87, 106, 192, 214,
225, 227–229, 248

exploration, 19, 27, 36, 68, 253
explosion, 52, 103
export, 46–48, 190
exposure, 80, 86
expression, 63, 84, 113, 191, 206, 260
extent, 86
extraction, 208
extremism, 246, 248

fabric, 219, 223
face, 13, 45, 73, 95, 96, 98, 101, 102, 104, 108, 125, 168, 169, 172, 174, 181, 194, 198, 199, 201, 202, 206, 211, 213–216, 224, 232, 250, 259
Facebook Messenger, 101
fact, 152, 160
factor, 129, 193, 223, 258
failure, 23, 54
fairness, 164
faith, 49
fall, 13, 30–33
family, 101, 124, 216, 218, 262
farming, 38, 74, 192
fashion, 86, 206, 224
father, 18
favor, 63, 180, 193, 202
fear, 20, 23, 25, 28–30, 68, 131, 227, 231, 246, 249
feedback, 140
feminism, 64
feminist, 64, 67, 68
Fidel Castro, 22
field, 93, 115, 128, 135, 137–139, 147, 165, 170, 265, 267, 271

fight, 20, 64, 65, 67, 68, 228, 260, 261, 263
fighting, 21
figure, 62
film, 191, 224
finance, 182, 196, 198, 199
financing, 54, 197
finding, 207
fix, 34
flexibility, 122, 123, 168, 170
flow, 113, 114, 180, 188, 196–198, 207
fluidity, 65
focus, 10, 46, 50, 59, 68, 161, 178, 216, 221, 231, 258
following, 16, 19, 36, 67, 81, 121, 183, 204, 242, 267
food, 4, 39, 87, 136, 195, 206, 211, 212, 214, 224, 229, 241, 254
footing, 174
footprint, 84, 190
force, 22, 23, 67, 155, 207, 209–211, 225
forecasting, 189
foreclosure, 54
form, 46, 52, 72, 88, 113, 138, 209, 225, 267
formation, 5, 80, 160, 208, 209
fossil, 74, 208, 241
Foster, 232, 267
foster, 38, 69, 74, 79, 152, 175, 190, 195, 221, 224, 231, 237, 238, 246, 263, 266, 267
foundation, 3, 35, 39, 52, 63, 67, 70, 91, 267
fragmentation, 173
framework, 6, 19, 34, 60, 136, 208, 248, 268

Index 285

francas, 87
France, 248
fraud, 142, 152
freedom, 30–33, 49, 62, 68–70, 106,
    195, 258–260
freelancing, 120, 121, 123
frenzy, 51, 53
frequency, 210
Friedrich Hayek, 49
fuel, 211, 231, 241, 246
fulfillment, 60, 68, 83, 99
Fulgencio Batista, 22
functionality, 90, 103
functioning, 5, 113, 153
fund, 194, 197
fundamental, 28, 45, 61, 106, 147,
    195, 227, 249, 258, 261,
    264
fundamentalism, 246
funding, 5, 27, 51, 60, 175, 196, 202,
    215, 243
fusion, 205, 224
future, 10, 24, 27, 33, 45, 51, 52, 58,
    72, 75, 85, 97, 99, 100,
    102, 116, 118, 120, 126,
    128, 134, 137, 140,
    147–149, 170–173, 207,
    209, 222, 224, 231, 236,
    237, 239–241, 244, 247,
    250, 258

gain, 21, 64, 72, 73, 100, 141, 152,
    155, 160, 172, 188, 228,
    232, 251, 265
game, 124
gaming, 138
gap, 101, 109, 111, 124, 125, 170,
    173–176, 193, 238, 261,
    262, 265

garment, 191
gas, 45, 73, 192, 237, 240, 241
gathering, 144, 246
Gavi, 243
Gavi, 243
gender, 4, 64–68, 87, 258, 259,
    261–264
generation, 82, 83, 104, 146, 240
genetic, 135–137
George C. Marshall, 38
Germany, 32
Ghana, 16
gig, 120–123
glass, 67
globalization, 40, 43, 86–88,
    182–187, 190–193,
    196–199, 202, 205–209,
    216, 222–225, 234, 264,
    267
globe, 231, 239
go, 127, 260
goal, 64
gold, 34
Golden Rice, 137
good, 164, 215, 247
goodwill, 242
governance, 24, 58, 71, 73, 129, 196,
    199–201, 229, 243, 244,
    247
government, 7, 17, 18, 20, 22, 23,
    25, 31, 45–49, 54, 71, 114,
    153, 155, 176, 202, 218,
    230, 231, 236, 267
grant, 65
gratitude, 82
green, 72–75, 208, 209
greenhouse, 73, 192, 208, 237, 240,
    241
grid, 146

ground, 22, 246
group, 22, 70, 71, 169, 210, 213, 261
growth, 7, 35, 38–40, 42, 43, 45–55,
    58–61, 81, 82, 91, 93, 113,
    121, 123, 172, 174, 176,
    180, 185, 187, 188, 190,
    192, 193, 197–199, 202,
    205, 207–209, 216,
    220–222, 225, 232, 236,
    238, 241, 255, 258, 262,
    264–266
guerrilla, 22
guidance, 137, 139, 163
guide, 163
Gulf, 224

habitat, 208
hacking, 125, 140, 141, 143
Haiti, 213
half, 46
hand, 6, 10, 52, 60, 82, 137, 139,
    161, 202, 223
handling, 99, 136, 162
happiness, 81–83
harassment, 65, 69, 84, 102, 232
harboring, 225
hardware, 127, 138, 140, 141
harm, 208, 209
harmonization, 243
harmony, 152
Hashtags, 156
hassle, 98
hate, 84, 102, 232, 233
hatred, 231
head, 138
headquarters, 40, 182
headset, 138
health, 65, 69, 74, 80, 82, 135–137,
    164, 165, 174, 194, 208,

211, 240, 242–244, 263
healthcare, 4, 65, 66, 112, 138,
    164–167, 174, 193–195,
    210–212, 214, 219–222,
    230, 235, 242–244, 254,
    255, 261, 263
heart, 90
hegemony, 88
help, 4, 35, 38, 43, 60, 74, 98, 99,
    105, 136, 143, 164, 181,
    189, 194, 195, 198, 199,
    212, 215, 218, 221, 224,
    237, 238, 242, 247, 254
heritage, 63, 206, 207, 223–225, 260
high, 21, 24, 29, 46–49, 51, 52, 72,
    99, 117, 138, 146, 165,
    172, 216, 236, 241, 265,
    266, 270
Hillary Clinton, 161
Hillary Clinton's, 161
hip, 205
Hiroshima, 28, 248
history, 9, 17, 19–22, 24, 27, 30, 33,
    39, 45, 53, 55, 58, 61, 70,
    72, 85, 91, 105, 106, 124,
    131, 165, 218, 236, 261,
    271
hobby, 93
Hollywood, 87, 191, 206
home, 17, 40, 43, 212, 213, 219,
    221, 223, 224, 234, 236
homeland, 17
homogenization, 86–88, 191, 193,
    206, 207
Hong Kong, 46
hop, 205
hope, 17, 32, 63
host, 40, 43, 61, 211, 212, 214–217,
    219, 223–225, 231,

Index 287

237–239, 260
hostility, 232
hosting, 214
household, 234
housing, 53, 54, 194, 232, 235, 255
Howard M. Sachar, 19
human, 3–6, 32, 46–48, 60, 67, 71,
72, 85, 106, 114, 115, 131,
135, 136, 167, 212, 214,
216, 220, 225–228, 232,
236, 240, 247, 248,
258–261, 264, 269, 271
humanity, 32, 260
humidity, 144
hybridization, 88, 205–207, 223
hype, 52

Ian J. Bickerton, 19
ice, 240
idea, 3, 16, 28, 49, 259
identification, 215
identity, 16, 63, 80, 82, 142, 152,
153, 205, 206, 210, 211,
223, 231
ideology, 7, 9, 23, 24, 48, 73, 247
image, 80, 139
imagery, 270
imagination, 31
imaging, 167
immersion, 138, 140
immigrant, 218, 231–233
immigration, 18, 216–219, 232,
233, 237
immunization, 243
impact, 10, 13, 21–23, 27, 33,
35–38, 42, 43, 45, 48–50,
53–55, 58, 60, 61, 63, 64,
67, 69, 70, 72, 74, 78,
80–83, 88, 93, 96, 99, 100,

102, 103, 105, 113, 116,
118, 120, 122, 124–126,
131, 132, 135, 142, 144,
147–152, 155–157,
159–161, 164, 168, 171,
174, 177, 178, 185, 187,
189–193, 196, 199, 201,
204, 205, 210, 211, 213,
215, 219, 221–225, 227,
229, 231, 234–237, 242,
244, 271
imperialism, 39, 86, 88, 206
impetus, 61
implement, 44, 60, 98, 114, 125,
146, 155, 164, 175, 190,
208, 215, 221, 222, 239,
255, 259
implementation, 38, 49, 72, 73, 141,
146, 167, 181, 243, 264
importance, 22, 32, 34, 44, 47, 49,
52, 55, 60, 73, 104, 108,
111, 140, 142, 161, 187,
206, 239, 242–244, 251,
260
improvement, 38, 178
in, 3–7, 9, 10, 13, 14, 16–25, 27–30,
32–40, 42–56, 58–72, 74,
75, 79–88, 90, 91, 93, 94,
96–98, 100–106, 108,
109, 112–116, 118, 120,
123–127, 129, 131, 132,
134–143, 146–149, 151,
152, 155–178, 180–183,
185–194, 196–203, 205,
206, 208–214, 216,
218–250, 254, 256–267,
269–271
inadequacy, 82
inception, 104

incident, 126, 252
inclusion, 175, 198, 216, 218, 219,
231, 261, 263, 266
inclusivity, 69, 79, 80, 88, 112, 195,
218, 224, 225, 232
income, 46, 50, 55, 58, 59, 122, 123,
174, 180, 181, 187,
190–194, 202, 230, 238,
243, 244, 255
increase, 38, 44, 47, 66, 190, 198,
229, 237, 240, 262
independence, 13, 15–17, 45, 228
indexing, 104, 105
India, 225, 248
individual, 24, 49, 51, 60, 68, 80, 82,
106, 129, 160, 164,
194–196, 228, 248, 258,
264
Indonesia, 36, 42
industrialization, 46–48, 208
industry, 38, 47, 48, 52, 54, 60, 96,
122, 124, 138, 171–173,
191, 224, 225
inequality, 22, 23, 43, 50, 55, 58, 59,
61, 64, 65, 82, 109, 112,
181, 185, 187, 191–196,
199, 210, 221, 227, 230,
246, 247, 259, 262, 264,
265
inflation, 44, 45
influence, 6, 22, 38, 39, 44, 58, 71,
72, 79–81, 86, 88, 102,
152, 159–161, 182, 185,
193, 205, 236
influencer, 102
influx, 212, 214, 235
information, 51, 79, 83–85, 89,
91–94, 98, 100–108,
113–115, 125, 139–142,

144, 149, 152, 155, 156,
160, 162, 164, 174, 176,
180, 188, 189, 191, 197,
199, 207, 215, 236, 238,
242, 243, 246, 251, 254
infrastructure, 38, 47, 51, 52, 58, 98,
99, 112, 126, 127, 129,
153, 155, 174–176, 197,
210–212, 214, 219, 220,
229, 230, 240–244, 246,
251, 266, 267, 270
infringement, 113, 172
initiation, 6
initiative, 39, 43, 47, 257, 265
injustice, 61, 62, 246
innovation, 47, 53, 55, 85, 91, 93,
113, 120, 129, 134, 137,
140, 162, 170, 189, 197,
205, 206, 221, 222, 238,
239, 248, 267, 271
insecurity, 50, 229
insight, 64
insolvency, 54
inspiration, 23, 70
instability, 16, 34, 50, 123, 196, 198,
199, 219, 220, 229, 231,
248, 260
instance, 46, 79, 93, 114, 126, 134,
167, 189, 190, 206, 213,
240
institution, 54, 68
instruction, 168
insurance, 196
integration, 48, 86, 140, 170, 181,
185, 187, 196, 197, 211,
212, 214–219, 232,
237–239, 260
integrity, 141, 160, 161, 207
intellectual, 93, 113, 172, 244, 262

Index 289

intelligence, 85, 102, 115, 132, 237, 246–248
intensity, 210
interaction, 98, 100, 169, 233
interactivity, 138
interconnectedness, 40, 50, 54, 196, 198, 207, 223
interdependence, 40, 188, 240
interest, 54, 86
interface, 111
interference, 3, 49, 160
internationalization, 196
internet, 51–53, 79, 84–87, 91, 93–97, 109, 113–116, 118, 124, 125, 144, 149, 152, 155, 156, 168, 169, 171, 172, 174–177, 197, 206, 236, 238, 265
interoperability, 146
intersection, 117, 118
intervention, 48, 49, 60, 167, 202, 246, 263, 268
intimacy, 101
intimidation, 245
introduction, 91
invasion, 23, 113, 153
invention, 124
inventory, 99, 189
investing, 45, 47, 61, 127, 134, 198, 209, 230, 236, 241
investment, 39, 43, 46–49, 51–55, 120, 192, 196, 197, 222, 236
investor, 54
involvement, 253, 270
Iran, 44, 249
Iraq, 44
isolation, 169, 227
Israel, 17–19, 44, 253

issue, 5, 18–20, 61, 65, 98, 106, 109, 113, 125, 137, 149, 152, 160, 161, 172, 193, 202, 209, 210, 213, 226, 230–232, 236, 240, 254, 259, 261

jazz, 205
Jerusalem, 18, 19
Jim Crow, 61
Jimmy Carter, 19
Jimmy Carter, 19
job, 50, 54, 58–61, 65, 116, 118, 131, 133, 134, 168, 174, 176, 181, 191–193, 196, 209, 212, 219, 232, 236, 238, 241
journal, 69
journalism, 93, 101
journey, 56, 149, 261, 263
Juan Williams, 64
Julius Nyerere, 16
justice, 50, 61–64, 66, 71–73, 75, 193, 195, 196, 233, 258, 262

Kate Millett, 69
Kim Il-sung, 20
kind, 258
knowledge, 40, 84, 91, 93, 94, 109, 113, 135, 143, 168, 170, 188, 190, 207, 208, 219, 221, 223, 224, 230, 244, 264, 265, 267, 270
Korea, 20
Kuwait, 44
Kwame Nkrumah, 16

label, 171
labeling, 136

labor, 43, 50, 120, 131, 134, 181, 185, 187, 190, 191, 195, 216, 218, 225, 232, 238, 239

lack, 16, 22, 54, 58, 59, 73, 101, 123, 174, 210, 211, 214, 215, 219, 220, 228, 229, 246, 254

ladder, 194

laity, 71

land, 23, 210, 229, 230, 241, 260

landmark, 34, 39, 62

landscape, 5, 9, 13, 20–23, 28, 29, 33, 37, 47, 48, 61, 94, 97, 100, 102, 104, 115, 118, 120, 123, 124, 136, 137, 158, 161, 163, 172, 173, 178, 183, 198, 250, 253, 254

language, 87, 115, 177, 188, 218, 224, 225, 231, 237, 238

Latin America, 16, 23

launch, 25, 27, 152

laureate, 257

law, 49, 152, 246

lawyer, 22

leader, 22, 55, 62, 74, 189

leadership, 62, 188, 261

learning, 47, 93, 94, 115, 138, 139, 149, 165, 167–170, 174, 176, 177, 189, 194, 207, 238, 253, 265, 266

leave, 210, 213, 219, 222, 262

ledger, 189

legacy, 22–24, 26, 27, 64

legality, 71

legislation, 108, 114, 155, 228, 233, 262, 264

legitimacy, 71

lending, 53, 54

lesson, 52

level, 7, 59, 82, 83, 97, 138, 195, 222, 229, 230, 232, 234, 240

leverage, 44, 55, 97, 100, 105, 123, 160, 174, 175, 267

liberalization, 55, 190, 196, 197

liberation, 68

library, 171

life, 69, 70, 123, 138, 194, 210, 214, 220, 261

lifespan, 209

lifestyle, 165, 191

light, 62, 70

limit, 5, 29, 50, 88, 181, 193, 249

limitation, 98, 164

linkage, 104

liquidity, 54, 197

listening, 173

literacy, 84, 94, 101, 111, 112, 126, 152, 160, 161, 174–178, 236, 239, 265–267

literature, 165, 224

live, 118, 125, 213, 227

livelihood, 214, 228

living, 4, 27, 62, 70, 135, 190, 193, 211, 220, 229, 236, 237, 255

load, 90, 146

location, 125, 144

logistics, 60, 98, 99, 188, 242

loneliness, 101

loss, 49, 52, 59, 87, 132, 192, 206, 208, 211, 220–222, 229

love, 70

lure, 220

machine, 115, 149, 165, 189

machinery, 71, 139

Index 291

mainstream, 70, 87, 88, 101, 117, 223
maintenance, 21
majority, 6
makeup, 135
making, 5, 6, 29, 35, 55, 60, 66, 73, 80, 86, 93, 98, 101, 103, 129, 135, 137, 144, 146, 152, 162, 165, 169, 175, 178, 194, 224, 229, 230, 244, 262
Malcolm X, 63
malnutrition, 255
malware, 152, 155
mammography, 167
man, 25, 267
management, 40, 54, 55, 98, 99, 125, 146, 167, 169, 188–190, 197–199, 208, 209, 214, 215, 230, 237
mandate, 18
manipulation, 135, 160, 161, 246
manner, 163
manufacturing, 42, 47, 48, 59, 81, 182, 188
mapping, 270
Margaret Thatcher, 49
marginalization, 88, 211, 232
market, 10, 39, 43–45, 47–55, 58–61, 120, 131, 134, 137, 168, 171, 180, 185, 187–189, 191, 195, 202–205, 216, 218, 232, 238, 239
marketing, 81, 99, 102, 106, 139
marketplace, 188
marriage, 67, 68
Martin Luther King Jr., 62, 63
Martin Luther King Jr., 62

Mary Dore, 67
Maryland, 71
masculinity, 263
mass, 18, 78–81, 211, 213, 237
matching, 238
material, 6, 81–83, 135, 172, 174
materialism, 70, 81–83
matter, 139, 168
maturation, 53
means, 5, 28, 49, 63, 102, 160, 169, 172, 174, 212, 225, 246
mechanism, 90, 181
media, 52, 62, 78–81, 84–86, 88, 93, 100–102, 106, 114, 124, 125, 149, 152, 155, 156, 159–162, 171, 173, 191, 206, 208, 233, 236, 246, 264
mediation, 212
medicine, 139, 140
medium, 102, 117
melting, 240
member, 3–6, 34, 35, 44, 181, 250, 259
membership, 5, 213
mentorship, 60, 228, 263
messaging, 101, 124, 161
microcosm, 30
microcredit, 257
microfinance, 238, 239, 257
Middle East, 19
might, 7, 213
migration, 205, 210–213, 216, 219, 223, 228–231, 236–239
milestone, 25, 124
military, 4, 8, 18, 21–23, 29, 44, 83, 246, 247, 251
million, 142
Milton Friedman, 49

minority, 261
misinformation, 80, 84, 94, 101, 102, 113, 160, 161
misinterpretation, 85
mission, 35
mistrust, 10
misuse, 114
mitigation, 42, 73, 237
mixing, 223
mobile, 97, 139, 215, 236
mobility, 50, 165, 174, 193, 194
mobilization, 93, 158
model, 74, 104, 105, 127, 218
modernization, 38
modesty, 68
moment, 27, 33, 45
momentum, 13, 17, 65, 70
monetization, 52, 106, 171, 173
money, 97, 193, 234
monitoring, 4, 43, 113, 165, 167, 189, 201, 246, 264
monopoly, 101
Montgomery, 61, 63
moral, 69, 71
morality, 71
mortality, 263
mortar, 51, 97, 169
mortgage, 53
motion, 117, 138, 140
motivation, 152, 169, 251
move, 100, 143, 194, 236
movement, 13, 16–18, 63–68, 70–75, 144, 189, 196, 197, 202, 210, 211, 216, 219, 223, 228
Muhammad Yunus, 257
multiculturalism, 218
multimedia, 139, 168
multitude, 106

music, 63, 79, 86, 87, 171, 224
Myanmar, 213, 270

Nagasaki, 28, 248
napalm, 71
narrative, 83
nation, 17
national, 5, 16–18, 63, 73, 86, 87, 113, 114, 152, 153, 155, 196, 199, 202, 216, 231, 233, 246, 258, 265
nationalism, 17, 232, 246
nationality, 213, 258
native, 232
nature, 43, 75, 120, 152, 160, 188, 198, 245, 248
need, 5, 29, 32, 34, 38, 41, 45, 52, 53, 55, 60, 65, 67, 73, 81, 97, 98, 101, 118, 127, 129, 134, 136, 138–140, 145, 147, 155, 168, 169, 171, 181, 182, 189, 192, 197, 198, 212, 224, 237, 239, 241, 242, 244, 253, 259, 267
negative, 43, 50, 54, 59, 83, 133, 186, 190–192, 194, 197, 205, 207–209, 219, 222, 223, 231, 233
negligence, 142
neighboring, 5, 18, 20, 212, 213, 270
neoliberalism, 49–51
net, 96, 194, 196
network, 52, 72, 89–91, 124, 144, 146, 175, 186, 187, 189
networking, 52, 100, 149, 174, 228
neutrality, 96
New Hampshire, 33

Index 293

news, 93, 94, 100–102, 114,
 149–152, 160
Nicaragua, 23
niche, 172
Nina Simone, 63
node, 90
non, 3, 29, 45, 67, 68, 71, 73, 175,
 245, 246, 248, 250, 259,
 265
north, 20
North and, 21
North Korea, 20–22, 248–250
notion, 49, 67, 68, 87
novel, 140
number, 51, 104, 172, 212, 230, 249
Nuremberg, 260
nutrition, 270

object, 25, 140
objectification, 69
objective, 3, 44
off, 23
offensive, 20, 114
offer, 41, 58, 87, 98, 116, 140, 143,
 146, 171, 175, 176, 188,
 220, 228, 235, 239
offering, 51, 97, 100, 104, 129, 158,
 167, 170, 173, 175, 199,
 221, 222
office, 71
oil, 44, 45, 72
one, 5, 20, 27, 37, 40, 45, 47, 53–55,
 82, 90, 93, 114, 126, 144,
 176, 182, 205, 223, 224,
 228, 236, 240, 245, 259
online, 51, 52, 69, 80, 84, 85, 93, 94,
 96–103, 105–108, 113,
 114, 143, 149–152, 155,
 156, 158, 160, 162, 168,

 171–176, 178, 208, 238,
 246, 260
onset, 229
opening, 140
opinion, 62, 63, 71, 79, 93, 101, 152,
 155, 158, 210, 213
opportunity, 6, 16, 105, 169, 208,
 209
opposition, 70, 73, 113, 114
oppression, 33, 64, 246
optimism, 51
optimization, 149
order, 9, 33, 35, 49, 58, 59, 99, 210
organ, 225
organism, 135
organization, 3, 5, 271
origin, 63, 258
other, 4, 6, 10, 17, 21, 23, 24, 27–29,
 36, 44, 52, 54, 60, 63, 72,
 86, 90, 100, 113, 118, 124,
 137, 139, 155, 161, 191,
 195, 202, 205, 208, 210,
 219, 223, 225, 229, 242,
 248, 249, 258, 259
out, 5, 21, 45, 54, 125, 174, 191,
 193, 215, 245, 257
outage, 146
outbreak, 20
outcome, 86
outrage, 72
outreach, 181
overconsumption, 82
overload, 84, 85, 94, 105
oversight, 50, 55, 136, 137
overvaluation, 52
overview, 19
ownership, 175

pace, 85, 168, 265

packaging, 100
packet, 89–92
page, 104, 105
Pakistan, 248
Palestine, 17, 18
pandemic, 177, 242, 243
paradigm, 90
parallel, 20, 21
parity, 66
part, 45, 152
participation, 27, 47, 64, 112, 137, 174, 175, 216, 261
partition, 18
partnership, 192, 243
passenger, 61
past, 55, 97, 159
path, 52
patient, 139, 164, 165, 167
pay, 65, 127, 262
payment, 98, 172, 197
peace, 3–6, 19, 40, 70, 213, 245
peacebuilding, 212
peacekeeping, 4, 6
people, 31, 38, 51, 72, 73, 79, 84, 86, 93, 97, 102, 124, 126, 142, 191, 210–213, 216, 219, 223, 228–230, 236, 237, 254, 257, 258
perception, 51, 113, 139, 140, 215, 232
performance, 46, 99
period, 7, 8, 10, 13, 17, 18, 30, 34, 40, 51, 68
perpetuation, 80
persecution, 210, 213, 223, 236, 261, 270
person, 125
personnel, 176, 242
perspective, 19, 49, 188, 202, 265

pesticide, 74
petition, 156
petroleum, 44
phenomenon, 43, 86, 87, 101, 131, 160, 219, 220, 222, 231, 237
Philippines, 235
philosophy, 70
phone, 125
pill, 68
pilot, 196
piracy, 172, 173
place, 6, 19, 20, 24, 54, 79, 82, 236, 237
placement, 139, 232
plan, 18, 39, 270, 271
planet, 72, 241
planning, 177, 215
platform, 16, 63, 72, 83, 88, 93, 100, 104, 122, 124, 156, 161, 181
player, 45, 48, 55, 191
playing, 93, 94
pleasure, 68, 69
plight, 214
pluralism, 23
point, 22, 30, 50
polarization, 194
police, 62
policy, 23, 35, 46, 71, 73, 79, 195, 199, 202, 218
policymaking, 51, 55
pollution, 72, 82, 208
pool, 262
pop, 78–81, 87
popularity, 87, 97, 120, 171, 205, 224
population, 18, 22, 23, 164, 194, 211, 214, 237, 270

Index

populism, 232
portion, 18, 194, 262
position, 21
positive, 43, 93, 94, 102, 164, 186,
190–192, 197, 205, 207,
209, 223, 232, 233, 235,
236
possibility, 29
post, 10, 40, 159, 177
potential, 28, 29, 43, 46, 51, 52, 58,
60, 80, 85, 87, 94, 102,
109, 111, 112, 114, 117,
131–135, 137, 140, 144,
146–149, 155, 157,
159–162, 164, 165,
167–170, 173, 174, 177,
180, 181, 190, 196, 198,
206, 207, 209, 213,
215–219, 221, 225, 231,
234–238, 242, 244, 247,
253, 256, 261, 262, 266,
267
poverty, 4, 27, 35, 180, 192–195,
198, 210, 211, 229, 230,
235, 236, 238, 247,
254–258
power, 5–7, 9, 13, 16, 22–24, 28, 31,
32, 44, 46–48, 51, 58, 62,
72, 74, 79, 82, 85, 87, 88,
100, 113, 129, 155, 156,
158, 167, 170, 172, 176,
193, 195, 208, 225, 257
powerhouse, 6
practice, 138, 140
precedent, 260
precipitation, 240
precursor, 137
prejudice, 232
preparedness, 230

presence, 42, 102, 138, 161
present, 19, 72, 74, 80, 103, 104,
138, 171, 172, 188, 211,
215, 234, 235, 240, 241
preservation, 72, 88, 109, 191,
205–207, 216, 224
preserve, 74, 192, 223, 225, 241
pressure, 82, 93, 181, 209, 223, 229,
238
prevention, 73, 212, 227, 260
pride, 63
principle, 28, 180, 260
priority, 255
privacy, 60, 84, 98, 101, 102,
105–109, 113, 116, 125,
126, 146, 153, 161, 164,
167, 248
privatization, 49, 50
privilege, 263
problem, 59, 103, 137, 149, 193, 225
process, 6, 13, 16, 17, 19, 43, 60, 88,
98, 102, 105, 160, 165,
183, 188, 191, 196, 216,
223, 237, 264
processing, 99, 115
procreation, 67, 68
product, 27, 98, 99
production, 38, 44, 45, 74, 81, 82,
88, 171, 188, 190, 202,
209, 244
productivity, 38, 47, 49, 58, 125,
131, 134, 180, 188, 220
professional, 60, 93, 168, 174, 221,
222, 262, 265
proficiency, 218
profile, 72
profiling, 97, 106
profit, 50, 175, 265
profitability, 52, 53, 188, 189

program, 38, 177, 206

progress, 4, 19, 25, 69, 73, 137, 218–220, 224, 256, 259, 261, 263, 264

project, 7, 83, 111, 112

proliferation, 29, 84, 149, 150, 206, 248–250

prominence, 48, 104

promiscuity, 69

promise, 83, 148, 149, 166, 170, 189

promotion, 16, 34, 38, 72, 208, 224, 230, 264

propaganda, 160, 246, 247, 251

property, 49, 172, 244

propose, 74, 177, 261, 271

prosecution, 227

prosperity, 40, 50, 82

protecting, 4, 49, 66, 106, 113, 125, 140, 195, 205, 259–261

protection, 50, 55, 63, 72–74, 113, 115, 129, 136, 161, 209, 210, 212–214, 227, 230, 238, 239, 260

protectionism, 34, 202, 204, 205

protest, 62

protocol, 136

provision, 35, 238, 265

prowess, 24

proxy, 9, 21

prudence, 53

public, 49, 50, 61–63, 71, 72, 79, 80, 93, 101, 113, 136, 137, 149, 152, 155, 158, 160, 164, 175, 181, 215, 216, 232, 233, 238, 243, 267

publication, 72

pull, 219

purchase, 97–99

purchasing, 80, 82, 97

purpose, 89, 155, 164, 225, 228

pursuit, 21, 50, 64, 73, 81, 82, 192, 193, 195, 196, 208, 232, 255

push, 21, 27, 211

quality, 60, 80, 104, 124, 167, 189, 193, 194, 210, 220, 222, 262, 263, 265, 266, 270

quantum, 147–149

quarantine, 242

query, 105

quest, 258, 260

quo, 23, 68, 70

race, 9, 63, 210, 213, 248, 250, 258, 263

Rachel Carson's, 72

racism, 61, 63, 195

radicalization, 246

radio, 79, 159

rainforest, 192

range, 4, 38, 81, 82, 93, 97, 101, 115, 139, 140, 144, 152, 156, 165, 171–173, 197, 198, 216, 226, 240, 251

ranking, 105

ransom, 155

ransomware, 155

rapport, 161

rate, 34–36, 208

re, 91, 105

reach, 51, 79, 87, 88, 91, 102, 105, 125, 159, 171, 172, 190, 191

reaction, 49, 54, 70

reading, 187

reality, 85, 102, 140, 147, 213, 236

realization, 259, 260

Index 297

realm, 106, 194
reassessment, 53
receipt, 225
recession, 44, 53
recipient, 39
recognition, 68, 73, 139, 140, 191, 263
reconstruction, 35, 38
record, 171
recovery, 37–40, 209
recruitment, 225, 238, 246
recycling, 209
redefinition, 68
redistribution, 194
reduction, 4, 35, 44, 50, 131, 167, 229, 236, 238
redundancy, 129
reevaluation, 36
refinement, 167
reform, 5
refuge, 210, 212, 213
refugee, 212, 214, 215, 260
regard, 242
reggae, 205
regime, 10, 20–22, 34
region, 17, 20, 22, 23, 37, 38, 126, 177, 212
regulation, 55, 137, 161, 187, 198
rehabilitation, 228, 247
reintegration, 228, 247
rejection, 31, 71
relation, 164
relationship, 9, 68, 125, 222
relativism, 258
release, 73, 155
relevance, 24, 103, 202
reliability, 146, 147
reliance, 36, 113, 152, 155, 191, 220
relief, 4, 30, 267

religion, 63, 210, 213, 231
relocation, 181
reminder, 32, 53, 55, 64, 142
removal, 190
remuneration, 221
repair, 139
reporting, 80, 142, 233
repository, 113
representation, 65, 66, 79, 80, 88, 202, 261, 262, 264
repression, 210, 246
research, 35, 47, 82, 89, 92, 93, 113, 164, 177, 208, 220, 221, 244
reserve, 34
resettlement, 214
resilience, 32, 190, 206, 230, 231, 237
resistance, 16, 18, 62, 63, 71, 73, 88, 135, 241, 263
resolution, 5, 6, 18, 138, 140, 212, 270
resonance, 161
resource, 49, 82, 190, 209, 244
respect, 3, 195, 247, 258, 259, 264
response, 4, 23, 36, 44, 45, 61, 68, 146, 187, 206, 214, 216, 230, 231, 242–244, 248, 252, 260, 267, 268, 270, 271
responsibility, 43, 74, 167, 187, 195, 259
rest, 25, 44, 129, 191
restoration, 74
restraint, 68
restriction, 114, 135
result, 16, 30, 86, 113, 142, 144, 160, 172, 193, 195, 198, 211, 213, 224, 229, 230

Index

resurgence, 21
retail, 51, 59, 96–98, 100
retaliation, 28
return, 19, 98
reunification, 30–33, 216, 218
revenue, 51, 52, 104, 194, 220
review, 168
revitalization, 38, 88, 206, 207
revolution, 22–24, 67–69, 83–85,
    100, 171
revolutionary, 22–24, 45, 93
rhetoric, 232
richness, 125
ride, 122
right, 19, 49, 65, 106, 164, 259, 264
rise, 6–9, 22, 34, 40, 42, 43, 45, 46,
    49–53, 55–58, 60, 72, 73,
    75, 81–85, 87, 97, 100,
    102, 120, 121, 123, 134,
    140, 149, 171, 173, 196,
    197, 199, 202, 205, 206,
    229, 231, 237, 240, 245,
    250
risk, 28, 29, 53–55, 59, 125, 136,
    165, 189, 190, 197, 198,
    206, 207, 224, 229,
    248–250
rivalry, 23, 24, 248
rocket, 27
role, 4, 5, 16, 18, 21, 24, 33–37, 40,
    46, 49, 55, 60, 62, 63, 66,
    70–72, 75, 79, 80, 83, 93,
    94, 96, 104, 113, 124, 137,
    140, 156, 158–161, 167,
    175, 177, 178, 181, 182,
    185, 187, 193, 197,
    199–202, 210, 212–214,
    219–221, 223, 224, 227,
    236, 238, 242–244, 247,
    249, 259, 262, 264, 267,
    270, 271
Ronald Reagan, 49
room, 88
root, 210, 212, 213, 215, 228,
    246–248, 258, 264
Rosa Parks, 61, 63
Rosa Parks, 61
route, 90
routing, 90
row, 20
royalty, 172
rule, 13, 16, 17, 20–22
Russia, 114, 250

sabotage, 251
safety, 43, 50, 60, 102, 135–137,
    178, 192, 194, 196, 210,
    212, 215, 220, 270
salespeople, 98
Sam Cooke, 63
Sam Cooke's, 63
sanitation, 270
Santa Barbara, 72
satellite, 10, 25, 86
satisfaction, 81, 82, 98
Saudi Arabia, 44
saving, 214
scalability, 90, 127, 149, 177
scale, 21, 36, 48, 59, 73, 83, 93, 100,
    109, 114, 124, 177, 192,
    196, 229, 245
scan, 139
scarcity, 220
scenario, 5
schedule, 168
school, 207
science, 27, 219
screen, 139

Index   299

screening, 167, 214
sea, 105, 210, 229, 240
search, 52, 103–105, 210, 221, 229,
  230, 236, 237
searching, 105, 176
seat, 61
second, 64, 82
section, 20, 58, 64, 72, 78, 143, 147,
  161, 231
sector, 47, 52–55, 60, 175, 185, 186,
  221, 222, 227, 267
securitization, 53, 197
security, 3, 4, 6, 19, 29, 39, 45, 98,
  100, 101, 106, 108, 109,
  113, 125, 126, 129, 136,
  142, 146, 152, 153, 155,
  160, 164, 195, 202, 211,
  213–216, 220, 241,
  244–250
seed, 137
segregation, 61, 62, 260
seizure, 22
selection, 172
self, 15–18, 45, 60, 79, 80, 82, 84,
  168, 169, 228, 263
selling, 97
Selma, 63
semiconductor, 47, 48
sensationalism, 233
sense, 25, 51, 63, 71, 74, 79–82, 88,
  124, 138, 140, 161, 175,
  224, 228, 231, 232, 237,
  246, 265
sensitivity, 167
sensor, 162
sentiment, 22, 71, 202, 216,
  231–233
Seoul, 21
separatism, 246

series, 14, 19, 21, 23, 43, 44, 55, 62,
  72, 249
service, 129, 189
set, 3, 8, 9, 17, 40, 74, 125, 127, 180,
  260, 265, 267
setting, 79, 201, 202
settlement, 3, 10, 181, 218
sex, 63, 68
sexism, 64, 195
sexuality, 67, 69, 263
shaping, 21, 33, 48, 60, 70–72,
  78–80, 87, 88, 99, 102,
  126, 128, 137, 140, 149,
  155, 158, 160, 185, 187,
  199, 215, 216, 219, 223,
  224, 236
share, 80, 84, 85, 93, 94, 100–102,
  124, 129, 156, 160, 207,
  212, 215
sharing, 51, 89, 93, 98, 101, 113,
  122, 144, 172, 174, 189,
  199, 208, 221, 230, 238,
  242–244, 246, 247
shelter, 4, 195, 211, 212, 214, 254,
  270
shift, 13, 21, 35, 44–48, 51, 55, 59,
  66, 67, 71, 82, 120, 129,
  173, 177
shipping, 98
shopping, 51, 97–100
shortage, 220, 222
show, 149
sickness, 117
side, 191, 192
significance, 24, 30, 33, 61, 142, 206
Simone de, 67, 69
Singapore, 46, 47
sit, 62, 71
site, 250

situation, 5, 205, 259, 260, 270

skill, 120, 131

slavery, 61, 225, 228

smartphone, 48, 105, 139

socialism, 24

society, 24, 26, 27, 30, 31, 33, 43, 55,
  60, 63, 64, 66, 67, 69–71,
  78–83, 86–88, 93,
  111–114, 124, 131, 132,
  134, 135, 150, 152, 158,
  159, 176, 185, 186, 193,
  195, 196, 210–212, 216,
  217, 222, 227, 228, 232,
  247, 255, 258, 262, 264

socio, 22–24, 68, 176, 177, 219,
  220, 224, 262

software, 52, 60, 103, 127, 138, 139,
  141, 142, 155

soil, 74, 209

solidarity, 16, 63, 232

solution, 19, 103, 239, 270

solving, 59

song, 63

sophistication, 253

source, 19, 21, 23, 137

south, 20

South Africa, 63, 260

South Korea, 20, 21, 36, 46, 87

South Korea's, 48

Southeast Asia, 42

sovereignty, 16, 39, 181, 202

space, 25, 27, 113, 118, 138

span, 46, 85

specialization, 47, 188

specificity, 167

speculation, 52, 53

speech, 38, 62, 84, 102, 113–115

speed, 147, 172

spending, 49, 54

spike, 44

spill, 72

sponsor, 246

sponsorship, 246

sportswear, 42

spotlight, 44

spread, 20, 22–24, 29, 36, 50, 54,
  69, 80, 84, 86–88, 101,
  102, 113, 114, 149, 155,
  160, 161, 182, 191, 206,
  211, 242, 247, 248, 250,
  260, 264

Sputnik, 25, 27

stability, 4, 22, 34, 36, 38, 44, 49, 55,
  155, 194, 198, 199, 220,
  227, 236, 239, 245, 247

stabilization, 44

stage, 6, 8, 9, 16, 17, 24, 40, 167

stagflation, 49

stakeholder, 215

stalemate, 20

standard, 34

standardization, 87

standoff, 10

start, 49, 60, 228, 248, 257

state, 18, 19, 23, 24, 29, 49, 114,
  245, 246, 251, 259

status, 6, 7, 19, 23, 68, 70, 194, 195,
  232, 258, 263

stem, 86

step, 138, 139

stigma, 69

stigmatization, 211

stimulus, 54

storage, 126–129

store, 126, 129

story, 79

storytelling, 191

strain, 211, 214

Index

strategy, 63, 161, 189
streaming, 171–173
strength, 6, 9
stress, 82, 232
stricter, 195
strike, 28, 115, 125, 137, 206
structure, 40, 104, 169
struggle, 10, 13, 24, 61, 62, 67, 169,
    174, 193, 211, 214, 222,
    259
study, 13, 16, 17, 24, 43, 155, 161,
    164, 187, 265–267, 271
Stuxnet, 253
subject, 93, 139, 168, 202, 258
subscription, 172
subsection, 6, 10, 13, 17, 22, 24, 30,
    33, 46, 48, 53, 55, 61, 67,
    70, 81, 83, 96, 100, 103,
    106, 109, 118, 120, 124,
    126, 131, 140, 147, 149,
    152, 156, 159, 168, 171,
    173, 190, 193, 196, 199,
    202, 205, 207, 210, 213,
    216, 219, 222, 225, 228,
    234, 236, 242, 245, 251,
    254, 261, 264, 267
success, 39, 46–48, 50, 63, 87, 169,
    190, 218
suffering, 267, 271
sufficiency, 263
suffrage, 64
suit, 20
summary, 193, 267
superpower, 6, 7, 55–58
supplier, 190
supply, 44, 45, 48, 98, 100, 146,
    187–190, 270
support, 4, 17, 18, 20–23, 34, 38,
    44, 46, 47, 52, 54, 60, 63,

    71–73, 79, 102, 125, 175,
    203, 207, 211–215, 218,
    228, 230–233, 237–239,
    243, 244, 246, 247, 266,
    267, 270
suppression, 113
supremacy, 24
surge, 51, 60
surplus, 197
surprise, 20
surrounding, 22, 51, 65, 67, 69, 161,
    164, 216
surveillance, 35, 106, 113, 242, 244,
    250, 260
survival, 167
survivor, 228
sustainability, 35, 45, 53, 70, 73, 74,
    172, 190, 196
sustenance, 246
switching, 89–92
symbol, 30, 32
Syngman Rhee, 20
Syria, 212
system, 33–37, 48, 54, 55, 62, 194,
    198, 218

tablet, 139
Taiwan, 46, 47
taking, 19, 53, 55, 137, 176, 231
talent, 188, 220, 262
talk, 124
Tanzania, 16
tapestry, 225
target, 153, 159, 161
task, 5, 216
taste, 87
tax, 46, 47, 54, 193–195, 220
teach, 71
teaching, 222

teamwork, 169

tech, 47, 60, 152

technology, 24–27, 29, 40, 48, 51–53, 58–61, 85, 86, 88, 91, 95–97, 100, 102, 105, 106, 109, 111, 112, 117, 118, 124, 133, 135, 140, 147–149, 152, 155, 156, 158, 164, 165, 169, 170, 173–175, 182, 187, 189, 190, 192, 196, 206, 209, 215, 219–223, 225, 230, 236, 238, 239, 241–244, 248, 250, 264–266, 270, 271

telecommunication, 124

telecommunications, 124–126

telegraph, 124

telemedicine, 165, 174

telephone, 124

television, 79, 80, 86, 101, 159, 171

temperature, 144, 210, 240

tension, 10, 29, 30, 73

term, 36, 39, 73, 74, 133, 177, 196, 211, 212, 214, 215, 231, 239, 240

territory, 18

terror, 246

terrorism, 29, 199, 245–248

testament, 32, 47

testing, 196

textbook, 9, 143

textile, 191

Thailand, 36, 42

the Democratic Republic of the, 16

the Eastern Bloc, 10

the Middle East, 17, 44

the Middle East Conflict", 19

The Soviet Union, 6, 10, 20

the Soviet Union, 3, 6–10, 13, 16, 21, 23–25, 27–30, 38, 39, 248

the Soviet Union's, 9, 27

the State of Israel, 18

the United Kingdom, 3, 224, 248

The United States, 6, 10, 21, 23, 29, 39, 45

the United States, 3, 6–10, 13, 16, 20–25, 27–30, 38, 44, 45, 61, 71, 224, 248, 250, 253

The United States', 6, 9

the United States', 39

the Western Bloc, 10

the Western Hemisphere, 22–24

theft, 140, 142, 152, 153

Theodor Herzl, 18

theory, 20, 28

thinking, 59, 84, 94, 101, 113, 158, 169, 178, 187, 264

thought, 259

threat, 18, 29, 38, 39, 113, 115, 152, 155, 206, 214, 231, 241, 245, 247, 248, 250, 251, 254

Thurgood Marshall, 62

time, 18, 21, 24, 25, 27, 35, 46, 51, 55, 61, 70, 97, 101, 103, 105, 124, 125, 138, 139, 146, 159, 165, 168, 189, 197, 216, 228, 270

today, 13, 18, 32, 45, 53, 63, 72, 106, 108, 109, 112, 113, 124, 134, 156, 159, 173, 187, 199, 225, 236, 240, 242, 250, 251

tolerance, 191, 247, 266

tool, 39, 102, 125, 161, 165, 238

top, 67, 105

Index 303

topic, 19, 84, 143, 234
tourism, 74, 206, 230
traceability, 189
track, 99, 152, 189
tracking, 106, 138, 140, 246, 247
traction, 100, 160
trade, 34, 35, 38, 39, 44, 47, 48, 50,
        51, 180, 181, 188, 191,
        192, 197, 202–205, 209,
        223–225
trading, 180
traffic, 99
trafficking, 225–228
training, 43, 59, 60, 112, 143,
        174–177, 194, 214, 215,
        218, 220, 222, 228, 232,
        236, 237, 244, 252, 263,
        266
trajectory, 17
transaction, 98, 236
transfer, 40, 135, 136, 187, 190, 208,
        209, 225, 230, 234, 241,
        244
transformation, 39, 48, 55, 83, 85,
        120, 125, 140, 168, 171,
        191, 231
transit, 129
transition, 45, 59, 60, 74, 134, 218,
        241
transmission, 90, 146, 207
transparency, 54, 58, 71, 93, 113,
        137, 152, 161, 164, 180,
        181, 189, 244
transportation, 40, 59, 60, 81, 86,
        122, 155, 192, 223, 225,
        236
travel, 31, 86, 242
treatment, 63, 164, 165, 167, 242,
        261

treaty, 136
trend, 100, 219
triumph, 15, 31–33
truce, 6
Trump, 161
trust, 54, 98, 101, 137, 152, 167,
        232, 242, 270
tsunamis, 229
Turkey, 114
turn, 54, 246
turning, 22, 30

U.S., 6, 7, 34, 38, 45, 71
UK, 49
Ukraine, 155
understanding, 24, 27, 33, 58, 64,
        67, 69, 73, 79–81, 88, 92,
        113, 139, 161, 168, 176,
        181, 196, 206, 207, 219,
        224, 225, 232, 233, 237,
        238, 248, 265, 266, 271
unemployment, 54, 59, 60,
        131–134, 194, 246
uniqueness, 206
United States, 53
unity, 16, 32, 63, 224
universe, 27
unrest, 50, 59, 191, 194, 211, 220
up, 25, 51, 55, 61, 82, 83, 91, 104,
        140, 194, 197, 209, 253,
        265
update, 155
upheaval, 17
upskilling, 47, 168
urbanization, 230
urgency, 25, 73, 212
US, 49, 161
usage, 178

use, 28, 29, 39, 60, 72, 74, 80, 82, 91, 92, 103, 106, 109, 118, 122, 126, 136–139, 141, 147, 155, 161, 162, 164, 167, 188, 198, 202, 241, 245, 248–251, 270

user, 52, 92, 98, 102, 103, 105, 117, 138, 139, 144, 161, 171

utility, 146

utilization, 90, 126, 127

vaccine, 242, 244

validation, 167

valuation, 51, 53

value, 34, 48, 49, 53, 54, 73, 80, 97, 206

variety, 98, 162, 171, 180, 188, 232

Venezuela, 44

venture, 51

verification, 250

veto, 5

viability, 52

victim, 228

victory, 22, 260

video, 86, 101, 124, 169

Vietnam, 42, 71

view, 138, 139

viewership, 171

vigilance, 55

violation, 260

violence, 5, 18, 62, 65, 73, 210, 214, 227, 229, 245–247, 259, 262, 263, 269

visa, 237

visibility, 171

vision, 115, 139

vitamin, 137

voice, 99, 101, 124, 125

volatility, 53, 199

volume, 93, 104

voter, 160

voting, 65

VR, 139

vulnerability, 44, 155, 198, 228, 229

wage, 65

waiting, 222

wall, 30–32

Walter Laqueur, 19

want, 122

war, 3, 6, 10, 13, 19–22, 28, 29, 35, 39, 40, 44, 71, 210, 212, 213, 248

warfare, 250, 251, 253, 254

warning, 230, 231

Washington, 62

waste, 74, 82, 83, 208, 209

water, 208, 209, 211, 214, 230, 240, 270

wave, 17, 64, 65, 70, 131

way, 33, 53, 55, 69, 70, 75, 79, 83–85, 91, 94, 97, 99, 100, 102–105, 118, 123–126, 138, 149, 159, 170, 173, 192, 196, 222, 236, 239, 264, 271

wealth, 50, 82, 142, 171, 193–195

weapon, 248

weather, 229, 230, 237, 240

web, 84, 103–105, 248

webpage, 93

website, 99

welfare, 50, 51, 180, 196, 205, 232

well, 13, 34, 49, 60, 74, 82, 83, 97, 141, 160, 167, 194, 196, 207, 210, 211, 222, 228, 231, 232, 247, 253, 262, 263

Index 305

West Berlin, 30, 31
West Germany, 30, 33
Western Europe, 30
whole, 60, 81, 83, 93, 210, 224, 227, 262
Wilhelm Reich, 69
will, 6, 9, 10, 17, 22, 28, 30, 43, 45, 46, 49, 53, 55, 58, 78, 81, 83, 96, 97, 102, 103, 106, 109, 116, 118, 124, 126, 140, 147, 149, 159, 161, 171–173, 190, 193, 196, 199, 202, 205, 207, 213, 216, 219, 222, 225, 231, 234, 236, 237, 239, 242, 244, 245, 250, 254, 259, 267
wind, 74, 208
wing, 49
withdrawal, 71
work, 5, 58, 61, 91, 112, 118, 120, 122, 123, 125, 140, 169, 176, 177, 181, 186, 192, 196, 207, 208, 213–215, 218, 221, 225, 228, 231, 233, 237, 238, 240–242, 247, 248, 258, 261, 271

workforce, 47, 59, 261
working, 22, 43, 168, 190, 191, 219, 221, 222, 234, 236, 242, 271
workplace, 65, 67, 139
world, 5, 8–10, 13, 14, 17, 19, 20, 24, 25, 29, 30, 32–34, 40, 43–45, 48, 54, 55, 58, 67, 72, 74, 75, 79–81, 83, 86, 88, 89, 100, 106, 108, 109, 112–114, 124, 125, 138–140, 142, 143, 146, 147, 151, 152, 155, 156, 158, 170, 173, 176, 177, 186, 187, 190, 191, 193, 196, 199, 201, 204, 205, 207, 213, 215, 216, 219, 225, 228, 236, 237, 239–242, 244, 245, 248, 250, 251, 254, 258, 261, 264, 265, 267, 271
worth, 82, 258

xenophobia, 211, 215, 231–233, 237

year, 61

zone, 10

306   Index

Milton Keynes UK
Ingram Content Group UK Ltd.
UKHW021927151124
451262UK00014B/1646